Advice for Advisers

The Development of a Residence Hall Association

Second Edition

Norbert W. Dunkel
Cindy L. Spencer
& Associates

Published by
The Association of College and University Housing Officers-International

Columbus, Ohio
June 1998

TABLE OF CONTENTS

ACKNOWLEDGMENTS

We wish to thank the advisers who give of their time and talents to assist hall governments, area councils, and residence hall associations become learning communities for students. Support, resources, and services for hall governance have been increasing steadily in the past decade. We believe that, with the support of the senior housing officers, this pace will quicken and the doors for hall governance will continue to open.

We wish to thank the authors who maintained a very tight production schedule. In an era when we are doing more with less, those individuals found the time to share their experience and skills. They are true teachers and educators. We thank Joanna Jennie for proofreading and copy editing the book. Our thanks also go to Mary Ellerbrock, the ACUHO-I Communications Coordinator, for her publications expertise and support of this project. Finally, our thanks are extended to George Peach for the cover design.

Norb wishes to thank his wife Kim and son Nicholas for their support of his travel and writing to educate others regarding the role of the adviser. Also, he wishes to thank Jim Grimm, Director of Housing at the University of Florida, for his continued support of students, their needs, and their desires. Finally, he thanks the University of Florida Inter-Residence Hall Association for continuing to provide the most gratifying experience an administrator and educator could enjoy — advising.

Cindy wishes to thank her colleagues and friends for their continued support, encouragement, and guidance. She would like to thank the students with whom she has worked with on various campuses and within NACURH for continuing to challenge her to grow as an adviser. She wants to thank Julie Moody and Peggie Love for their assistance with the many tasks associated with this project. Also, she would like to thank Dr. Jack Collins, Director of Housing and Residence Life at Ball State University, and Alan Hargrave, Associate Director, for their support of the students and their leadership development as well as the professional development of the staff who advise students.

ABOUT THE EDITORS

Norbert W. Dunkel is Associate Director of Housing for Staff and Student Development at the University of Florida, Gainesville, Florida. He has worked in housing and residence life positions at South Dakota State University, the University of Northern Iowa, and Southern Illinois University at Carbondale. He has served as the co-founder and co-director of The National Housing Training Institute for the past eight years. Norb has written almost forty articles or chapters concerning students and student development. He served as co-editor of the first edition of *Advice for Advisors: The Development of an Effective Residence Hall Association* and he is the co-author of the Jossey-Bass book, *Advising Student Groups and Organizations* with John Schuh. He served as the Editor for *The Journal of College and University Student Housing* and Associate Editor for *The College Student Affairs Journal.* He currently serves on the ACUHO-I Executive Board as the ACUHO-I Publications Coordinator.

Norb has served as an adviser to hall governance organizations for the past nineteen years, and he currently serves as the adviser to the University of Florida Inter-Residence Hall Association. He served as the founding adviser to the Florida Association of Residence Halls (FARH). He received the SAACURH and NACURH Daniel Hallenbeck Awards for Career Service in 1996. He was inducted into the SAACURH Adviser Hall of Fame, into the Association of Alumni and Friends of NACURH by SAACURH, and was the first recipient of the FARH Adviser Award named in his honor in 1992.

Cindy Spencer is the Director of Residential and Greek Life at the University of Nebraska at Kearney. She has worked in housing and residence life positions at Ball State University, the University of Tennessee at Knoxville, the University of Georgia, and Western Kentucky University. Cindy is chair of the ACUHO-I Housing Internship Committee. She served on the GLACUHO Executive Board and on a wide range of committees within ACUHO-I, GLACUHO, and SACSA (Southern Association for College Student Affairs). She served as co-editor of the first edition of *Advice for Advisors: The Development of an Effective Residence Hall Association.*

Cindy has served as an adviser to student organizations for the past 15 years. She currently serves as the adviser to the Ruth Peter's Chapter of the National Residence Hall Honorary at Ball State University. She served as the founding adviser for the Tennessee Association of College and University Residence Halls (TACURH). As an adviser, she was the SAACURH recipient of the Daniel Hallenbeck Award for Career Service in 1993. Cindy was inducted into the Association of Alumni and Friends of NACURH in 1996. She received the Indiana Residence Hall Association Adviser of the Year Award in 1997. Cindy was elected as the NACURH Conference Resource Consultant in 1995. She continues to serve in this position.

FOREWORD

Advising Student Groups is a Fantastic Experience!!

Advising residence hall student government groups is a wonderful opportunity to participate in student development at its finest. The responsibility of advising should not be taken lightly or viewed as a secondary or "add-on" responsibility, because it is at the very heart and soul of preparing students for the challenges of life. Advising is a dynamic process which is both challenging and rewarding.

The success of this book's first edition is testimony to the fact that all of us — veteran, rookie, and "wanna-be" advisers — are always looking for information and techniques that will assist us in developing, improving, and refining our advising skills. The editors, Norb Dunkel and Cindy Spencer, both extraordinarily effective advisers, recognized the need for this book and committed to making it a reality. We are grateful to them for filling this need and, as a result, helping us to become better advisers. The chapter authors were selected for their experience and proven effectiveness as advisers. They have each "walked the walk." The skills and techniques discussed can be practiced, learned, and perfected. I am confident you will rank this book as one of your most valued resources.

While serving as an adviser, you will realize many "teachable moments" and opportunities to integrate student development and group dynamics theory with practice. Your behavior and approach to people, problems, and programs will provide a model for the group's officers and individual members. You have a golden opportunity to develop a close working relationship with the organization's officers. While you observe the strengths, weaknesses, and struggles with which to officers are dealing, you will find yourself in the roles of coach, teacher, confident, and mentor. You will be challenged with deciding when to confront, console, challenge, and correct. This is student development at its best! Balancing appropriate growth-producing interventions for the individual officers with the "good of the organization" will be a frequent struggle.

One of the greatest challenges for advisers is learning when to speak up and when to keep quiet. This is particularly true when the group is heatedly discussing an issue for which you see the obvious answer. As veteran advisers will attest, the line between providing advice and support versus providing direction and control is thin and, at times, elusive. Is the process or the solution more important? Is it possible the group might arrive at a better decision or solution than the one on which you have settled? Should the adviser make sure every undertaking of the group is successful? Is it appropriate, on occasion, to watch a group struggle and fail? How do you respond when you feel the group is making a grave mistake? What is the role of the adviser and how to do you communicate that to the group?

Assisting the group in goal setting is vitally important for the adviser. All too often organizations fall into a rut of repeating the same programs and projects year after year. This approach provides a high level of comfort for the officers, but requires little thinking, creativity, or ingenuity and eventually leads to apathy and complacency on the part of the membership. To be viable, organizations must be responsive to the needs and the desires of both members and constituents. The process of setting goals and developing programs to realize their accomplishment infuses an organization with new life and enthusiasm. Organizations that are moving toward a common, clear, specific goal are vibrant and alive with members who are excited about the organization and supportive of each other's efforts.

From my own advising experience, I can remember sitting in numerous meetings and wondering whether anything of value was taking place. Was the discussion and, at times, the bickering leading somewhere or just a waste of time? Was anything of value happening? Was I helping the group reach its goals? Was I doing anything to positively stimulate the growth of even one student? At other times I marveled at the wisdom, intelligence, and maturity exhibited by the group. Yes, it is possible to experience frustration, dejection, and elation all within the space of a single meeting!

I highly recommend the advising experience to each of you. It is an exciting educational venue where student growth and development is the order of the day. I am confident you will find advising to be a gratifying, rewarding professional experience.

This book is dedicated to all of you who have devoted or will devote yourselves to working with students in the capacity of adviser. The significance of your role cannot be overstated. Your contributions to the group and to individual students are unparalleled. I salute you and congratulate you as you carry out this important assignment.

Daniel A. Hallenbeck, Ph.D.
Former NACURH Adviser

PREFACE

As undergraduate or graduate students, residence life staff may have been given opportunities to supervise employees or facilitate meetings with student volunteers. Training opportunities abound and bookshelves are full of materials to support training and meeting facilitation. Additionally, many courses and seminars are geared to providing information on supervising using the most contemporary methods and tools. Similarly, many staff may have been given the opportunity to advise an organization, perhaps a student governing organization in housing. What type of training or experience does a staff member bring to the advising responsibility? For most staff, adviser training is the experience one receives on the job.

During the past twenty years several publications have begun to provide a basic understanding of the role and responsibilities of advising. Those publications continue to provide an excellent overview of advising and, with the addition of formal training recently initiated at conferences and on campuses, begin to create an intentional training and knowledge approach. The publications include Bowling (1980), Dunkel and Porter (in press), Dunkel and Schuh (1998), Dunkel and Spencer (1993), Osteen and Tucker (1997), Rasche and Stoner (1989), Schuh (1984), Terrell and Cuyjet (1994), Werring (1984), and Wyatt and Stoner (1984).

This second edition of *Advice for Advisers: The Development of an Effective Residence Hall Association* is intended to be used as a training manual or resource book. Many of the chapters include practical applications in the form of case studies or vignettes. These applications make excellent training opportunities for hall, area, or campus-wide organization advisers. The authors have collected current information to update their chapters. By doing so, the chapters continue to be relevant to both new and seasoned advisers.

The first chapter is a reprint of the NACURH "White Paper" on residence hall government by Stoner and Wyatt. We continue to believe that the "White Paper" provides an historical benchmark for many of the publications on advising.

In Chapter 2, Boersig and Wallington provide information on the characteristics and thoughts of transitioning from student to adviser. Additionally, advice is presented for new advisers regarding their role, styles and techniques, group development, and advising issues.

Chapter 3 includes the responsibilities of advising. Porter reports the results of a national study of RHA adviser responsibilities. She also compares the top ten most important adviser responsibilities as indicated by advisers with the top ten as indicated by RHA presidents.

Chapter 4 is a reprint from the first edition of the book. Komives and Tucker conducted a national study of effective RHA structures and systems and provided a qualitative summary of their findings. Common themes of successful RHAs provide a template with which other RHA structures and systems might be compared.

In Chapter 5, Cawthon and Underwood provide a brief overview of organizational theory to prepare the reader to understand the varied structures that an RHA might assume. The chapter presents formal and informal structures as well as centralized, decentralized, and blended structures. Additionally, the authors discuss the governing documents of RHAs.

The motivation of students is presented in Chapter 6. Extrinsic and intrinsic motives are described, as well as motivation theory and research. Mitchell and Munro-Krusz also offer recommendations for working with individuals and groups.

Chapter 7 is a lengthy and useful presentation of group development concepts and ethics. Sampson expands on the chapter in the first edition by including additional theories and models. The treatment of ethical principles as an integral component of RHA member training is included. The chapter concludes with ten excellent scenarios for discussion.

Chapter 8 challenges the reader to examine the role of the RHA in developing inclusive communities. Papish and Wall explore how an RHAís mission, values, and purpose inform its position regarding diversity. Additionally, information on inclusivity and the RHA diversity quotient are provided.

In Chapter 9, Miller and Blattner review the importance of establishing positive relationships with numerous campus constituencies. Information on learning communities and service learning is included.

Chapter 10 addresses the topic for which most advisers continually seek information. Schuh discusses legal issues that impact advisers and RHAs, reviewing current areas of legal responsibility and how various case law applies to situations involving RHAs.

Chapter 11 presents information on how RHAs can manage their money, account for their money, and audit their accounts. Hudson, Hudson, and Tattershall share the results of their national study of RHA financing practices.

Information on raising money is presented in Chapter 12. Grandpré and Kimble review how to conduct a successful fund-raising campaign, how to generate institutional and departmental funds, and how to work with vending and other contractual services.

Chapter 13 provides information on how to work with companies whose purpose is to sell merchandise for profit and return a percentage to the RHA. Dumhart and Schoen provide guidelines for working with companies, including what to look for in an outside company, and advantages and disadvantages of working with an outside company.

The history and services of NACURH are included in Chapter 14 by Stoner, Berry, Boever, and Tattershall. They review the organizational purpose and structure, outline the development of the Association of Alumni and Friends of NACURH, discuss the relationship of NACURH with ACUHO-I, and detail the history of NACURH from 1954 to 1998.

In Chapter 15, Spencer discusses the structure of the various conferences. She addresses the benefits of attending conferences, receiving conference awards, preparing a delegation, and bidding for conferences. Checklists are provided for advisers working with their delegations.

Professional development for RHA advisers is presented in Chapter 16. Averill and Bradley challenge readers to identify resources, services, and strategies to advance professionally and become more knowledgeable regarding their role.

In Chapter 17, Dunkel challenges the reader to look to the future of RHAs, their roles and responsibilities, and their relationships with housing operations and the larger institutional community.

It is our belief that these authors provide the reader with excellent information and resources to advance the level of knowledge of RHAs and advising. There are few roles more gratifying than serving as an adviser. Please remember:

"To Advise Is To Touch A Life Forever More"

References

Bowling, S. R. (1980). Student government and leadership. In D. A. DeCoster & P. Mable (Eds.), *Personal education and community development in college residence halls.* Washington, DC: American College Personnel Association.

Dunkel, N. W., & Porter, J. D. (in press). Residence hall association adviser responsibilities. *Journal of College and University Student Housing.*

Dunkel, N. W., & Spencer, C. L. (Eds.). (1993). *Advice for advisors: The development of an effective residence hall association.* Columbus, OH: ACUHO-I.

Dunkel, N. W., & Schuh, J. H. (1998). *Advising student groups and organizations.* San Francisco: Jossey-Bass.

Osteen, J. M., & Tucker, G. L. (1997). Authority, accountability, and advice: Understanding the unique roles of residence life staff and hall government leaders. *Journal of College and University Student Housing, 27*(1), 34-40.

Rasche, C. M., & Stoner, K. L. (1989). Working with students and student government. In J. Schuh (Ed.), *Educational programming in college and university residence halls.* Columbus, OH: ACUHO-I.

Schuh, J. H. (Ed.). (1984). *A handbook for student group advisers,* No. 37. Alexandria, VA: American College Personnel Association.

Terrell, M. C., & Cuyjet, M. J. (1994). *Developing student government leadership.* New directions for student services, No. 66. San Francisco: Jossey-Bass.

Werring, C. J. (1984). The purpose of residence hall student government: One conceptual model. *Journal of College and University Student Housing, 14*(1), 7-13.

Wyatt, K., & Stoner, K. L. (1984). A NACURH "White Paper" on residence hall government. *Journal of College and University Student Housing, 14*(1), 3-6.

Norbert W. Dunkel
University of Florida

Cindy L. Spencer
University of Nebraska at Kearney

A NACURH "White Paper" on Residence Hall Government

Ken Stoner
University of Kansas

Kevin Wyatt
Past NACURH Chairperson, 1981-82

A NACURH "White Paper"

During the 1982 mid-year meeting, the Board of Directors of the National Association of College and University Residence Halls (NACURH) adopted a long-range goal of aiding the development of residence hall associations (RHAs) on campuses across the nation. As the first step in the process, NACURH contacted 42 housing professionals across the country. Twenty-seven replied, for a response rate of 64.3%. All surveyed were professional housing staff members at member institutions of NACURH and the Association of College and University Housing Officers-International (ACUHO-I). The persons contacted had been specifically identified by the student leaders of NACURH as individuals who were considered consultants in the field on student organizations and leadership. Because student leaders were seeking and heeding the advice of those individuals, the NACURH officers decided to write each resource person identified and produce a compilation of their comments as a "White Paper" on residence hall government.

The following "White Paper" was prepared to share the professional advice of our colleagues on a broader basis with the constituencies of both NACURH and ACUHO-I. Those individuals surveyed were asked simply to provide an open-ended commentary on what they considered to be the two or three most fundamental principles in organizing and maintaining a residence hall association on campus. An RHA was defined as a leadership organization representative of the various halls on each campus. Related articles have been referenced only if specifically identified by one or more of the respondents. The information obtained was organized in a fashion that produced a hierarchy of five sequential criteria for the initial development of an RHA or for the reevaluation and improvement of an existing RHA:

1. Determine the need for the organization.
2. Identify support for the organization.
3. Obtain a source of income for the organization.
4. Ensure effective leadership within the organization.
5. Develop methods of system maintenance within the organization.

Although specifically dealing with campus-wide residence hall governments, this information is applicable to any self-governing student organization from an individual living unit to university-wide student government.

Determine the Need

The first criterion to consider when establishing or strengthening an RHA is need. It is essential that students within a particular residence hall system express the desire for the establishment of an association. Too many organizations are initiated without recognizing the needs on which to build the future which, in turn, hinders essential early success. It is possible for administrators to facilitate this need or desire in students by expressing interest in obtaining input from a representative council. Yet the decision to establish an RHA must be based on the students' conviction that the RHA can meet expressed needs of the residents.

From these needs, the RHA shapes its future by clearly defining its purpose and identifying long-range as well as short-term goals. It is through this process that students, as well as staff, gain a broad understanding of the purposes of the RHA.

Time spent in constructing a statement of purposes is most crucial during the early stages of development. Many new RHAs waste their first years trying to justify their existence. If the organization's mission is defined, students will better understand the parameters of their involvement and will have some built-in direction for setting and achieving goals.

Appropriate long- and short-term goals of any organization can be evaluated on five bases: purpose compatibility, practicality, feasibility, attainability, and measurability. In addition, fledgling organizations should be encouraged not only to work on major issues and projects of greatest importance to the students, but also to work on items that will bring the organization early accomplishments. These early successes will keep people involved and excited and will establish credibility not only with residents but also with staff. The goals statement should lay out a plan of action for the future. The plan must be tempered with the understanding that growth will be slow. Often it is a temptation of newly formed organizations to attempt to conquer the world rather than focus on smaller, although no less significant, goals. The successful residence hall student governance program will rise to the top in an environment that promotes goals, priorities, and plans (Werring, 1981).

Identify Support

The second criterion needed for a successful RHA is support. This support is best when it comes from all levels of the institution, rather than being limited to student constituents. It is the staff and higher administrators that give student organizations, particularly new ones, the needed sense of real importance. An effective RHA will be obligated by those it serves to review any and all institutional policies applicable to student residential life, and this input should be fostered and welcomed by the staff as one means of improving the environment cooperatively with the student consumers (Nettles, 1976). Sincere administrative support will allow students to disagree with the housing staff or higher institutional administrators without fear of reprisal. Allowing students to exert their independence and autonomy can facilitate individual development and increase organizational productivity for the system. Both staff and students are working in their own ways toward the improvement of the residential living environment. If students feel the issues they raise in a mature and responsible manner are accepted, they will be much more effective and will learn the skills and techniques associated with responsible leadership.

Staff support alone is not sufficient to maintain the student organization. The RHA must also have the support of the subordinate hall governments within its jurisdiction. A strong base of grassroots student support is essential if the organization is to continue over a long period of time. If hall leaders view their building associations as separate entities from the RHA, and not as part of a centralized system with common needs, goals, and objectives, it will be difficult for the RHA to function as a body that provides leadership for all of the halls. It is also important for each subordinate governing unit within the residential environment to have a unique mission to minimize jurisdictional difficulties and to provide clear guidelines for the residents. By combining resources, skills, and ideas the entire residence hall system will benefit. It is imperative that the RHA continuously solicit support and cooperation from the various hall associations, other student organizations, and individual students.

Consistently open channels of constructive communication are critical to the perceived credibility of the RHA (Stoner & Yokie, 1969). Openness on the part of both students and staff will quickly develop solid relationships and reinforce the team or "we" concept. It behooves the housing staff to foster this credibility whenever possible; the credibility of the RHA will increase the effectiveness of the housing staff by having a representative parallel organization.

This principle of two-way communication serves as the base of interaction not only between the RHA and the housing staff, but also between the RHA and other students and student groups. Moreover, this communication process can be expanded to become a major force of interaction with other institutions in the state and region, and eventually across the nation. A diverse exchange of ideas will strengthen any student government organization; communication is the first step in this exchange.

For both new and old RHAs the most important message the staff communicates to students is encouragement. Student leaders easily become discouraged by working between a transient "now"-oriented constituency and the long-range departmental planning and administrative timetable. Thus, a pat on the back or a simple thank-you note will often keep people involved and productive. Every student needs some type of positive stroke or reward for taking the time to work with the RHA. There are many ways to do this, and careful thought should be given to this form of support (see also Chapter 6).

Without a doubt, the most effective means of administrative support is the leadership and commitment provided by the professional staff member serving in the role of adviser to the RHA. This staff member will not only clarify direction for students, but will also serve as a role model and an active physical reminder of the institution's commitment to the development of both student government and individual leaders. The adviser must be willing to devote many hours and to expend a good deal of energy toward the creation and development of the RHA, often with minimal personal recognition in the process.

As long as there is an annual turnover of officers within the RHA, the need for a professional in an advisory role remains critical. The framework and underlying awareness of the RHA's role on campus comes from having an adviser who provides for an orderly transition from year to year.

Obtain a Source of Income

The third criterion for consideration when organizing a residence hall association is an independent and guaranteed source of income. This funding often comes from the housing office through some type of monetary allotment, such as a per-person amount based on occupancy, paid directly to the RHA at the beginning of each academic term. Some housing operations contractually guarantee dues collection or provide another means of raising money. Other funding sources for RHAs often include a percentage of vending commissions, refrigerator rentals, and/or solicitation of individual memberships in the association. Regardless of source, the monies must be guaranteed and the source of income reliable (see also Chapter 11).

RHA finances should be totally separate from those of any other campus group. Monetary control provides the autonomy needed to ensure that the efforts of the RHA are directed toward the goals of the residents and are free from the influence of other governing bodies. A method for periodic audits of students' accounts should be established to ensure that the use of monies is appropriate and in the best interests of all residents. Audits which correspond with officers' terms or the academic calendar are usually considered most useful.

Ensure Effective Leadership

Leadership is the fourth criterion necessary for the RHA to be a responsible, well-functioning unit. When starting an RHA, there is opportunity to carefully select officers and co-workers. The initiators of the RHA should consider selecting a group with a common goal of meeting the needs of students and serving them in the best way possible. Care should be taken to ensure that this group is representative of the campus residence hall system and encompasses a wide variety of individual interests and talents. This core group will set the stage for future years, and it would be helpful if those selected also possessed charisma, some knowledge of student government, an awareness of student needs, and a high level of energy. Above all else though, they must be responsible to their constituents and to each other. It does not take long for residents and administrators alike to distinguish between leaders who first serve others and leaders who serve themselves first.

Once an RHA is established, development of student leadership is essential to the maintenance of a stable, functional, and effective organization. Students with decision-making authority must be taught to assess the needs of constituents, to formulate skills, and to implement programs and activities in a timely manner. Where students do not have final authority, they must be taught the strategies of influencing change (Bowling, 1980). This commitment to growth and development must be accepted by the staff and transmitted not only to, but also by, the students themselves. Through a system of overlapping or staggering terms, experienced leaders can and should be encouraged to assume the roles of mentor and teacher. Topics for both formal and informal training could include group dynamics; leadership styles; team building; how to run a meeting, set an agenda, and motivate volunteers; and other self-governance-oriented material. Although the primary purpose of student leadership training is to facilitate an RHA, individual student growth is no less important. Thus, sessions in communications skills, assertiveness training, time management, and other interpersonal-skill-building areas are equally important to the development process.

Develop Methods of System Maintenance

The fifth criterion for organizing and maintaining an RHA is system maintenance. Maintaining an organization over time will require as much, if not more, energy as periodically modifying or changing the organization (Fredericksen, 1980). Even the most efficient and stable organization will progressively deteriorate and become disorganized in the absence of constant and personal attention.

The best method to ensure that system maintenance will occur is to define an appropriate structure that maximizes student participation and involvement while accomplishing organizational objectives that are fundamental to the success of the RHA. In addition, developing an organizational structure parallel to that of the sponsoring administrative body provides natural communication links at all levels while fostering mutual support between the two organizations.

The key to organizational success is flexibility. The RHA must have the flexibility and commitment to deal with concerns, issues, and proposals as they arise. These may range from the perceived impact of enrollment fluctuations on the RHA to student demands for more visitation hours or coed housing. Also, successful RHAs must be prepared to positively channel the spontaneous release of energy associated with such events as the winning of a key ball game, the first snow on a relatively warm day, or a power outage in one of the halls.

Continuous and comprehensive assessment of student needs provides the basis of the most widely used methods for determining actions needed to maintain the system. A direct by-product of any assessment should be a master plan serving one to three years to be used when setting long- and short-term goals. Through assessment, the staff of the RHA can gain valuable insight into timely programming and useful organizational change, thus keeping the RHA fine-tuned to meet the students' needs.

Other forms of system maintenance, often considered more practical, are equally important. Providing office and meeting space for the students is essential during their initial search for organizational identity. An office can add to group cohesiveness by providing a place the officers can call their own. Encouraging regular meetings, appointing an adviser, and giving the RHA access to such services as duplication and typing will serve as daily reminders of the administration's support of student government and the RHA.

Finally, a form of system maintenance being recognized more and more for both immediate effects and long-term impact is attendance and participation at residence-hall-oriented conferences. These conferences range in size from specialty conclaves of three or four institutions to nationally endorsed conventions of over 100 institutions. The program list is impressive, including educational "swap shops" and forums that range from organizational foci on hall representation and financing to such individual topics as communication skills and motivation. Small informal discussions among residence hall leaders at these conferences will have a positive impact on those present. Residence hall conferences are geographically dispersed; at least one will occur in a location close to virtually every college or university in the United States. Attendance at these meetings will certainly enhance system maintenance.

In summation, a successful RHA will determine needs, identify support, obtain a source of income, ensure leadership, and develop system maintenance. These five criteria constitute the thoughts and ideas which are actively being solicited by student leaders of RHAs across the country and which are being expressed by professional staff members on the member campuses of NACURH and ACUHO-I. NACURH has surveyed and compiled the responses of these consultants in order to share them in a "White Paper" on residence hall government.

References

Bowling, S. R. (1980). Student governance and leadership. In D. A. DeCoster & P. Mable (Eds.), *Personal education and community development in college residence halls.* Washington, DC: American College Personnel Association.

Fredericksen, C. F. (1980). The future is now. *Journal of College and University Student Housing, 10*(2), 3-6.

Nettles, M. (1976). Toward governance of the students by the students. *Journal of College and University Student Housing, 5*(2), 25-27.

Stoner, K. L., & Yokie, J. A. (1969). Residence halls and the future. *Journal of the National Association of Student Personnel Administrators, 7*(2), 72-75.

Werring, C. (1981). Student government: A priority? *Residential Sharing Via Proposals, 11*(1), 1-2.

Wyatt, K., & Stoner, K. (1984). A NACURH "White Paper" on residence hall government. *Journal of College and University Student Housing, 14*(1), 3-6.

This article was revised and reprinted with permission of the *Journal of College and University Student Housing.*

The First Advising Position

Pam Boersig
Adrian College

Evelyn Wallington
Clemson University

The First Advising Position

Advising can be a frustrating, challenging, and rewarding experience. Staff often take on advising duties with limited experience and understanding of what advising is and what it means to be a residentially-based student government adviser. Furthermore, advising a student group is very different from being a student member. This chapter presents advice for a new adviser in several areas including what an adviser is, roles of an adviser, advising styles and techniques, importance of group development, and several advising issues.

What An Adviser Is

According to the *American Heritage College Dictionary* (Costello, 1995), an adviser is a person who gives advice or makes a recommendation as to a decision or course of action. In a residence hall setting, an adviser's duties vary. Typically, the residence hall association (RHA) makes decisions with input from the adviser rather than vice versa. Common themes shared by RHA advisers include:

1. Advisers suggest and provide input but do not have decision-making authority.
2. Membership is made up of any resident who lives on the floor or in the hall. Executive officers are voted into the position by the student membership, not selected by the adviser.
3. Advisers do not share in the group limelight. The group exists to serve students and not the adviser. With training, students should facilitate meetings and coordinate programs. The adviser will be in the background, encouraging and supporting students' efforts.
4. Rewards are generally intrinsic in nature and depend upon the accomplishments and personal growth of the group. Advisers are not guaranteed that personal growth will occur and student appreciation may not be apparent for several years.
5. The adviser is not a voting member of the group. With the adviser's input, students must decide what the issues are.
6. Advising responsibilities are assigned by a third party, usually the supervisor or department director. For most advisers, this component is part of their position description.

Roles of the Adviser

The role of the adviser is not parental. He or she needs to establish a good working relationship with the group based on respect and genuine caring and concern. Several adviser roles demonstrate care and concern (Schuh, 1984).

Educator/Trainer

The adviser has a responsibility to educate group members about the mission and purpose of the organization, including knowledge regarding the department and institution, and to provide training for group members, particularly executive members. The success of the group may depend on the scope of training provided by the adviser. Most groups require basic training. This effort takes time but the payoff is well worth the time commitment. The challenge for advisers is how to stay motivated with a new group when the training topics do not change. What is old hat for an adviser is a new ground-breaking issue for the group. Advisers would do well to recognize their training limits and stay in touch with their own developmental needs.

Resource Person

Students will often bring their concerns to advisers first, due to their established relationship. The adviser should be knowledgeable of campus and community resources including human resources, audiovisual resources, and unanticipated resources. Review the purpose, functions, and activities of the group to make sure they are empowered with the appropriate information to succeed with the goal at hand. A group cannot be expected to program successfully if they are not knowledgeable about speakers, food service, facilities, publicity, and audiovisual information.

Continuity Source

The adviser provides the historical perspective. The adviser is the informal historian and provides the rationale for past goals and projects. This role should not be ignored or minimized. Perspective from the past provides the group with critical background information that it may need to move forward. As an adviser, encourage the group to keep good records and preserve accurate files so there is a sense of history for future students.

Fiscal Agent

This role is becoming more important as student groups are held accountable to student members and to the institution regarding fiscal responsibility. Budgets and other fiscal matters should be voted on by the constituents. Fiscal decisions should be preserved in writing and made public to members. At many institutions, students provide recommendations to the department staff who make final fiscal decisions. Advisers need to be very knowledgeable of financial guidelines.

Counselor

Student members will approach advisers with a variety of issues that may be personal, academic, or organizational in nature. Students may also approach advisers with concerns about other group members. Advisers are discouraged from giving advice, but instead should provide objective options and appropriate referrals. At times, students will self-disclose personal information the adviser may not be ready to hear. Be a good listener and reflect back to them. Understand personal counseling limits, making certain to refer students when appropriate.

Group Facilitator/Conflict Mediator

Group members will not always agree or see eye to eye on the issues. An adviser can be assured that conflict is a regular, ongoing part of the position. What is an appropriate adviser response? Let group members confront each other and work through the concern with their peers. Students are less fragile than might be believed. Effective conflict resolution is a basic training topic that should be covered early in the year. Advisers can role model and role play effective confrontation techniques with group members.

Negative Adviser Roles

There are also some negative adviser roles that should be avoided, including becoming the boss, parent, manipulator or center of attention. The group does not exist to serve the adviser. It is fairly common for a new adviser to resort to negative advising roles when times get tough. Becoming the boss or telling the group what to do and how to do it might take care of the immediate problem but it fails to foster autonomy or personal development. As the adviser, one is not the parent. It is not appropriate to take on personal issues or concerns as if the students were children. Students should be treated with respect and as mature adults. Furthermore, manipulating the group by serving as the center of attention while in the adviser role is counterproductive at best and could result in personal damage to the students. These negative roles are self-serving and fail to foster the development of students.

Adviser Do's and Don'ts

How can an adviser stay positive and energized? By following some simple techniques, advising can be enjoyable and rewarding.

1. An adviser should establish good rapport with the group while maintaining professionalism. An adviser should not become such a student advocate that the objective viewpoint is lost.
2. An adviser should attend the organization's meetings and programs. An adviser should not assume the group will handle everything and does not need an adviser in attendance at events.
3. An adviser should suggest, not impose.
4. An adviser should work with the executive board. An adviser should not do the work of the president or executive board.
5. An adviser should help ensure that the group examines all sides of an issue by being a devil's advocate.
6. An adviser should help develop team spirit and cooperation. An adviser should not allow the organization to become a one-person operation.
7. An adviser should help group members develop assertiveness. An adviser should not allow the group to be laissez-faire or autocratic.
8. An adviser should have a relationship with the group that allows growth and development. An adviser should not be the parent or reactive administrator.
9. An adviser should treat members as individuals. An adviser should not assume that group attitudes, needs, issues, and personalities will remain the same year to year, or semester to semester.

Advising Styles

Advising roles and do's and don'ts are important basics to promote adviser effectiveness. What about the person who wants to be an exceptional adviser? What techniques separate a good adviser from an excellent adviser? Advising styles and techniques help differentiate between good and great advisers. This section will elaborate on effective communication styles including availability, serving as a consultant/coach, guidelines for effective advising, and important personal qualities that an adviser should possess.

Advisers should be aware that no single communication or leadership style is most effective. An effective style is dependent upon many variables, including the maturity level of the group, motivational factors affecting student leaders, and the communication styles of student leaders. Are students new to their positions? Do they have a basic understanding of the system and how it works? Are the students motivated by tasks, people, or both? Do they prefer to operate with a structured schedule or a more flexible one? In order to be successful, advisers will need to adjust their style and adapt to the students. As students mature, they may adapt more to the adviser's style. In the beginning, advisers need to be more directive and less developmental. As student leaders become more comfortable in their positions, advisers can modify the structure and direction. Advisers should attend house and executive meetings on a regular basis as a participant, not as the facilitator. A weekly meeting with the president individually will encourage regular communication and provide a safe environment to discuss concerns and issues. Additionally, monthly meetings with each executive member allow the adviser to establish individual relationships with those students as well. Furthermore, attendance at programs demonstrates concern for the group. Attendance also affords valuable insight when it is time to evaluate a project or program.

Availability

Availability is always an issue for the busy adviser. Regular meetings minimize a crisis intervention mode of thinking. Students should know that an adviser is available for important matters, but most issues can wait until regularly scheduled meetings. Moreover, students should have a clear understanding of the distinction between issues that necessitate consultation with the adviser and decisions that can be made independently. If an adviser must be consulted on every matter, students will question their own ability and effectiveness.

Consultant/Coach

Acting as a consultant/coach is a significant focus of advising and ultimately where an adviser wants to be with their group. Consulting is not a skill that is learned overnight. There is a delicate balance between providing input and encouraging the group to make independent decisions. Ensuring that the group is on track with the mission or goals is a critical component of coaching. Additionally, encouragement of group members will vary from person to person. Some members will need lots of support, while others will need only a little. Finally, written notes of appreciation are always welcome.

Guidelines For Effective Advising

1. Be an educator. Make sure the group is functioning and understands group dynamics.
2. Help the group develop a realistic plan of action relevant to their mission statement and goals.
3. Know group members and their individual and group needs.
4. Be sincerely committed to the organization. Let members know the adviser cares about their well being.
5. Be approachable and available to the students. Attend their meetings and activities.
6. Provide appropriate critical feedback through individual meetings. Participate in the evaluation of programs and activities.
7. Share in the group's successes and failures. Help guide the group to success.
8. Be ready for new experiences. Be open to learning.
9. Know available resources and provide this information readily.
10. Have fun!

Personal Qualities

Several personal qualities will bolster an adviser's effectiveness. There is no substitute for honesty and an assertive interpersonal style. A sense of humor and openness to new ideas and approaches will be beneficial. Patience, genuine concern for students, and flexibility will go a long way toward increasing an adviser's enjoyment of the position. Advisers who need a lot of structure and order should adjust their style or it will be a long year for the students and the adviser!

Importance of Group Development and Training

One of an adviser's most important duties is the growth and development of the individual and the group. Training must be ongoing and must focus on group members as individuals as well as the positions they hold within the organization. Additionally, group development activities should help the group maximize its potential while allowing for creativity and fun. Residence hall government provides an avenue for students to be successful. This will occur if they are provided opportunities to learn from their own life experience. Training must be adjusted so that student needs are met. Therefore, if adviser and student government training needs are not congruent, the training should focus on students' needs. Basic training should provide information about policies and procedures. Students also need to understand how they fit into the big picture and what their purpose is in relation to the RHA. Training provides an opportunity for students and staff to interact with each other.

Training Components

An effective training model may consist of several components, including post-election training, pre-fall workshop, retreats, leadership conferences, personal development, and leadership class for credit (Boersig, 1989).

Post-election training involves a transition with outgoing officers, including goal setting and planning for the new year, team-building activities, and budget preparation. This training component may take place in one day or over the course of several weeks. New officers will also need individual time with outgoing officers. Sorting through and organizing files, as well as reading program activity evaluations and reports will contribute to the effectiveness of this transition.

Pre-fall training may be co-sponsored by the RHA and the residence life department or with other student organizations. Topics that should be covered include position expectations, goal setting, budgeting, motivation and recognition, programming, running a meeting, campus resources, policies and procedures, and leadership conferences.

A pre-fall workshop may last two days or a week. Team building, group icebreakers, meals, and social activities are critical to the success of this event. Personal invitations may be issued to hall government leaders, staff members, and other interested students. A variety of facilitators conducting interactive activities will make pre-fall workshop more enjoyable. Co-sponsoring the pre-fall workshop with other campus organizations provides an excellent opportunity to develop communication among groups and may facilitate program co-sponsorship later in the year. This is also an excellent way to pool resources and minimize costs.

Off-campus retreats are a great way to strengthen group bonds. Freedom from interruptions allows the group to focus on critical issues. Retreats may occur at any time during the year but may be more effective when the group has been together for a few weeks or months. Team building that relies on self-disclosure and/or physical challenges such as a teams course or trust exercises may be appropriate. Properly interpreted assessments, such as the Myers-Briggs Type Indicator (MBTI; Lawrence, 1993) or the Communicating Styles Survey (Mok, 1975), provide members with insight into how they can work more effectively with each other.

Leadership conferences such as NACURH or regional affiliations are great opportunities for learning. These gatherings offer individual and institutional interaction including programs, meals, and social activities. Conferences serve as motivators and energizers for returning student leaders. For new student leaders, opportunities abound for program idea exchanges. Conferences are also a great opportunity for advisers to share concerns and renew themselves (see also Chapters 13 and 15).

Several institutions offer leadership courses for academic credit. At The University of Iowa, a leadership class for new students is provided through the College of Education. The course encompasses theory development, interpersonal skill building, group interaction, and current leadership issues. The Center for Creative Leadership located in Greensboro, North Carolina, distributes a sourcebook that contains a leadership course syllabus, suggested textbooks, and audiovisual resources. Group projects, written tests, a world leader reaction paper, and leadership interviews are some of the typical leadership class components. Academic classes may provide an additional training opportunity for interested students.

Personal development activities exist in various forms including individual assessment and ongoing support groups. Typical personal development activities may include skill-building topics such as assertiveness, stress management, and conflict resolution. Individual assessment allows for personalized skill development such as public speaking, meeting facilitation, budget preparation, and self-esteem. Personal development encourages an adviser and student to focus on specific issues and to develop a one-on-one relationship. Trust and risk taking must be present for personal development to be successful.

Resource Information

Information and knowledge are valuable resources that empower students. Print and human resources are often overlooked as training components. Manuals that include financial guidelines, programming tips, support data, and campus and community resources are staple items. Parliamentary procedure that includes bills, resolutions, and constitutional or bylaw changes should be a part of representative training.

Advisers should help students learn about print, human, and audiovisual resources in the campus and community via newsletters, training programs, effective student task delegation, and individual or group meetings. Newsletters could focus on a different campus or community resource in each issue. Campus and community resource persons can be invited to house meetings. An ongoing speaker series could be established. Students learn by doing. Effective student task delegation that focuses on these resources is the best teacher. Encourage students to utilize campus resources. Allow students to make their own arrangements rather than doing it for them. Students can then teach each other and feel an important part of the training process.

What role should the adviser play in relation to training and group development? Is the adviser the coordinator, promoter, or trainer? Should the adviser be involved with training or should the students decide what the training focus will be? The adviser's role is dependent on the student group, its membership, and members' maturity. No two groups or individuals require the same training program.

The adviser has a responsibility to promote the concept of training with the students. Ideally, the adviser and students decide together the relevant topics and most effective format for those topics. Facilitating group development is a chance for students to observe the adviser in another venue. Furthermore, utilizing other presenters allow students to experience first-hand other campus resources and introduces them to a variety of learning formats.

Issues Advisers Face

First-time advisers face a number of issues as they adjust to their new role. These issues can be grouped together in three broad categories: being an adviser versus being a participant, becoming comfortable with the adviser role, and creating a balance within the group.

Being an Adviser versus Being a Participant

One of the major adjustments new advisers face is the transition from being an active participant in a group to taking a less active role. Advisers often experience a struggle in going from being hands-on to a more hands-off approach. In learning to be more of an adviser and less of a participant, the new adviser may deal with feeling a loss of control and learning how to let students fail.

Feeling a loss of control. The adviser may have been the student who was in charge and got things done. Now as the adviser, he or she does not control group members or the decisions they make; instead, the adviser assists students in making their own decisions. The adviser does not make decisions for the group, but is responsible for providing feedback, interpretations, and guidance so that group members can make their own decisions. For some advisers, being less directive and more of a coach can be very difficult.

Since the adviser does not select the membership, this can add to the feeling of loss of control. The adviser must adjust to the fact that those who want to participate will choose to do so. The election of officers is also beyond their control. Here is another example of being the coach and then learning to accept results.

The adviser must also give up control in expressing personal opinions. Advising is not a vehicle to voice one's personal opinions to influence the group. Since they do not have voting rights, advisers must learn to deal with the decisions of the group. The goal is to assist students in making a sound decision, not making it for them. Student leaders who become advisers often struggle with the use of their voice in an appropriate manner.

Letting students "fail." Often, this is one of the hardest challenges, since many advisers want to protect students from failing. Advisers often do not want to risk allowing something to fail so that students can learn from the experience. Detaching oneself from the desire to reach in and save a program is difficult to do. Advisers learn to follow up with progress, but do not actually do the work to ensure a program's success.

Advisers may experience pressure from the institution to have successful groups and programs. New advisers may not feel comfortable in letting students or supervisors know that it is often best for students to learn from mistakes. More learning and future successes can come from these valuable teachable moments, but how does an adviser explain that to a supervisor or students who want to know why he or she did not tell them what to do? Educating others on the value of not reaching in to save the program is important.

Suggestions for the New Adviser:

1. Utilize an assessment tool to help discover where the need for control is. This will assist an adviser in discovering more about one's style, as well as giving more of a definition of what control means. Available tools include the Adviser's Inventory (Jones & Banet, 1978), LEAD model (Hersey & Blanchard, 1988), and the MBTI (Lawrence, 1993).

2. Set expectations with the group. Talk with them to find out how they want or need adviser input. Explain to them an adviser's role in decision making.

3. Discuss why an adviser may not be able to save a project. Utilize teachable moments to help students explore what they have learned in the situation and how they can make changes in the future. Discuss their definitions of success and failure. An adviser may have a very different definition than students.

4. Talk privately with the supervisor to find out what types of advisers the group previously had. Knowing about the styles of previous advisers may make transitioning smoother.

The First Advising Position

Becoming Comfortable in the New Role

Advisers need to allow time to learn more about the group and the institution and their expectations, and to adjust to the new role. This process can be facilitated in several ways.

Know resources. This is a challenge for the adviser at a new institution, who may feel that students know more than he or she does. Be open (and smart) enough to acknowledge that they have more knowledge and that a lot can be learned from them. Take notes on resources and pass them along to others. Knowing resources empowers the students.

Learn the philosophy and policies of the group and the institution, including formal and informal structures. The adviser will be called upon to help interpret policies and to provide the staff interpretation of issues. Learn about the history of the group within the institution. This can assist an adviser in the direction to take with the group.

Learn to be patient. This slow process does not take place overnight. The adviser and the group need to take the time to understand how the group forms, its expectations, and its limitations. An adviser must be able to sit back, listen, and process. Knee-jerk reactions will create an impression of the adviser as a reactive administrator instead of one who helps students solve problems.

Learn to accept feelings of incompetence. It can be difficult for the new adviser to gauge how the group is progressing. Lack of feedback from supervisors, as well as not having colleagues at the institution, can add to this. Set up evaluation times with supervisors and students to get feedback from them. This is a learning process and, once again, patience is important.

Suggestions for the New Adviser:

1. Meet with the group to develop an understanding of each person's roles. Utilize the adviser do's and don'ts list and the Adviser's Inventory (Jones & Banet, 1978) to develop roles and expectations.
2. Talk with the supervisor to find out the supervisor's — and the institution's — expectations and philosophies. Share any of the above tools that have been used with students. The supervisor or colleagues may also complete a questionnaire to better understand their perspectives. The adviser can thus acquire more direction on whom and how to educate (see Chapter 3 for more strategies on discussing adviser responsibilities).
3. Realize that there will be setbacks at times. Group development is a process that takes time.
4. Meet with other departments, such as student activities and student services, to learn about available resources. Initiate contact to develop a positive rapport with them. Advisers can be on the same side and not in competition.

Creating a Balance

Often, the new adviser needs to balance the adviser role with other job responsibilities. There are very few professionals or even paraprofessionals who are "just" advisers. In their zeal to become the best adviser ever, advisers can often get in over their heads and neglect other job-related functions. Learning to give appropriate amounts of time and energy to all parts of the job is important. Issues in this category include being a student advocate without losing professionalism and being an adviser versus being a friend.

Being a student advocate without losing professionalism. Be wary of creating the impression that one can only think like a student and not an administrator. As a professional, an adviser needs to help students understand the role within administration and that there are two sides to issues (student vs. professional). New advisers often come close to crossing the line of professionalism to gain the respect of the students.

Being an adviser versus being a friend. Learning to tell students "no" is not easy. The adviser has the hard task of keeping a professional distance with students and knowing when to say "I cannot help." Many new advisers are seeking the support of students and may know more about how to be a friend than how to be an adviser. Being an adviser means informing or educating students about what their relationship will be and where the boundaries are.

Suggestions for the New Adviser:

1. Write out expectations of the students. Be specific.
2. Make a commitment not to spend every free moment with students or on the job.
3. Utilize role plays or games to address issues. This can be less threatening with students and have more positive effects.
4. Have students write out their expectations of an adviser. Be willing to make expectations a two-way street.
5. Work to develop professional peer relationships within the office environment. Seek advice from more "seasoned" professionals and supervisors.

In the end, advising can be a rewarding experience. Advisers have an opportunity to see student development in action. Students become self-actualized and experience success right before our eyes. Advising is a wonderful opportunity not to be missed. Get ready for the experience of a lifetime!

References

Boersig, P. (1989). *RH Positive: Effective residence hall government training models.* UMR-ACUHO Pre-Conference Workshop, Lincoln, Nebraska.

Costello, R. B. (Ed.). (1993). *American heritage college dictionary* (3rd ed.). Boston: Houghton Mifflin.

Hersey, P., & Blanchard, K. H. (1988). *Management of organizational behavior.* Englewood Cliffs, NJ: Prentice-Hall.

Jones, J. E., & Banet, A. E., Jr. (1978). Critical consulting incidents inventory. In J. W. Pfeiffer & P. Jones (Eds.), *1978 Annual handbook for group facilitators.* LaJolla, CA: University Associates.

The First Advising Position

Lawrence, G. (1993). *People types and tiger stripes* (3rd ed.). Gainesville, FL: Center for Applied Psychological Types.

Mok, P. (1975). *Communicating Styles Survey.* Richardson, TX: Training Associates.

Schuh, J. (Ed.). (1984). *A handbook for student group advisors.* Publication number 37. Alexandria, VA: American College Personnel Association.

The Adviser's Inventory

Instructions: Following are 19 critical incidents that require the adviser to respond in some manner. For each incident there are three alternative actions that the adviser might consider. Rank order the options in each item to indicate what you would probably do in each of these situations. Write "1" in front of your first choice, "2" in front of your second choice, and "3" for your least preferred choice. Do not omit any items.

1. You receive a phone call that is a request for you to make a third-party intervention between the caller and another person. You say:
   a. ___ "How do you feel about the situation?"
   b. ___ "I should talk to the other person first."
   c. ___ "Can you give me some background information?"
2. During a training event, a participant interrupts by criticizing your "Mickey Mouse activity." You say:
   a. ___ "I'm concerned that you're upset."
   b. ___ "Let me reiterate the goals of the activity."
   c. ___ "Let's check it out with others and see what they think."
3. Three hours before a training event that is expected to be difficult, you meet your facilitator. You...
   a. ___ Get acquainted on a personal level.
   b. ___ Instruct the other person regarding your strategy.
   c. ___ Share data and negotiate roles.
4. Asked to attend a staff training day when you had something else planned, you ...
   a. ___ Indicate your appreciation of the scheduling problem.
   b. ___ Quote your time schedule, justify it, and offer to make a referral.
   c. ___ Explore alternatives regarding how an acceptable time can be negotiated.
5. In a confidential conversation, the hall president discloses that a committee chairperson's position is in jeopardy. You ...
   a. ___ Explore the hall president's dilemma and feelings.
   b. ___ Test the hall president's willingness to deal with the situation openly.
   c. ___ Explore alternative actions with the hall president that he or she might consider.

6. In planning your activities for the coming year with your colleagues, you uncover a basic disagreement on priorities. You ...
   a. ___ Make sure that your colleague's needs and feelings are acknowledged and carefully considered.
   b. ___ Let your needs be known and propose a planning strategy.
   c. ___ Approach the planning as an exercise in logical problem solving.
7. A supervisor calls you to ask your assessment of an RA who has recently attended one of your training sessions. You say ...
   a. ___ "I feel good about you taking an interest in your people."
   b. ___ "You're talking to the wrong person."
   c. ___ "Let's explore the implication of evaluating a person this way."
8. You have spent a significant amount of effort with your student organization in preparing a bid for a project for the Vice President for Student Affairs. Afterwards, you learn that the winning project had inside information that was not made available to your group. You...
   a. ___ Chastise yourself for your naiveté.
   b. ___ Request a full explanation.
   c. ___ Reconstruct the bidding process to look for possible learning for yourself.
9. You are discussing with the RHA president a proposed team-building session for the officers. When pressed to specify the concrete outcomes that you can guarantee, you ...
   a. ___ Affirm the person's concerns that the event will be productive.
   b. ___ Indicate that you can promise no particular results.
   c. ___ Work with the person on a statement of goals and strategy for evaluation.
10. Immediately prior to implementing a highly important activity, you experience a personally traumatic experience. You ...
   a. ___ Say to yourself, "The show must go on."
   b. ___ Postpone the activity.
   c. ___ Consult with others to explore the options.
11. You have had personal conversations with all the members of a student group and each has voluntarily expressed negative feelings about the behavior of a certain group member. In a team- building session, that person solicits feedback, but others have nothing to say. You ...
   a. ___ Reassure the other person in a light-hearted way that the silence could be positive.
   b. ___ Confront the group with the collusion.
   c. ___ Work with the person to make a specific request of individuals.
12. In planning a training event, your co-facilitator argues strongly to incorporate a favorite structured experience. You have serious reservations about it since the particular design involves deceiving the participants. You ...
   a. ___ Agree to go along with it in spite of your concerns.
   b. ___ Insist on the necessity of undoing the possible effects of deception.
   c. ___ Explore with your partner how the design furthers the goals.

13. In an RHA meeting, the members are ganging up on one person and bombarding that person with negative feedback. You say to the individual ...
    a. ___ " You must be feeling under attack."
    b. ___ "You don't have to be the target now unless you want to."
    c. ___ "What would be useful for you right now?"
14. In a problem-solving meeting of a group of student leaders, one member, whose work is far behind schedule, begins to cry. You ...
    a. ___ Assure the person that it's understandable to be upset.
    b. ___ Announce a break so that you can work with the person individually.
    c. ___ Explore with the entire group what can be done to work with the situation.
15. You have become increasingly concerned that the student organization you are advising is engaging in unethical practices in selecting committee personnel. In a meeting of the executive committee, sexist and racist attitudes are expressed. You ...
    a. ___ Say nothing lest you be perceived as judgmental.
    b. ___ Confront the group with your concerns about its policies.
    c. ___ Suggest that the group discuss ways that the organization might ensure fairness in selecting committee members.
16. In planning a team-building session, you become concerned that the student leader's major motivation for having the activity is to provide a basis for removing a student member. You ...
    a. ___ Reflect the student leader's feelings of frustration about the person.
    b. ___ State your misgivings and explain that you are unwilling to do a hatchet job.
    c. ___ Look for ways to resolve the conflict.
17. You have advised an organization's new president on how to conduct meetings. During the questions and answer period, the new president puts down one of the members for asking a stupid question. You ...
    a. ___ Attempt to help the member's feelings by making a joke of the situation.
    b. ___ Confront the president's behavior as detrimental to open inquiry.
    c. ___ Help the member phrase the question in order to get useful information from the president.
18. After hearing your academic and experiential credentials misrepresented during an introduction, you ...
    a. ___ Let the incident go unnoticed to avoid embarrassment to the person(s) talking about you.
    b. ___ Set the record straight.
    c. ___ Analyze with the other person(s) later how the data about you were distorted.

19. You are advising the hall president to conduct an open forum to discuss some improprieties in the management of the hall activities fund. The president becomes anxious and considers canceling the forum. You say ...
    a. ___ "I understand your reluctance to give bad news in public."
    b. ___ "It is important for you to consider the possible long-term consequences for such a decision."
    c. ___ "Let's look at some ways you might want to minimize the threat."

Scoring Instructions: Sum the points you assigned to the alternative "a" for the 19 items, and then do the same for "b" and "c." Enter those totals in the spaces below.

a. Support __________

b. Direction __________

c. Problem Solving __________

Interpretation: The major options available to the adviser in response to critical situations can be classified as follows:

Support: Being sensitive to the feelings of the person(s).

Direction: Controlling situations through confrontation and leadership.

Problem Solving: Assisting others through exploring facts, options, and strategies.

Look at your lowest score. This is your most probable, or knee-jerk response in difficult advising situations. Your middle score represents your most likely back-up posture. Your highest score, of course, indicates your least-used strategy or posture. Although this rank ordering may be situation-specific, it can give you an overall picture of your advising style in conflict situations.

Consider the distances between your scores. These can be thought of as a crude index of the thickness of your initial and back-up responses. A large score gap can indicate that you will persist for some time before changing to the approaches represented by higher scores.

Go back to the Adviser's Inventory items to study ways that one might more effectively manage strengths in critical advising situations. An adviser may wish to practice or plan new behaviors when these types of conflicts arise in the future.

The Adviser's Inventory relies heavily on the Critical Consulting Incidents Inventory (Jones & Banet, 1978).

Responsibilities of a Residence Hall Association Adviser

Diane Porter
University of Florida

Responsibilities of an RHA Adviser

Introduction

Have you ever seen a job description for a residence hall association (RHA) adviser? Or is "RHA adviser" just one line within a job description? Too often residence life staff members are given the role of adviser because someone has to do it, or it is just the nature of their position, and they are not given any direction in how to be an adviser. The purpose of this chapter is to identify the most important adviser responsibilities as determined from RHA advisers and RHA presidents. By identifying these responsibilities, training programs and position descriptions can be developed and enhanced to prepare staff to become effective advisers.

Dr. Ken Stoner (1988), former adviser to the National Association of College and University Residence Halls, Inc. (NACURH), identified the following responsibilities of an RHA adviser:

1. Advisers should serve as a source of support to the officers.
2. Advisers should keep their respective association's executive committee informed of new research developments and trends relating to residence halls and residential life.
3. Advisers should serve as role models, emphasizing the importance of student contributions to residential life programs across the country.
4. Advisers should be listeners and motivators.
5. Advisers should transmit historical information and assist their associations in maintaining an accurate historical perspective.
6. Advisers should assist in ensuring a smooth transition of new officers.
7. Advisers should serve as stimulators, generating new ideas for services and programs.
8. Advisers should serve as overseers of the association's budget and finances, making every effort to ensure solvency.
9. Advisers should be aware of the awards given out by the various regional and national associations. Recognition is one of the foundations of a residence hall association and advisers should make sure that appropriate recognition of individuals is not overlooked.
10. Advisers should also participate in their respective regional or national conferences and should submit program proposals for consideration.
11. Advisers should provide support to the various officers to make sure that their student responsibilities are being fulfilled. For example, advisers should provide instruction on time management and stress management while reinforcing the leaders' responsibilities to the RHA.

Dunkel and Porter (1996) expanded upon Stoner's list, creating a list of 30 potential responsibilities of RHA advisers. RHA advisers and presidents from 350 NACURH-affiliated institutions rated the importance of these adviser responsibilities. Before reading any further, please rate the responsibilities in Activity One, list your top five in rank order, and compare your rankings to the national norm. Later in this chapter, the top five responsibilities selected by both advisers and students will be explored in depth.

Activity One

For each item listed below, rate its importance as a responsibility of an RHA adviser on a scale of 1 (low) to 5 (high).

It is the adviser's responsibility to:

	Low Importance				High Importance
1. Serve as an information resource	1	2	3	4	5
2. Motivate and encourage members	1	2	3	4	5
3. Be a problem-solving agent	1	2	3	4	5
4. Maintain organizational records	1	2	3	4	5
5. Set goals	1	2	3	4	5
6. Provide vision	1	2	3	4	5
7. Attend meetings and activities	1	2	3	4	5
8. Run an RHA meeting	1	2	3	4	5
9. Reward and recognize others	1	2	3	4	5
10. Evaluate student volunteers	1	2	3	4	5
11. Orient new officers to their roles and responsibilities	1	2	3	4	5
12. Provide continuity for the organization	1	2	3	4	5
13. Recruit and retain members	1	2	3	4	5
14. Guarantee success of programs and activities	1	2	3	4	5
15. Be responsible for officer elections	1	2	3	4	5
16. Be an interpreter of university policies	1	2	3	4	5
17. Confront negative behavior	1	2	3	4	5
18. Know how to host a conference	1	2	3	4	5
19. Be a financial manager	1	2	3	4	5
20. Understand student/group development theories and models	1	2	3	4	5
21. Possess knowledge of legal issues	1	2	3	4	5
22. Know *Robert's Rules of Order*	1	2	3	4	5
23. Understand how diversity affects the RHA	1	2	3	4	5
24. Understand fund-raising	1	2	3	4	5
25. Know the national and regional bid and award processes	1	2	3	4	5
26. Possess knowledge of NACURH and its services	1	2	3	4	5
27. Attend regional and national conferences	1	2	3	4	5
28. Meet with RHA executive board	1	2	3	4	5
29. Know how to conduct a programming needs assessment	1	2	3	4	5
30. Know the steps to develop a program	1	2	3	4	5

Responsibilities of an RHA Adviser

Based on your answers, select the five most important responsibilities of an RHA adviser. List them below in order of importance:

1
2.
3.
4.
5.

Activity Two

Have your RHA president complete the same survey and then compare the rankings. Based on both sets of responses, answer the following questions:

1. What does your president perceive to be the most important adviser responsibilities?
2. Which responsibilities did you agree upon? Disagree?
3. How did your top five responsibilities compare? Top ten?
4. What issues do you need to address together now that you have this information?

This is a good activity to stimulate conversation between you and your president, to set expectations early in the year, or to identify and address problem areas later in the year.

Most Important Adviser Responsibilities

Based on the results of their survey of RHA advisers and presidents, Dunkel and Porter (1996) identified the ten most important adviser responsibilities.

Advisers

1. Meet with RHA executive board
2. Serve as an information resource
3. Interpret university policies
4. Attend meetings and activities
5. Motivate and encourage members
6. Understand student/group theories and models
7. Know the steps to develop a program
8. Provide continuity for the organization
9. Orient new officers to their roles and responsibilities
10. (tie) Reward and recognize others
    (tie) Understand how diversity affects the RHA

RHA Presidents

1. Meet with RHA executive board
2. Attend meetings and activities
3. Serve as an information resource
4. Interpret university policies
5. Motivate and encourage members
6. Understand how diversity development affects the RHA
7. Know the steps to develop a program
8. Attend regional and national conferences
9. Understand student/group development theories and models
10. Possess knowledge of NACURH and its services

How did you and your RHA president compare to other advisers and presidents across the country? The focus should now fall on those responsibilities that students indicated are important for the adviser. Interestingly, RHA advisers and presidents have agreed on the top five. The following is a detailed look at each of those five responsibilities and a list of questions for the RHA adviser and president to discuss in order to help the adviser fulfill the responsibilities and meet the expectations and needs of the president and general RHA membership.

Meeting with the RHA Executive Board

It is important to both advisers and executive board members to meet on a regular basis. These meetings can be with the entire executive board as a group and with individual board members. As a group, the adviser and executive board ideally would meet prior to the general RHA meeting. This should be a time when the executive board reviews what will be discussed in the general meeting, the adviser is invited to give input, and any questions or issues are addressed in preparation for the general meeting. This is the adviser's time to ask the difficult questions if it is perceived that questions may arise in the RHA meeting that board members may have to address. The adviser should also give the board enough information so the board is able to run the meeting without having to rely on the adviser. When this pre-meeting is adjourned, the adviser should feel comfortable with the executive board's ability to facilitate the general meeting; subsequently, the adviser can truly act in an advisory capacity during the general meeting.

The adviser should schedule individual weekly meetings with the RHA president. During this time, the president and the adviser may set goals and expectations, evaluate the progress of the executive board and the RHA membership, discuss solutions to potential problems, and plan for upcoming programs and events. This also gives the president an opportunity to discuss new ideas with the adviser, clarify information before sharing it with the executive board, and discuss concerns (e.g., executive board, RHA, academic, personal). Through a regularly scheduled individual meeting, the adviser and president continue to establish and develop their relationship. The format of this individual meeting could also be a model for the RHA president in meetings with other executive board members.

Questions to Address with the RHA President about Meeting with the Executive Board

1. When is a convenient time for the adviser and executive board to meet prior to the general RHA meeting?
2. What is the role of the adviser in meeting with the executive board?
3. When is a convenient time for the adviser and the RHA president to schedule an individual meeting? What is the format of this meeting?

Attending Meetings and Activities

Attending meetings and activities was ranked fourth in importance by advisers, but second by students. Every effort should be made to schedule these meetings during a time when both the adviser and the executive board can attend. However, there should also be a level of trust and empowerment present in the executive board when an adviser cannot attend every meeting. This can be established through the weekly individual meetings and pre-meetings. The high ranking of this adviser responsibility by

RHA presidents indicates that it is very important to students for advisers to be visible and show support for their events and programs. This also brings up an issue that must be addressed early in the year with the executive board. What are the students' expectations of the adviser for attending programs and activities? Are they realistic? This is an area in which the adviser and board may need to find a compromise and decide how often the adviser will attend programs and which programs are especially important to the board and warrant adviser participation. Participation in activities provides the adviser a chance to visit with RHA members and other students in informal settings, thus helping them establish a positive relationship with a housing administrator. The adviser should view this time as an opportunity to see the students on their own turf and to keep in touch with the student perspective on campus. It is also important that the adviser or a designee attend programs and activities to be of assistance if problems arise with contracts, facilities, performers, police, etc. As an institutional representative, the adviser must ensure the health and well-being of the students who attend programs or activities.

Questions to Address with the RHA President about Attending Meetings and Activities

1. When and where is the general RHA meeting? Is the time convenient for the adviser?
2. What is the role of the adviser at these meetings?
3. What expectations does the executive board have of the adviser about attendance at RHA programs and activities?
4. What is the role of the adviser at programs and activities?

Serving as an Information Resource Person

One of the primary roles of the adviser in meetings with the RHA president, executive board, and RHA membership is to serve as an information resource person. When executive board members need information or clarification in meetings, they should be able to turn to their adviser for assistance. If a question is asked during an RHA meeting, the executive board should first be allowed to answer the question or address the issue on their own. If they need additional information or clarification, they should ask the adviser to participate in the conversation. When this does happen, the adviser should be recognized by the board and then given the opportunity to speak. The adviser must be careful not to undermine anything the board has said previously and should offer just enough information to answer the question or address the issue. Remember, general meetings are facilitated by the president and the executive board; the adviser's role is to advise.

The adviser should also serve as a liaison to the housing office and student affairs division in the role of information resource person for the RHA. As pertinent information is received, it should be shared with the group. It is the role of the adviser to keep the RHA informed of upcoming events, projects, or decisions that may impact students in the residence halls.

In order to reply to questions, advisers should be well versed in several areas, including the housing operation's rules and regulations, forums and authorizations needed to hold programs and activities, budget approval processes, campus legal counsel, directors of various campus departments, and other student leaders and advisers of organizations on campus.

Questions to Address with the RHA President about Serving as an Information Resource

1. When and how will the adviser contribute with information during an RHA general meeting?
2. Will there be a signal between the president and the adviser in RHA meetings if the president needs some help or information? What is the signal?
3. Who is privy to information from other university entities which may or may not be appropriate to share with all students? How is this determined?
4. What are the most effective and efficient ways to share information with the RHA president, executive board, RHA membership, or residence hall students?

Interpreting University Policies

Interpreting university policies is similar to serving as an information resource person. As information is shared and events are planned, it is the adviser's responsibility to point out any potential violation of university policies if the executive board fails to recognize the violation. This requires the adviser to be knowledgeable regarding housing and university policies and to be aware of available resources if questions should arise that the adviser cannot answer (e.g., Director of Housing, Vice President for Student Affairs, the institution's legal counsel, etc.). It is also important to empower the students by sharing this information-gathering process so that they may become more self-sufficient decision makers in the future.

Questions to Address with the RHA President about Interpreting University Policies

1. What is the role of the adviser in interpreting policies? What is the best way for the adviser to address these issues with the RHA president, executive board, or general RHA membership?
2. How can the adviser empower the RHA president and other students to find answers for themselves?
3. What is the students' role in the policy revision process?

Motivating and Encouraging Members

According to Dunkel and Schuh (1998, p. 77), "Understanding what motivates students may be your single most desirable skill." RHA presidents and advisers ranked this responsibility fifth. It is the adviser's responsibility to motivate and encourage the executive board; in turn, it is the executive board's responsibility to motivate and encourage RHA members. If the adviser is effective in this area, the board will do a better job of recognizing the needs of members in terms of motivation and encouragement. It is important that both advisers and board members know how their respective groups are motivated and to which forms of encouragement they are most receptive. Most importantly, the adviser must be seen by board members and students as a motivated individual. (See Chapter 6 for additional information on motivation.)

Questions to Address with the RHA President about Motivation and Encouragement

1. What motivates the president to stay involved with the RHA? What motivates other executive board members?
2. How does the president prefer to be encouraged or recognized? Other executive board members?
3. What are some effective strategies for motivating and recognizing students involved in the RHA?
4. How will the adviser know when the RHA president is not feeling very motivated? What is the role of the adviser in this situation?

Additional Roles

While the focus of this chapter has been on the top five adviser responsibilities as identified by advisers and RHA presidents, it is important to note that the RHA adviser may fulfill a variety of roles throughout the course of a semester, an academic year, or even during the term of an executive board. Each group will have different needs, levels of individual development, and group dynamics. What works one time may not necessarily be effective with the next group or situation. While this leads to somewhat ambiguous roles for the adviser beyond the top five listed here, there are some constants to keep in mind.

Advisers do not run the RHA. The RHA is a mechanism students should be able to use to voice concerns, make policy suggestions and changes, and provide services and programs for fellow residents. Advisers have different forums to voice their own concerns about university policies, programs, and services on a more professional level and it is not appropriate to use the student organization for personal gain.

Students have the right and the capability to make their own decisions. An adviser should seldom reverse a decision made by the students. If the decision violates a university policy or breaks a law, the adviser should help the students make an alternate decision. If the decision has serious financial ramifications for the organization, the adviser should help students think through their decision. An adviser may ask challenging questions in order to get students to think about the implications of their decisions. This can be done without making the decision for them. Most of the time the students will make the right decision if the adviser guides them through it, empowers them to make the decision, and trusts them.

The adviser should be actively involved in helping student leaders acquire and develop the skills they need and desire to be successful. According to Astin (1977, 1985), Boyer (1987), Kuh and Schuh (1991), and Pascarella and Terenzini (1981), student success and satisfaction in college are directly related to student involvement in extracurricular activities. They also contend that students get involved in organizations and take on leadership roles for a variety of reasons (e.g., to satisfy a sense of belonging, purpose, or accomplishment; to make a difference; to develop transferable career skills; for personal growth in leadership abilities, etc.). It is the role of the adviser to know the executive officers well enough to determine what motivated them to get involved and then find ways to meet their needs or develop desired skills.

Advisers are the silent supervisors of the executive board. Dunkel and Schuh (1998) proposed a flowchart in which advising shares a number of characteristics with supervising. Advisers work with the executive board in team building; setting expectations and goals; communicating regularly and effectively, both verbally and nonverbally; recognizing one another's strengths and weaknesses; reflecting on organizational, academic, and personal issues; and evaluating programs and processes. Most advisers are initially hired and trained to be supervisors of staff and are usually quite comfortable in that role. The difference with advising is usually the type of students in the organization and the motivation behind their involvement. It is important for the adviser to take the time to get to know the students and their reasons for getting involved in the organization.

Conclusion

Although the primary focus of this chapter has been the top five of the 30 adviser responsibilities reported by RHA advisers and presidents (Dunkel & Porter, 1996), it is crucial that each adviser and RHA president meet to discuss which roles and responsibilities are most important for them and for the needs of their organization. Each advising experience with an RHA will be unique. If there were a job description for advisers, it would need to be flexible to encompass the needs of the RHA. It might include 5, 10, 15, or all 30 responsibilities, depending on the institution and the students involved. Whatever the case, the RHA adviser now has a foundation for the most important responsibilities as reported by colleagues and student leaders.

References

Astin, A. (1977). *Four critical years.* San Francisco: Jossey-Bass.

Astin, A. (1985). *Achieving academic excellence.* San Francisco: Jossey-Bass.

Boyer, E. L. (1987). *College: The undergraduate experience in America.* New York: Harper & Row.

Dunkel, N. W., & Porter, J. D. (in press). Residence hall association adviser responsibilities. *Journal of College and University Student Housing.*

Dunkel, N. W., & Schuh, J. H. (1998). *Advising student groups and organizations.* San Francisco: Jossey-Bass.

Kuh, G. D., & Schuh, J. H. (1991). *The role and contribution of student affairs in involving colleges.* Washington, DC: National Association of Student Personnel Administrators.

Pascarella, E. T., & Terenzini, P. T. (1991). *How college affects students.* San Francisco: Jossey-Bass.

Stoner, K. (1988). *Residence hall advisor outline.* Unpublished manuscript.

Successful Residence Hall Government: Themes from a National Study of Select Hall Government Structures

Gardiner Tucker
University of Northern Colorado

Susan Komives
University of Maryland

Successful Residence Hall Government

College residence halls are widely recognized as student living and learning communities. Communities are collections of people living in close proximity who have a shared purpose and who recognize their interdependency. Individuals within a community can probably have a pleasant living experience and not be personally bonded to their neighbors. Indeed, many citizens live that kind of life in our towns and cities. Community structures still exist, however, to deliver services, to provide security, to teach children, and to offer such programs as recreational opportunities in each of those communities. Communities are more successful when citizens take responsibility for shared problems, volunteer their time for shared purposes, participate in shared governance, and uphold collective responsibilities. Indeed, volunteers in communities are essential for success. Likewise, residence hall structures and processes are essential to support, develop, and involve residents who live within those communities. Resident involvement in their own communities is therefore essential both for successful community development and for the individual leadership development and empowerment of involved students.

Student Governance

The nature of residence life government structures that support resident communities is largely unmapped. After a flurry of position statements in the early 1970s promoting student inclusion as partners in shared campus governance, there has been a surprising dearth of research and scholarly writing about student involvement in any level of campus governance, whether in the campus senate, student government associations, or residence government.

In one of the few studies of residence hall associations (RHAs), Wyatt and Stoner (1984) identified five components for organizing and maintaining a system-wide RHA from a national sample of 27 residence hall association advisers (see also Chapter 1). These fundamental components were: "determine the need for the organization, identify support for the organization, obtain a source of income for the organization, ensure effective leadership within the organization, and develop methods of system maintenance with the organization" (p. 3). Werring (1984) elaborated on the purposes of RHAs, envisioning the intersection of student involvement, facility personalization, and positive atmosphere and attitude which he termed the "created environment" (p. 41). Komives (1980) proposed a multilevel residence life governance model based on a principle of resident accountability for issues and responsibilities at the floor and hall levels.

More attention has been paid to developing, motivating, and involving volunteer student leaders in residence halls and other student activities. Boatman's GRAPE theory (1975) has wide appeal. Boatman identified five factors which she believed activated most volunteers to get involved and stay active in leadership roles: growth, recognition, achievement, participation, and enjoyment. Boyd (1985) advocated training for student government officers which would raise their awareness and commitment to representing student diversity among their constituents and identified specific structural and programmatic interventions at one campus. Few writings, however, link the nature of the system to its role in empowering and involving those leaders.

Advising

Advising for campus groups originally was begun to increase the amount of institutional control within organizations. Eventually, as student activities expanded, the adviser's role was perceived as educational and aligned with the institutional mission (Marine, 1984). Today advising has expanded to many levels with multiple responsibilities. "The specific mix of activities performed by advisers varies among groups and within groups over time, but generally includes product-oriented functions, development-oriented functions, and linkage-oriented functions" (McKaig & Policello, 1984, p. 57). In order to be effective, these multiple roles need to be guided by theory. This theory should include both student and group or organizational development (Komives, 1984).

There is little research on the nature of residence government advising. Hall directors are typically the advisers to hall-based government systems. They are encouraged to stress educational and coaching roles with students, using such tools as group building, role negotiation, reality testing (by being a devil's advocate), mentoring, and problem solving (Butler & Leighton, 1993). Effective adviser-advisee relationships are thought to be based on such assumptions as shared responsibility for setting role expectations, open communication, identification of the impact of other duties and roles, honoring individual styles and humanness or mutual sharing, and continual growth and learning (Gwost, 1982). Both advisers and advisees are encouraged to engage in self-assessment, to spend the time needed, to be human, and to be responsible (Gwost, 1982, p. 36).

Professional staff who advise student governance groups have a clear need for training and information in these areas. Numerous workshops, convention programs, and opinion pieces appear in the literature targeting enhanced advising effectiveness (Butler & Leighton, 1983). Further, many student leaders in residence halls receive training and exchange ideas through the National Association of College and University Residence Halls, Inc. (NACURH).

Purpose

The purpose of this study was to illuminate factors that identify strong, sustained resident student governance systems. This study sought sample campuses which are not exhaustive of all systems but have stories to tell about their experiences. These results may not be generalizable; at best they describe the institutions involved in the project. Readers should carefully assess their own contexts to determine if these factors and themes illuminate their own situations.

Methods

Ten expert nominators who are current or former Association of College and University Housing Officers-International (ACUHO-I) presidents or board members were asked to nominate campuses that they regarded as having a strong, sustained resident student governance system. These panelists nominated 39 different campuses. Thirteen campuses were nominated by two or more panelists and one campus was included for its thoughtful redesign of its governance structure. Thirteen of those identified agreed to participate in the study. At the conclusion of each interview, researchers used a snowball sampling procedure to seek other campuses the interviewee might suggest and all 14 of the original campuses were endorsed by one or more interviewees. One additional campus was added to the study as a result of the snowball sampling. As a screening question, all interviewees were asked if their resident government system was as strong as others' perceptions. All but one interviewee agreed with that analysis to some degree; however, one campus interviewed was excluded from data analysis because the adviser stated the system was not strong and that it was an incorrect perception. Therefore, a total of 13 campuses were included in the analysis of data. The campuses interviewed were all public institutions: Eastern Illinois University, Iowa State University, Mississippi State University, Oklahoma State University, Texas Tech University, University of Akron, University of Florida, University of Georgia, University of Kansas, University of North Carolina at Chapel Hill, University of North Dakota, University of Northern Iowa, University of Tennessee-Knoxville, and the University of Wisconsin-Eau Claire.

Researchers designed a telephone interview protocol which involved open-ended discovery questions (e.g., "Why do you think your resident government system works as well as it does?"), as well as questions that sought factual information about all levels of resident governance (e.g., "What is the authority and responsibility of the hall level of government?"). A letter was sent to each chief housing officer (CHO) inviting participation and requesting an informed contact to be the interviewee. In two cases the CHO (who may or may not have been the RHA adviser) was the interviewee and 11 interviewees were the adviser to the RHA. Interviews ranged from 105 to 180 minutes in length. Member checks included sending transcripts of interviews to interviewees for corrections and clarifications. Interview transcripts were unitized and analyzed for relevant themes. A document analysis included materials submitted from each campus, including organizational charts, constitutions of all levels of residence life governance, training materials, NACURH bid materials, and residence life handbooks.

Factors Involved in RHA Success

All themes of success revolve around this basic question: What makes Residence Hall Associations (RHAs) effective? Five major areas of effectiveness were identified: (a) staff values and beliefs regarding students, (b) the role of the adviser, (c) the purpose of the RHA, (d) the organizational structure, and (e) leadership development.

Staff Values and Beliefs Regarding Students

The transcendent theme that may surpass all others in impact is that in these systems, students matter and are highly valued. Students were seen as capable, mature, and responsible adults who deserve the autonomy to make their own decisions. Staff held a deep respect for students and their abilities. One researcher noted the staff's "respect for students jumped right out of the phone!" Staff members also showed a belief in and an understanding of the importance of RHAs to the overall residence life program, believing a positive relationship between the staff, adviser, department, and student in the RHA must exist.

Staff saw the students as unique. The staff must be able to articulate the characteristics of their students which set them apart or distinguish them from students in general. These descriptions expressed staff pride concerning their students. "Something very special about the students [here] ... is they come from very hard-working, diligent backgrounds and when challenged with a task or whatever in front of them, they do a tremendous job of rising to the occasion." "[Our student are] from strong family backgrounds. Traditional and homogeneous. This lends stability." "Many [students are] from farm families, all part of a working group." "We get a very, very talented, articulate, bright, globally concerned student." "They [students] come with lots of leadership experience. I'm amazed; they already know parliamentary procedures." "[Our students are] very willing to get involved almost in a political sense. They see Residence Hall Associations as the place that that can happen."

Staff are committed to student involvement. Staff have a strong philosophy and commitment to the role of student involvement. They view involvement as crucial to the educational process. "'Involvement' — that's my catch word — my job is involvement." "We have a strong grassroots commitment to student involvement from the level closest to the students ..." "[We have a] philosophy of community that revolves around community involvement and student working together ..."

A *strong government system is essential for residence life program success.* This theme developed from the voices of the advisers, who described students and the importance of the Residence Hall Association in glowing terms. "We value it [RHA] very highly. It's very evident to our staff that it's important to us. We put in a lot of time ourselves on it and we have everyone that works in our operation involved in it. It's just understood, if you're working here, you value that process of students being involved in their community." "We have people all up and down the line, all the way from RAs to the President's office who believe we have a strong residence hall program and RHA." "[The former president] said that the development of the leadership opportunities in the residence halls has been so tremendous over the last ten years that it has become as respected as any organization on campus in developing strong student leaders." "[The staff] have to believe that students are capable and able to do tremendous things." "... we are a one-party system — everyone is in it for the same mission and purpose, to provide service and programs for residents. Staff are committed to the success of the resident student governance system. Staff are communicative, inclusive, and act with congruity." "... we stay in touch [with the RHA]." "... [we] walk the walk and talk the talk." "... top down support is essential ...." "... say 'we' not 'they'."

Staff commitment is endorsed in resource allocation. These views maintained by staff are translated into actions in a variety of ways, including the contribution of support via resources, ongoing communication, and staff hiring practices. Other resources included clerical support, reserving meeting space, and compensation for executive board members. "We support our student groups big time. We respect their abilities, [give them] office space and pay their way to all conferences out of our travel budget." "We recognize how well they support us in their program and we support them financially."

Multidirectional communication is expected. Staff ensure regular communication between the resident student government system and staff. The topics centered around policy and residence life issue reviews, among others. The structures set up for communication brought the student voice to the department. "[The RHA performs] policy review and makes recommendations. The Division of Housing goes to IRHA meetings regularly to get recommendations on policy changes or budget." "We solicit feedback because we never want to do anything that we don't feel like we've got the support of the student leaders, the student staff, and the students. We try to create as many avenues as possible to solicit feedback." "The IRHA president attends housing professional staff meetings." "IRHC coordinating body is the voice of the institution for students with the administration." "We advise in a way that puts issues in their laps.... if we put them in a situation and they are successful, they are more likely going to want to come back and try something else and test their boundaries." "They [RHA] are involved in a very high level of decision making. The president gets to sit on the Housing Advisory Board."

The nature of student input sought is clear and predetermined. All RHAs have either recommending power, authority to decide issues and policies, or a mixture of both at different levels of influence. "[The hall government] has recommending power, a voice, and [can make] decisions over multipurpose areas and times." "[The area government decides] permanent improvements, programming money, use of space in the area, training, retreats they take, and how they set up area recognition. They can make lots of recommendations on rules, budgets, etc." "... they are effective because we listen to what they say. They are not a body that sets policy for us, thought they make recommendations to us, but if they have worked through the process with us, there are not many times when we have not taken their advice and moved in their direction." "Whenever we get ready to make some major changes, we also create focus groups where we contact students and student leaders."

Finally, these beliefs, values, and actions lead to a resident student government system led by students who feel they have the ability to have an impact. "We have a student group that feels empowered."

The Role of the Adviser

The role, placement, and commitment of the adviser is central to the success of the RHA. The adviser was found to be a key person in the residence life organization. This theme was consistent across the campuses. The RHA adviser was usually a line member of the central office staff, positioned at a level high enough to take risks and to bring significant issues to the group. The adviser was at a level to ensure access to information concerning the department and to receive and carry student feedback forward. "It is important [for the adviser] to be a high level staff member." "I think many organizations fail to reach their potential when the advising responsibilities are delegated down to the lowest person on the totem pole."

Advisers are professional educators. Statements regarding personal qualities of advisers abounded in the interviews, centering around knowledge and abilities relative to individual students, organizations, and higher education. Participants on several campuses reported the importance of their philosophy in their hiring practices with such statements as: "We recruit professional staff when we interview who can articulate the importance of hall government." "[The adviser should have] thorough training in student development ... also a thorough understanding of student government and some organizational development, which helps the adviser to recognize organizational growth and see group dynamics when an organization is struggling." "We talk about student development, counseling, and management. We have a workshop on how to advise. This is why we have that reputation [as a strong system]." "A knowledge of group development and group dynamics is so crucial. I never thought that I would be continuing to use the course I took as a master's student in group dynamics." "[The adviser needs to have] commitment to housing; we try to pick CSP graduate students to be the adviser because they are committed to student development and housing."

Advisers understand how to work with volunteers. The staff recognized the need to understand the volunteer aspect of resident student governance systems. "The adviser should have a knowledge of situational leadership, a spirit of volunteerism, and an ability to identify motivations." "Other than discipline, hall government advising is one of the hardest things you will do. They are all volunteers and elected, so it may be hard to motivate them." "Working with students as volunteers means you have to be flexible; do lots of massaging, stroking, and positive reinforcement; and spend lots of extra time. Do a retreat and spend time with them — you just cannot throw them together and expect them to do it." "We offer carrots, those things out in front of people to say 'here are rewards.' ..." "You'll get lots to eat and lots of free T-shirts."

Advisers are flexible and have a high tolerance for ambiguity. Advisers had a successful advising philosophy that balanced direction and autonomy. "Channel, don't control." "We have a tremendous rapport with the students; we do not try to tell them what we think they should do. We do try to present issues to them so that they can make good decisions and recommendations.... We sit there and try to feed them information so they can make informed decisions and recommendations." "You do not want to over-advise but you don't want to under-advise either." "People have to be comfortable letting go of control to give autonomy." "... autonomy for each hall means all halls look different and don't have to have the same constitution. We don't dictate roles or positions [which causes] empowerment." "Autonomy means you get inconsistencies."

Advisers are highly engaged. The adviser's role was recognized as needing to be closely involved with the student organization and working to develop a two-way relationship. "Be visible, attending events, even briefly." "[The RHA members] have the opportunity to come by without an appointment and talk." "I have students out to my home on a regular basis." "Our staff is willing to put in the time on evenings and weekends to provide that one-on-one and group time to keep student leaders informed."

Advisers develop talent. Advisers saw encouragement of students as a high priority. "We have an obligation to encourage. I don't think we do that enough in the profession generally. We've got to get these brilliant nuggets who are being taken away from us all over the world and get them to work in higher education, student affairs, etc." "... what we like to do is encourage as many students as possible to grow through government involvement ... So we encourage students — freshmen — to get involved real soon." "The thing I have always tried to challenge staff or RHA people to do is to pull aside people who appear to show strong leadership skills and start working with them. I know I would not be in my position had someone not done that for me." "We identify good students and send them letters encouraging them to apply."

Hall level advisers face unique challenges. Staff articulated the difficulties faced by new hall directors, emphasizing the extra commitment they have to make to the importance of hall government. The challenge to new hall directors is often the pull or tug between advising the hall government and supervising the resident assistant staff. "Hall directors might put [hall government] on the back burner and spend more time and attention with the resident assistants." "Some of my hall directors are more comfortable with their staff. It is harder to work with [hall government] students because you can't make the final decision."

Advisers possess multiple skills, beliefs, and values. Other patterns emerged concerning advisers. The adviser was encouraged to maintain a global or big picture view of the RHA and the department of resident life. Participants felt that advisers should know their own advising styles, believe in teamwork, display good communication skills, and be approachable. A number of values were identified as important for an adviser to possess, including patience, dedication, enthusiasm, an open and positive attitude, and respect for students.

The Purpose of the RHA

A clear, focused purpose of the RHA emerged as a theme throughout the interviews. Several main areas or purposes emerged: (a) RHAs improve the residence hall environment, (b) RHAs provide activities for resident students, and (c) RHAs are seen as a leadership training ground for other campus organizations. "The win-win of it all is that their efforts in getting that leadership experience make the residence halls a better place to live." "[The RHA] has a major programming role ... [they sponsored] Hispanic awareness week, Black awareness month, rape and sexual assault week, and disability awareness week." "[The RHA] has been a body to be a leadership development type organization." "If you get freshmen involved, then they become hall president, on up — this is a good example that things are working well. This year the student body president was a former RA, a former hall president, a former house president, and so forth. The same thing with the vice president. We are a feeder group to prepare student leaders." "Individual hall governments feed to RHA roles; RHAs feed to resident assistants; resident assistants to graduate assistants and hall directors, and so forth."

Organizational Structure

This theme included successful strategies for elections, association involvement, design elements, recognition and reward systems, communication networks, and resource distribution.

Structural designs varied. The principle concept was that form follows function. Successful systems use organizing structures that resemble their facilities or their professional staff system. "... we've taken our facilities and basically said that facilities drive our governmental structure." "Our strength is that our structures are parallel to our organizational structure so you have a cross reference. They [RHAs] go wrong if they have an area government but no area director — you need parallel structures." Every campus had at least a floor or hall government system. Half of those studied had both. If there was an area, complex, or community director staff position, there was also a governmental unit at that level. Area governments, however, were the least well-developed units with less clear purposes and roles than the hall level or campus level units.

Each campus had a system-wide governance unit(s). These were most often called the Inter-Residence Hall Association (IRHA) or Residence Hall Association (RHA). Three campuses had two or more system-wide groups with clearly articulated roles and purposes. In addition to a policy-oriented RHA, they had a Residence Hall Programming Board, President's Council, Recognition and Involvement Board, Residence Hall Activities Board, or a National Residence Hall Honorary.

Whatever the system, it was perceived as coherently organized. The staff clearly articulated the idiosyncrasies of their systems and the rationale for the design. For example, if there is no floor- or area-level government, or if there is more than one central group, the adviser can explain why. Consistency in organizational structure between halls on a single campus was discovered to vary, suggesting that a single structural system for all halls was not central to effectiveness. Too much consistency was stated as stifling individuality, creativity, and a sense of ownership. The different structures allowed staff to avoid controlling details and gave students the leeway to choose their own process.

Each level of government had a central focus of activities. Floor levels have social activities as their predominant role. Hall levels had more variety of roles but were mainly social in nature. The area and system-wide governments had more variety in their activities, ranging from programming and leadership development to resource allocation and policy review.

There is a trend to shift emphasis toward decentralization. Several systems are increasing their focus on floor and hall governments to promote involvement and autonomy. "[We are] strengthening the floor or house level to emphasize the individuality rather than paying a lot of attention to the hall, complex-, or campus-wide system where the individual student doesn't get to be involved other than as an attendee at a program. Our desire is to have the individual program and from a procedural sense." "We put primary emphasis on house governments, on what most people would consider the lowest level. We elevate it to the highest level. And we see it as the most important thing." "We are decentralized at the hall level and each hall has its own constitution. Each hall is run its own way."

Successful governments provide continuity of officers. Elections were held primarily in the spring with spaces for new students saved and included in the fall cycle of elections. "Strong halls elect in the spring and freshmen halls elect in the fall.... some positions are saved for the fall." "They are elected in February as IRHA executives for two months to get transition training with outgoing execs." "We elect officers mid-December and have mid-year transition. We changed it to create a smooth transition. Brand new people coming in the fall flounder too much." "... we encourage freshmen to get involved from the very beginning. We have some positions in fact in some of the halls that are ... specifically new student positions.... Instead of electing them in April they put them off until August or early September to elect them."

Some systems provide summer continuity for the RHA. "[The RHA] is active over the summer. It is a nice refreshing time to get their feet on the ground and begin to understand the intricacies of parliamentary procedure and schedule of the year." "Initially I didn't give as much credit to historical practices that execs are elected in the spring, that presidents are elected in the spring, and then they are offered an internship for summer to work summer orientation. They see a whole different aspect! They see their constituencies and see their concerns, parents, and public. [They] get a bigger picture of the whole university — it broadens them out in a hurry."

Recognition and rewards are central to RHA success. Successful systems celebrate group and individual accomplishments and contributions. "... there is a hall and colony of the year contest that goes on throughout the year that is pretty reputable ... people really vie for that award because that's probably the most prestigious award we would give a hall or colony government at the end of the year." "[We have the] Gold Stars Award: the top reward system to get involved. The reward banquet is for all hall council people with a dessert buffet — gobs of dessert. Each hall council selects their member of the year. We have president of the year, treasurer of the year, communications coordinator of the year, activities representative of the year, and awards for outstanding programs in the hall, sponsored by the hall council." "They [RHA] do a lot of the recognition things on campus for the housekeepers and the dining center people and all that kind of stuff — trying to let the students tell those people how important they are to them. They do the end-of-the-year banquet that recognizes everybody for their accomplishments...."

Successful RHAs have a clear system for communication to all levels of governance units and to residents. Regular and predictable meeting times were highlighted as part of the communication system. "... we have worked diligently over the past several years — you'll notice a board on our flow chart there that is called our ARH Promotions Board ... they also do a number of ... 'Hall Street Sheets,' where they periodically, every six weeks or so, put out a sheet that gives updates as to what is going on. I think that is an ongoing process when you role over 1500 new students every year, so it takes a lot to get them all up to speed as to what is going on." "Every hall does a newsletter that student housing requests, every executive of RHA gets one through the RHA office. RHA minutes go to the hall directors, resident assistants, and student housing." "[We have] house mailboxes — information gets out to each house. [We also have] an IRHA monthly newsletter that goes to each house."

There is a clear source of adequate funding and budget authority. The staff commented on the de-emphasis on fund-raising to fund traditional programs because of the large amounts of time involved. This point is illustrated by the following statements: "... they can't fund-raise for money into their own coffers but they can raise money for philanthropy." "... they cannot just struggle to find money when they are also struggling to get the organization together..." Resources were developed from a variety of sources, including activity cards, allocations from rental income, vending percentages, hall dues, and allocations from the department of residential life. Budget authority was central to self-governance and helped groups feel empowered.

Leadership Development

Multiple levels of formal leadership training exist. Successful governments intentionally identify and develop student leaders. Each staff member recognized the role of the RHA in student leadership development. Formal training programs were found to be widely used and implemented regularly. They often help students become effective in their leadership position. "... number one, we see the individual students developing as leaders as a priority and what we do is encourage as many students as possible to grow through government involvement." "Leadership development is way out in front of everything they do. This is why I continue to do this, finding skill, nurturing that skill, and putting them into more leadership [opportunities]." "On Saturday, we dedicated a new building which was to have a major platform party with the Board of Regents and Chancellor. We insisted the president of the hall be right up there with those people. He was petrified, yet it was good for him. ..." "They plan the one-day leadership conference at the beginning of the year for training all student leaders." "They look around at who's going to fill their shoes. Students nurture others along." "Leadership development [makes us successful]. We brought up entering students as freshmen and placed them in a role to do something with their skills; they feel good about that and take on a greater role, staying with the organization because they feel so good about it." "Every year we bring in officers who are very interested in new ideas, focusing on leadership development." "We spin out of this housing operation some tremendous student leaders. Their abilities and where they end up in the business world is reflective of their leadership experience which they had in the halls." "It came down to let's affect the most number of students possible to help them be leaders or contributors beyond the university. If we can seed the ... Midwest with hundreds of people who have some confidence building in terms of their ability to be a leader, we think we're doing more...."

Strong commitment to develop leadership in underrepresented groups surfaced. In addition, affirmative action efforts are being made to include underrepresented resident groups in governance bodies. At one campus, the Black and Hispanic Student Union presidents have seats on the RHA Board. At another, the Minority Concerns Committee has representatives to the area governments. These are separate from the hall and floor representative system, where some underrepresented groups leave to lead other groups. "Minority floor representatives at the hall level rarely go on to become execs in the hall. Minority students go on to leadership in minority student unions."

Officers benefit from experiences from other campuses. Most campuses emphasized being involved regionally and nationally. This involvement can provide perspective, enhance leadership, and add meaning. "IRHA should be involved regionally and nationally. The role of the NCC [National Communications Coordinator] at regional and national doesn't determine the success of IRHA but gives them a chance to see the larger picture." "[We go] to the regional NACURH. We plan to bring new members to motivate them and educate them...and get them geared up for the rest of the semester." "[We are] consistently strong which seems to be because we are active in MACURH and NACURH."

Residence life promotes leadership education. As leadership educators, these advisers saw tremendous benefits to individual students, campuses, and students' future careers and communities from this residence life learning experience.

General Observations

RHAs are made up of many different components which allow them to work effectively. These vary in nature according to the context of the specific institution in which the RHA exists. What stands out from this study is the commitment of the institution and staff to the success of the RHA. This commitment is based on a clearly articulated philosophy that students matter and are highly valued both by the residence life department and by the campus in general. Students must lead, manage, and influence their own communities. These values are manifested in many unique ways within each institution. Every action or process which is implemented by the staff is evaluated by the criterion of student growth. All of the institutions involved sought a collaborative relationship between the residence life department and the RHA. Students were consulted on a variety of decisions which impacted the department.

The five principles in the Wyatt and Stoner study (1984) are supported in this research. Successful hall governments appear to have a clear purpose and meet a need, strong support exists at multiple levels, the income stream is assured, generative leadership systems exist, and renewal and maintenance of the structures and leaders is assured.

In this study, five areas of effectiveness emerged from current strong, sustained RHAs. They were: (a) staff values emphasize students as mature, responsible, capable adults; (b) the adviser develops a "mattering" relationship with the student leaders who are a part of the RHA; (c) the purpose of the RHA, at all its levels, is clearly understood and supported by the students and the department of residence life; (d) the organizational structure is set up to provide continuity, involvement, recognition and rewards, formal communication, and an income stream; and (e) ongoing leadership development takes place to identify emergent leaders and to ensure positional competence, student growth, and effective organizational maintenance.

The adviser's actions reflected these "mattering" values, resulting in a high level of involvement by all advisers. An ethic of care (Gilligan, 1982) was prevalent among all staff interviewed. Advisers need to be placed at a level within the residence life organization which allows them to take the risks in decision making associated with their level of the RHA, that is, the hall director advises the hall government, the area director advises the area government, and the director or associate director advises the campus-wide resident student government. This facilitates students' empowerment to make decisions during their meetings, rather than waiting for the adviser to check the central office for permission. In addition, this placement level allows the adviser to bring important issues to the students, letting students know their ideas will be heard at the appropriate level. This relationship reflects the trust which exists between the RHA and the residence life department.

Advisers were found to possess important personal and professional values which enhanced their effectiveness in relating to students. These values were translated into professional practices which developed a strong mentoring and coaching relationship with the RHA. Patience, dedication, enthusiasm, openness, positive attitude, and respect for students were demonstrated through adviser visibility, open-door practices, and accessibility through schedule adjustments to match student schedules, especially with time devoted on evenings and weekends.

Advisers also recognized their impact on students. Many advisers articulated the need to encourage students to become involved. Involvement is seen as an integral step in the developmental process. It is interesting to note that many advisers mentioned that they came into the profession due to a personal experience of being encouraged by an RA or staff member during their student years.

Clarity of purpose was of central importance, providing the necessary focus of RHA activities. Successful RHAs were clear in their priorities. The majority of advisers felt that leadership development was the primary role, with activities provided by the organization and the effect on the residence hall environment being secondary.

The thread of leadership development ties each campus together. All had programs designed to train student leaders in positional knowledge and leadership skills. These programs were often utilized to link the student to campus administration, enhancing the central importance of the RHA.

Organizational structure was found to vary between campuses. The organizational structure formalized the communication process between students and the residence life department. Having the structure in place appears to free the latter to experiment with various approaches to student involvement and development. The system works well because of its consistency. Simply put, each campus has created an organizational structure that works within its own campus context. Therefore, each campus had a clear structure in which the residence life department invested care, time, and resources.

RHAs had extensive bureaucracies, which encouraged consistency from year to year. Bureaucracy is a system of rules, regulations, and procedures set within a hierarchy (Certo, 1985). All RHAs had evidence of highly formalized systems. This included workbooks, manuals, constitutions, and forms. Formalization adds to the continuity of the governance system.

There is a trend among many of the campuses to decentralize, that is, to focus resources and emphasis on the organizational units lowest in the governmental hierarchy (floor and hall levels). The effort here is to increase attention to the areas that maximize individual student involvement. The process of decentralization in organizations leads to the greater division of labor which allows decisions to be delegated (Daft & Steers, 1986). Decentralization allows more decisions to be made at "lower" levels within the RHA , increasing the involvement and ownership of a greater number of students.

There are several limitations to this study. Informed and objective though they seek to be, these findings come through the lenses of advisers. Further studies can speak to student leaders as well. Method triangulation was not used, and there was only one source per campus. The study included public institutions only, which may differ from smaller private institutions in funding and other issues. These findings describe the participant institutions and goodness of fit must be determined by other users.

In summary, campuses seeking to strengthen their resident government systems are well advised to do one thing first: assign a central administrator the responsibility to develop, nurture, support, and provide continuity for the student governance system. Then, "walk the talk" and value that system.

Case Study One

Over the years RHA advising has been shifted to one of the most recently hired hall directors. While it used to be in the job description of the Associate Director, other pressing demands like facilities renewals, outsourcing food service, and a fire in a major residence hall meant that the Associate Director has to readjust duties and RHA advising was shifted to hall director staff. The responsibility has remained there ever since. The RHA has become quite activist in recent years. Members are showing signs of wanting to protest rising food plan fees and they are very dissatisfied with the limited serving hours during final exams. In addition, the RHA is considering recommending a major policy change regarding pets in the residence halls and using the fact that hall directors are allowed this privilege as one of their arguments. The hall director adviser to the RHA is very nervous. She knows that central administration does not like addressing these issues and she will be put in a tough spot being expected to defuse the agenda yet believing the students have a right to be heard. How should she approach this dilemma with her supervisors and with the students? What communication systems might be helpful if she remains the adviser?

Case Study Two

You are the new Director of Residence Life at Seesaw University (SU), which has 3,000 students housed on campus. The total student body is 10,000. The nine residential buildings on campus are divided into three distinct geographic areas. Each building has a full-time resident director (RD) and a part-time assistant hall director (AHD), and each geographic area has an area director (AD).

For resident student governance, each hall has a hall council advised by the AHD. The hall councils have two representatives who attend RHA meetings, but have no voting power. Hall council officers are elected once per year in the fall; RHA officers also are elected in the fall. The RHA maintains budgetary control and entertains budget requests from the hall councils.

Parule Foster is the adviser to this RHA. She is a graduate assistant, working on her Master's degree in college student personnel administration. She works on her assistantship responsibilities 20 hours per week, and also has responsibilities in the central office working with room assignments. She feels overworked and wants the students in the RHA to take leadership and run the organization themselves, consulting her only in emergencies. She meets with them when she has time.

When you arrive you discover several concerns brought forth by various students and staff. You find from the campus student governance association that the RHA is seen as a group that implements programs similar to the resident assistants on campus, only on a larger scale, and even then their first program of the year does not take place until Halloween. Several of the AHDs tell you that the hall councils have little respect for the RHA. The RHA president comes to you individually, saying she feels her officers do not take her seriously. During this same meeting you ask her if she has sought ideas from NACURH, and she responds with, "What's that?"

After gathering these opinions, you examine the past annual reports for the department and uncover a gradual reduction in funding for the RHA from resident student fees, and an increasing emphasis on the RHA raising their own money through fundraising activities on campus. You also see that the Department of Resident Life sponsors an annual recognition ceremony for RAs, and that RHA officers are invited to attend but do not partake in the actual ceremony.

To address these concerns you draw together your professional staff, including ADs and RDs, and the RHA president. Together you must (a) determine which aspects of the five factors involved in RHA success from this chapter are present, (b) figure out which aspects of the factors that are absent need to be in place to promote success for the RHA at SU, and (c) derive specific strategies to put needed aspects in place. Your group may create any information that is not presented in the case description. Choose someone in the group to act as the Director — this person facilitates the discussion. Choose someone to act as RHA president — this person reports the findings and strategies of the group. After each group has reported, have a general discussion on how this case applies to actual participant cases.

References

Boatman, S. A. (1975). *Motivating members: GRAPES for everyone.* Unpublished manuscript, University of Nebraska at Lincoln.

Boyd, R. (1985). Analyzing student government: Strategies for representing special interest groups. *Programming, 18,* 47-51.

Butler, D. G., & Leighton, K. (1993). *Advising residence hall student governments: No more dozing in the back of the room.* Paper presented at the annual conference of the Mid-Atlantic College and University Housing Officers, Baltimore, MD.

Certo, S. C. (1985). *Principles of modern management: Functions and systems* (3rd ed.). Dubuque, IA: William C. Brown.

Daft, R. L., & Steers, R. M. (1986). *Organizations: A micro/macro approach.* Glenview, IL: Scott, Foresman.

Gilligan, C. (1982). *In a different voice: Psychological theory and women's development.* Cambridge, MA: Harvard University.

Gwost, A. (1982). Effective student adviser relationships. *Programming, 15,* 34-36.

Komives, S. R. B. (1980). Student governance and leadership. In D. A. DeCoster & P. Mable (Eds.), *Personal education and community development in college residence halls* (pp. 229-249). Washington, DC: American College Personnel Association.

Komives, S. R. B. (1984). Applying theory to practice: Understanding student and organization development. In J. H. Schuh (Ed.), *A handbook for student group advisers* (pp. 23-44). Alexandria, VA: American College Personnel Association.

Marine, J. (1984). Student groups and advisers: Historical perspective. In J. H. Schuh (Ed.), *A handbook for student group advisers* (pp. 16-17). Alexandria, VA: American College Personnel Association.

McKaig, R., & Policello, S. (1984). Group advising — defined, described, and examined. In J. H. Schuh (Ed.), *A handbook for student group advisers* (pp. 45-58). Alexandria, VA: American College Personnel Association.

Werring, C. J. (1984). The purpose of residence hall student government: One conceptual model. *Journal of College and University Student Housing, 14*(1), 40-43.

Wyatt, K. W., & Stoner, K. L. (1984). A NACURH "white paper" on residence hall government. *Journal of College and University Student Housing, 14*(1), 3-6.

This research was supported in part by the Department of Resident Life at the University of Maryland-College Park, College Park, MD 20742.

The Organizational Structures of RHAs

Tony W. Cawthon and Susan J. Underwood
Clemson University

Introduction

Organizations can be seen as a number of individuals or groups, with identified responsibilities, who come together for a specific purpose (American Heritage Dictionary, 1992; Rogers & Agarwala-Rogers, 1976). The key function of organizational structure, as stated by Hanson (1996, p. 225), "is to define, channel, and give order to actions and events, thus providing stability and predictability."

University housing departments have attempted to foster this stability and predictability by providing for well-established structures within their organizations to include Residence Hall Associations (RHAs). RHAs have been established across the United States in virtually all colleges and universities with mature residential life programs. The specific purpose of these associations varies by institution but, in general, they formalize the involvement of residents in hall governance and they open communication channels between residents and their institutional leaders.

Brief Overview of Organizational Theory

To appreciate how and why RHAs have been structured, a basic understanding of organizational theory is needed. Beginning with the turn of the century and well into the middle of the century, theorists viewed organizational behavior as operating within closed systems. From this perspective, now known as the conventional view, institutions such as colleges and universities operated with little concern or influence from outside forces. The conventional view was predicated on the desire of organizations to maintain stability and predictability at all costs, creating structures which were highly hierarchical, rigid, formal, and controlling (Kuh, 1996).

Since the 1960s, the postconventional view of organizations has come into vogue. In this view, organizations such as colleges and universities are considered to be complex open systems shaped by many external influences and pressures. According to this theory, today's institutions of higher education not only are, but must be, ever-changing as they adapt to fluid environments. Roles, predictability, and stability are no longer paramount. Instead, open communication and responsive structures are valued (Kuh, 1996).

Although admittedly oversimplified, the primary difference in these organizational views might be summed up with two words: static versus dynamic. Conventional organizations have structures which preserve the status quo whereas postconventional organizations are dynamic and hold structure as secondary to goal achievement.

Hollingworth (1995) put these ideas in clear focus with a straightforward classification of organizations into five types: power, role, task, person, or matrix. Power organizations have the greatest control with their desire to dominate their environment. They refuse to subject themselves to external law or power. Role organizations are rational, orderly, and preoccupied with responsibility, legality, and predictability. Structure, roles, and responsibilities are well defined. Task organizations are centered around goal attainment and, to that end, structure is important only to the extent that it supports the achievement of the task at hand. Person organizations, such as research teams and support groups, exist to serve the needs of the members. Structure is a function of what pleases the members, and decisions are made in a consensual manner. Matrix organizations are combinations of two or more of the other types.

In Hollingworth's classification of organizational types, power and role reflect the conventional view, whereas task and person would be considered postconventional. The primary distinction between conventional and postconventional organizations is the formalization and responsiveness of the structure as it serves to support the purpose of the organization.

Organizational Structure

RHA organizational structures exhibit various characteristics based on the degree of formalization and centralization. Formalization is the significance of rules and regulations in the organization while centralization deals with the way power is distributed in an organization (Strange, 1993). Organizational structures of contemporary RHAs vary in the degree of formalization and centralization as a function of the history and personality of the institution and the student affairs program, the demographics of the students to be served, the physical characteristics of the residence halls, the current philosophy and goals of the housing department, available monetary resources, and strength of commitment to hall governance (Ambler, 1993; Verry, 1993).

Formal and Informal Structures

Highly formalized RHAs have well-defined roles and responsibilities for members and office holders. Governing documents are lengthy and attempt to define every conceivable situation. When new situations arise, members of highly formal associations are expected to react by evaluating their response in light of existing policies and procedures and to revise the bylaws to sanction unauthorized responses. Less formalized RHAs have brief constitutions and bylaws defining the primary roles and responsibilities of executive officers and members, and will allow for a more dynamic interpretation of these governing documents. New situations will be addressed with less formal means and members will be freer to react with innovation and creativity.

Highly formalized structures offer assurance of consistency and predictability. Every conceivable situation and appropriate response are clearly defined and little effort is needed to interpret policies and procedures. These formalized or rigid structures can lead to stagnation and reactivity, whereas less formalized structures may encourage dynamic decision making and creativity. Communication channels in organizations with informal structures often are more open and issues are addressed in a fluid and less controlled atmosphere. The shortcomings of the less formalized organizational structure are that decision making may take longer and new situations may require more thought and effort.

Centralized, Decentralized, and Blended Structures

RHA structures, as previously mentioned, may be viewed from the perspective of the degree of centralization and classified as one of three broad structures: centralized, decentralized, or blended. The degree of centralization suggests a great deal about the philosophy of the RHA as it strives to accomplish its stated purpose or goal. Of the three structures, the blended structure is by far the most prevalent and will be used to illustrate many of the topics in the remainder of the chapter. However, a full discussion of RHA structures would not be complete without the inclusion of a brief description of the centralized and decentralized structures.

Highly centralized structure: Central RHA with individual building or area representation. RHAs with a highly centralized structure have a strong central association and no individual building or area governments. Representatives from individual residence halls or areas are elected or appointed, as delineated in the constitution, to serve on a central RHA. This central or oversight RHA establishes policies and procedures to govern the overall residence life program for all residence halls or areas. The RHA has a constitution and bylaws detailing the structure of the executive council, membership, offices, responsibilities, and committees as appropriate. Building-level quality of life issues are handled through existing residence life staff or informal governing procedures or bodies.

Although less common than a blended structure for RHAs, the centralized structure might be suitable for a campus with a small residential program or one where administration desires to maintain tight control over residence life issues or greatly values consistency. The absence of building or area governments would limit the number of residents involved in residential governance. Additionally, the centralized structure is less appropriate for a campus which highly values diversity and flexibility in their residence life program. Individual areas or buildings might have a more difficult time expressing their individuality in this structure.

Decentralized structure: Building or area government with no central RHA. In the decentralized structure, individual buildings or areas have their own organizations with no central or oversight RHA. Each residence hall or area government operates independently of the others on campus. Each organization establishes its own governing documents, policies, and procedures. This structure affords no formal means of coordination between the buildings or areas. Theoretically, distinctly varied residential life programs could be generated in this structure. Regardless of the distinctiveness of each organization within the decentralized structure, invariably some building or area governments will be stronger than others, producing potential difficulties for residence life administrators.

The decentralized structure might be appropriate for a campus with a relatively small number of individual residence halls or defined areas, or where diversity is the overriding value in the residence life program. For example, a campus with a number of theme halls, or halls with distinct interests, might benefit from a decentralized approach to residence life governance. One drawback of this structure is the lack of formal avenues for dialogue among the building or area organizations. Little or no communication among them could create an environment of competition and unnecessary duplication of effort.

Blended: Building or area government with central RHA. The blended structure is by far the most common on today's campuses. Blended RHAs have individual building or area governments and a central RHA providing oversight and/or coordination among the individual organizations. Building- or area-level governments are made up of voting and nonvoting members. The majority of members have voting privileges and are elected to serve as representatives in the individual building or area governments. Nonvoting members, on the other hand, may include alumni members or advisers. The ability of each building or area organization to operate independently is detailed in the governing documents; however, a fairly significant level of independence is typical of a blended system. Furthermore, the individual organizations will elect officers who make up the governing body for the RHA.

The oversight or central RHA is made up of elected or appointed members from the individual governments. An executive council is comprised of elected officers from the body of representatives and oversees the operation of the central RHA. Through its members and executive council, the central RHA provides coordination, guidance, and direction for the building or area governments. This structure attempts to maximize the potential gain to be realized from building- or area-level organizations while minimizing the shortcomings inherent in the decentralized structure with its lack of coordination.

Governing Documents of RHAs: Constitutions and Bylaws

Historically, RHAs operate under policies and guidelines established in constitutions and bylaws. A constitution is defined as "the act of composing, setting up or establishing" (American Heritage Dictionary, 1992, p. 404). The RHA constitution serves as the overall governing document, containing the fundamental principles that prescribe organizational policies. For most RHAs, the constitution is established at the onset of the organization and remains intact for the duration of the organization. If a housing program is in the initial stage of establishing an RHA, the constitution will be presented to the membership at the initial meeting for ratification. The constitution itself should provide the necessary procedures for ratification.

For those campuses in the initial stages of RHA development, it may also be necessary to register the organization with the campus organizations office. Campuses typically have a detailed process for recognition of student organizations. Completion of the necessary paperwork and submission of a constitution are the first steps of this recognition process.

Organizational bylaws are very different from the organizational constitution. The *American Heritage Dictionary* (1992, p. 263) defines a bylaw as "a rule governing the internal affairs of an organization." In other words, bylaws are the working documents of RHAs. Bylaws attempt to create the kind of organization that the RHA hopes to become. As the organization grows, develops, and changes, these changes are reflected in the bylaws of the organization. For most organizations, bylaws can be viewed as amendments to the constitution. The procedure for proposing and ratifying amendments must be carefully defined in the constitution as well.

In an existing RHA with the constitution in place, needed changes will be made to the bylaws. Carver (1997) proposed several guidelines regarding the characteristics of bylaws, including length, membership, quorum, officers, committees, staff, and legal review. While most of these characteristics will be considered later in this chapter, length and membership will be examined here. For bylaws to be effective, Carver (1997) indicated that they should establish basic structure and avoid being lengthy. The same is true regarding the size of the RHA. As organizations become larger, members may assume less responsibility as individuals. In organizations with large numbers of members, logistics such as coordinating meetings, setting meeting dates, and staying focused in meetings become problematic.

The Organizational Structures of RHAs

In summary, a well-conceived constitution and bylaws are essential for the creation of a productive RHA. A strong constitution will summarize the organization's philosophical tenets, and an effective set of bylaws will inform all members about organizational operations and policies.

Elements of an RHA Constitution

The components making up RHA governing documents vary greatly. As discussed earlier, many factors have the potential to impact how these documents are organized. Despite differences in organizational structures, common components have been identified.

Name. The name is the official title of the association and should reflect the philosophy and purpose of the organization. Specific examples of RHA names include Residence Hall Association, Resident Student Association, United Residence Hall Councils, Association of Residence Halls, and the Campus Resident Student Association.

Purpose or preamble. This section describes the functions and mission of the RHA. RHAs have several purposes, but first and foremost is the objective of serving as the voice of residents by representing them to campus administration. Other functions include coordinating activities, assisting in the planning and execution of programs, serving as a liaison to other organizations and departments, and creating an atmosphere conducive to intellectual and educational pursuits.

Membership. The membership section details who constitutes the general membership of the RHA. Generally, all residents living in university housing constitute the membership of the RHA. Often this section includes a commitment to nondiscrimination against individuals or groups on the bases of creed, ethnic origin, gender, race, religion, or sexual orientation.

Also, information on the specific membership of the RHA will be included. Obviously, the specific members of the RHA vary depending upon the structure being used. Members may be the officers, area representatives, building representatives, or members at large. If building or area representation is used, the document should be explicit in defining the number of representatives allowed and the eligibility and selection of such representatives.

Organizational structure. The constitution should address the overall organization of the RHA. A detailed explanation of the organizational structure is included in this section. Specifically, this section focuses on the governing bodies, executive councils, and representatives comprising the RHA.

Power and duties of officers and members. This component is often lengthy and includes the roles of and detailed job descriptions for the officers of the organization. This section contains both elected and appointed members of the executive council. Elected executive council officers usually include president, vice president, secretary, and treasurer. The responsibilities of the vice president may be divided among vice presidents for administration, programming, finance, or public relations. Appointed positions to the executive council frequently include the adviser, a National Association of College and University Residence Halls (NACURH) National Communications Coordinator (NCC), a liaison to student government, and a liaison to the National Residence Hall Honorary (NRHH). It is essential that governing documents address the voting rights of appointed members of the executive council.

Qualifications for and removal from executive council. This portion of the governing document outlines the selection process for electing officers as well as the criteria officers must meet to serve. Terms of office and powers of the council should also be addressed. Additionally, this section contains impeachment or removal procedures for executive council members.

Meetings. This article summarizes the meeting structure to be used by the RHA. It discusses both regular and special meetings and frequency of meetings.

Attendance and quorum requirements. This section is an essential component in most RHA governing documents. It outlines the attendance policy and use of alternate representatives, procedures for removing individuals from the RHA, procedures for appealing the removal of individuals from office, and replacement of removed representatives.

For the organization to achieve its working potential, a quorum should be clearly defined. In most organizations, a quorum is defined as a simple majority which is one half of the representatives plus one. However, RHA constitutions may establish other definitions for a quorum, such as a three-fourths majority or a specific percentage.

Elections and election codes. Articles in this section outline the process by which officers are elected to serve the organization. Specific articles address nominating and voting procedures, qualifications for eligibility, and procedures for filling unexpected vacancies. Compensation for officers, if provided, would be included.

Voting rights. The constitution should be clear as to who has voting rights within the RHA. This section also addresses duties and responsibilities of the voting membership, how voting occurs, the use of proxies if applicable, and who coordinates voting procedures.

Funding and finances. This portion of the document discusses how the RHA generates its funding sources. Articles should also be included that discuss how the monies received are allocated to the budget, specific operating procedures for disbursement of monies, and how the budget is adopted or amended.

Parliamentary authority. Most RHAs follow the current edition of *Robert's Rules of Order* (Robert, 1996) as the basis for it parliamentary procedures. A common omission from governing documents of RHAs is information relevant to the role of the parliamentarian, for instance how the parliamentarian is elected or appointed.

Recall, impeachment, and removal of executive officers. Procedures should be clear in these areas. All members of the organization should understand the procedures to follow in removing one of its members. This section should clearly delineate the grounds upon which officers can be removed, recalled, or impeached. Unfortunately, many RHAs do not realize how inadequate this section of their governing document may be until faced with the necessity to take such actions.

Amendments and ratifications. This section outlines procedures RHAs must follow in making changes to its governing documents. For most organizations, changes in governing documents require a two-thirds affirmative vote of voting members to ratify the document. This section may also address relationships of the governing document to other documents such as housing contracts and university student handbooks.

The Organizational Structures of RHAs

Committees. The committee structure utilized by the RHA is outlined in this element of the constitution. The constitution should focus primarily on standing or ongoing committees. Task forces, ad hoc committees, or special committees with short-term, specific charges are ordinarily established in the bylaws. The governing documents should address the development and approval of committees, reporting structures utilized, responsibilities of committees, dissolution of committees, and procedures for establishing ad hoc committees.

Relationships with other organizations. Articles in this section discuss the RHA's relationships with organizations such as NACURH, regional associations, and the institution's student government associations.

Governing Bodies

The RHA governing body, also known as the executive council, is responsible for setting directional policy for RHA. The RHA executive council is responsible for the total leadership of the organization. As such, it is the ultimate group entrusted with the highest power or authority. The governing council has the charge of administering and overseeing all RHA business.

The governing body is usually elected by voting members of the RHA. Election procedures are clearly articulated in the governing documents. Typically, elections are handled by an elections commission, the president, or his or her designee. To be eligible for executive council positions, individuals must meet specified criteria. To qualify for such positions, individuals must be registered, have lived on campus for a minimum number of semesters, and be in good disciplinary standing with the university. Generally, office holders must maintain a minimum grade point average. It is also expected that potential officers will have had some prior RHA experience.

Officers are generally elected during the spring semester. Terms of office usually run for one year from the time of election and individuals are not permitted to hold more than one RHA position.

The composition of the governing council may vary from campus to campus. The size and complexity of the organization, tradition, and responsibilities are all factors that influence this composition. Generally, the governing council will consist of president, vice president, secretary, treasurer, NACURH National Communications Coordinator (NCC), and adviser. Of these positions, the vice presidential role reflects the most variety. It is not uncommon for large, complex RHAs to split this function into many positions.

As stated earlier, this list of governing body positions is not exhaustive. Other executive council positions might include a programming coordinator, foundations coordinator, student government liaison, historian, service learning coordinator, and NRHH liaison. The primary distinction of this list is that these position holders, although members of the governing council, are often not voting members. An overview of the most prevalent executive council positions is presented below.

President

The president is the highest ranking officer of the governing council. The president has the responsibility of preparing the agenda and presiding over all RHA regular and special meetings. He or she is the official RHA representative and serves as the official spokesperson for residence hall students. It is the president's job to represent RHA with the administration. An effective president meets regularly with university housing officials on both a formal and informal basis. Generally, the president makes all appointments to committees, serves as an ex-officio member of all committees, assists with budget preparation, and leads the organization toward achievement of its goals. In fact, it is the responsibility of the president to ensure that each governing body member is successful in fulfilling his or her job responsibilities. In most RHAs the president becomes a voting member only in tie-vote situations.

Vice President

In RHAs one or more individuals may serve in the vice presidential capacity, such as vice presidents for administration, finance, programming, recognition, public relations, and executive relations. Typically, the role of the vice president in most RHAs is to serve in the absence of the president and to coordinate the activities of all committees. Other responsibilities might include serving as the parliamentarian, coordinating residence hall appreciation week, overseeing hall or program recognition efforts, and chairing the judicial component of the RHA.

Secretary

The primary responsibility of the secretary is to record accurate minutes of all meetings and to distribute these minutes to appropriate persons. An effective secretary will also maintain a filing system for minutes. An additional function of this position is to maintain the database of RHA members. The secretary will also record meeting attendance and determine when a quorum has been met.

Treasurer

In many governing documents, this position is also referred to as the business manager, auditor, or finance director. The overall responsibility of the treasurer is to establish procedures for the coordination and recording of all RHA expenditures and business transactions. An effective treasurer is one who presents both oral and written financial reports to members. These reports may be prepared on a weekly, monthly, semester or yearly basis. Additional treasurer duties include depositing of monies, assisting with yearly auditing of records, and preparing the annual RHA budget and financial report. In complex RHAs, the treasurer assists individual halls with budget preparation and oversees the fulfillment of individual building treasurer responsibilities. It is the treasurer who often chairs the finance committee, leads fund-raising activities, and assist the university housing office with its budget preparation.

NACURH National Communication Coordinator (NCC)

The NCC serves as the RHA liaison to state, regional, and national organizations. The NCC is given the responsibility of organizing the RHA delegation for the various conferences. This responsibility includes coordinating delegate registration, serving as voting delegate, and handling all correspondence with the state, regional, and national organizations. The NCC prepares and submits all dues and reports requested by NACURH and its regional affiliates.

Adviser

The adviser, if applicable, serves on the governing council and is not a voting member. The adviser is generally a staff or faculty member designated by the residence life department. The primary role of the adviser is to attend RHA meetings, functions, and events to provide guidance, feedback, and support to RHA members.

Membership Types

For most RHAs, membership is comprised of students residing in university housing. The exact membership will be specified in the governing documents. Because one-on-one communication with all residential students, whether in large or small halls, is not realistic, most RHAs have developed procedures to determine active membership. Generally the voting structure of RHAs includes the executive council and representatives; however, the constitution and/or bylaws should specify members with voting rights.

In all the aforementioned RHA structures, the voting members are those individuals elected to the executive council and building or area representatives. The governing documents outline the number and method of selection of the council and representatives. More often than not, the size of the building or area determines the number of representatives. With some of the structures, the selection and number of representatives is quite simple, but in others it can become quite complex.

In the centralized structure, the number of representatives serving on the central RHA might be as straightforward as the number of residential buildings or areas in the university housing system. For example, if the institution has 12 residence halls, there might be 12 representatives to the central RHA, with each member representing a different hall. The executive council for the central RHA would be elected according to procedures detailed in the governing documents.

The decentralized structure does not have a central RHA and generally each floor is represented in the individual building or area government. Each building or area would have its own executive council and representatives. Again, size of the residence floor or apartment unit dictates the number of representatives. For example, in a nine-story residence hall, each floor might elect one voting representative to serve on the building or area government.

The executive council and representative structure in the blended structure is more complex. The blended structure allows for individual building or area governments with executive councils and representatives as well as a central RHA with an executive council and representatives. The individual building or area executive councils and representatives are most likely chosen similar to the decentralized structure, but the central RHA executive council and representatives selection is usually more complex. For example, the governing documents for a system of 12 buildings and 5000 residents might specify one representative for buildings with 1-250 residents, two representatives for buildings with 251-500 residents and three representatives for buildings with 501 or more residents. The elected executive council and representatives become the

RHA voting delegates in this structure. The central RHA council and representatives concentrate on issues impacting all resident students, whereas the individual building or area governments concentrate on issues specific to each building or area.

One special issue is whether or not resident assistant staff can serve as representatives to the RHA. This policy varies from campus to campus, as specified in the governing document.

Members-at-Large

At-large members can be either voting or nonvoting members. Voting members are afforded all the rights and responsibilities of full members. Nonvoting members, on the other hand, are permitted to participate in RHA processes but may not vote on RHA business. Regardless of the role, members-at-large should be expected to attend meetings, serve on committees, and participate in discussions.

There are advantages and disadvantages to having members-at-large. The primary advantage is that these members usually represent specific groups and can be invaluable in communicating issues to and from the RHA. Other advantages include allowing for more input, strengthening cooperative relationships with other organizations, and providing more leadership opportunities for student leaders. Despite these advantages, the obvious disadvantage is maintaining the motivation and enthusiasm of these members. For those without voting privileges inconsistent attendance may be a problem.

Examples of members-at-large include liaisons to the student government association, NRHH, Greek life, the housing advisory board, and food services.

Alumni and Corporate Members

This is the newest category of membership for RHAs. The governing document should be extremely clear in outlining the roles and functions of these members. Alumni member status is often awarded to individuals who have a history of interaction with the RHA, such as past RHA officers. Corporate members usually include those individuals with whom the RHA does business. RHAs seeking new revenue sources, for example, may work closely with marketing and T-shirt companies. Having such individuals serve as liaisons, or members-at-large, can go a long way to strengthen contacts. The governing document should describe fully the role and voting privileges of both alumni and corporate members.

Standing and Ad Hoc Committees

Like most organizations, the effectiveness of any RHA depends upon an effective committee structure. Large RHAs rely on committees to complete much of the work, but RHAs are cautioned to be careful in not creating too many committees. Most RHAs utilize two types of committees as part of their organizational structure: standing and ad hoc committees. The roles, responsibilities, and charges of standing committees should be clearly described in the governing documents. The charges of these standing committees should be reviewed periodically and revised if necessary. The most frequent examples of RHA standing committees are finance, budgets, nominations and elections, programming, constitution and bylaws, community service, judiciary, recognition, and dining.

Conversely, ad hoc committees, also known as task forces or steering committees, are developed for only a finite period of time. Their existence comes about as an RHA discovers a need to address particular issues or coordinate special events or programs. An RHA executive council can establish any number of ad hoc committees during its tenure. Although the charge, role, and responsibilities of these committees are not specified in the governing documents, those serving on such committees should have this information shared orally with them. Examples of RHA ad hoc committees include: (a) a committee to plan residence hall appreciation week, (b) a committee to investigate funding sources for RHA, and (c) a committee to examine vandalism in the residence halls.

Conclusion

The purpose of this chapter was to provide the reader with an overview of RHA organizational structures and the basic components of RHA governance. Three organizational structures and the conditions under which these structures are most effective were discussed. Key information on membership, constitutions, and bylaws was presented to assist individuals working with the mature RHA as well as those engaged in the initial stages of RHA development. Individuals seeking additional information about RHAs are encouraged to refer to the remainder of this book, talk with professional colleagues, or contact the National Association of College and University Residence Halls or the Association of College and University Housing Officers-International.

References

Ambler, D. A. (1993). Developing internal management structures. In M. J. Barr (Ed.), *The handbook of student affairs administration* (pp. 107-120). San Francisco: Jossey-Bass.

American heritage dictionary (3rd ed.). (1992). Boston: American Heritage.

Carver, J. (1997). *Boards that make a difference.* San Francisco: Jossey-Bass.

Hanson, E. M. (1996). *Educational administration and organizational behavior.* Boston: Allyn and Bacon.

Hollingworth, J. E. (1995, August). *Total quality management.* Paper presented at the College Business Management Institute, Lexington, KY.

Kuh, G. (1996). Organizational theory. In S. R. Komives & D. B. Woodard, Jr. (Eds.), *Student services: A handbook for the profession* (3rd ed., pp. 269-297). San Francisco: Jossey-Bass.

Robert, H. M. (1996). *Robert's rules of order.* Glenview, IL: Scott-Foresman.

Rogers, E. M., & Agarwala-Rogers, R. (1976). *Communication in organizations.* New York: Free Press.

Strange, C. C. (1993). Dynamics of campus environments. In S. R. Komives & D. B. Woodard, Jr. (Eds.), *Student services: A handbook for the profession* (3rd ed., pp. 244-268). San Francisco: Jossey-Bass.

Verry, B. (1993). The organizational structure of RHAs. In N. W. Dunkel & C. L. Spencer (Eds.), *Advice for advisors: The development of an effective residence hall association* (pp. 45-53). Columbus, OH: Association of College and University Housing Officers-International.

Author Notes

The authors wish to acknowledge the efforts of Bart Verry, whose chapter on organizational structures of RHAs was used as the foundation for this updated chapter.

The authors also wish to acknowledge the use of the constitutions and bylaws from the following institutions: Appalachian State University, Clemson University, Kansas State University, University of Arkansas, University of Florida, University of Michigan, University of Tennessee-Knoxville, and Wake Forest University.

The Motivation of Students: From Theory to Practical Application

Susan Mitchell
California State University, San Marcos

Kim Munro-Krusz
Ball State University

The Motivation of Students

The students were enthusiastic and full of ideas at the summer planning retreat. Now they seem to be focused on everything but their goals and the organization's success. This is not an uncommon scenario for any student organization. What does the adviser do? This chapter provides advisers with the insight, theory, resources, and practical approaches to get leaders motivated to fulfill their goals and plans.

Motivation, like leadership, is a concept that seems simple on the surface, but if looked at more deeply is found to be more complex, with a body of research that is sometimes contradictory and confusing. At face value, motivation is what causes human beings to act. As advisers, it is helpful to understand the role of motivation as it relates to bringing about actions which are in keeping with the educational missions of institutions.

Motivation is an important concept for advisers to understand for two reasons. First, as educators, advisers seek to facilitate the learning and development of student leaders. Second, advisers continually work toward the development of a student government organization which provides activities and programs to facilitate the development of all students in the residential communities, whether that be socially, educationally, spiritually, physically, or emotionally. Understanding how people are motivated provides advisers with a context for efforts in assisting student leaders, both as individuals and as groups, to accomplish specific goals.

The purposes of this chapter are (a) to provide key concepts for consideration in motivation theory and research, (b) to discuss intrinsic and extrinsic factors in motivation theory, (c) to identify specific ideas that can be used to facilitate the motivation of students both as individuals and in groups, and (d) to provide case studies for thinking further about the concept of motivation.

Motivation Theory and Research

Human motivation has been included in the behavioral sciences literature for many years. Employers and educators have a keen interest in learning how to assist employees and students in their ability to develop into people with satisfying and productive personal and professional lives. The following discussion of motivation research and theory offers advisers some key concepts that will be helpful in developing a context for better understanding the concept of motivation.

In the 1960s, three human motivation theories were most prominent in the literature. In the first of these, Drive Theory, Hull (1952) maintained that motivation is based on physiological need deprivation which "drives" organisms to engage in random activity until the need is satisfied and the drive is reduced. This theory was beset with problems such as the fact that not all motivation derives from physiological needs, and that some organisms, including people, often engage in activities that increase rather than decrease physiological needs, such as human rights activists who fast to make a political statement (Locke & Latham, 1994).

With his Reinforcement Theory, Skinner (1953) asserted that behavior was controlled by reinforcements, which were consequences that followed behavior, making future responses more likely to occur in similar situations. This behaviorist approach dominated the field of psychology for decades, but due to the fact that it was based on the premise that human action could be understood without reference to consciousness, it eventually was replaced by other theories which acknowledged the role of consciousness in human action (Locke & Latham, 1994).

The third prominent theory in the 1960s was Subconscious Motives (McClelland, 1961), which stressed the subconscious aspects of consciousness. McClelland maintained that subconscious motives guide human action. For instance, people with strong achievement motives are more likely to be successful in entrepreneurial occupations than those with low achievement motives. However, this theory did not take into account the individual's conscious convictions in the role of motivation (Locke & Latham, 1994).

In the last three decades several approaches to motivation have emerged that are particularly helpful to advisers. These are Goal Setting Theory, the Expectancy Theory of Motivation, and Sociocultural Theory. In the mid-1960s, Goal Setting Theory emerged as an alternative to the earlier theories of that decade. It is based upon the core concept that much human action is purposeful and that the simplest explanation of why some people perform better on specific tasks is because they have different performance goals (Locke and Latham, 1990). In over 400 research studies on Goal Setting Theory, researchers have consistently found that given sufficient ability and high commitment to the goal, the harder the goal, the better the performance because people adjust their effort to the difficulty of the task before them (Locke & Latham, 1994).

Researchers also consistently found that goals which are both specific and difficult lead to higher performance than vague but challenging goals, vague but unchallenging goals, or the setting of no goals. Over 40,000 people from varied cultural and work backgrounds in the United States and Canada, as well as in numerous other countries including Australia, the Caribbean, Israel, and Japan participated in these studies. The results suggested that goal setting is applicable in varying cultures and is characteristic of many human beings (Locke & Latham, 1994).

Intensity has also been found to be a factor regarding the accomplishment of goals. It has been found that those who thought most intensely about a particular problem were most likely to demonstrate their commitment to solving the problem (Gollwitzer, Heckhausen, & Ratajczak, 1990).

There is controversy regarding the assigning of goals by someone in authority versus setting goals participatively in increasing performance on the part of subordinates. Latham, Erez, and Locke (1988) found that goals assigned with a rationale are just as motivating as participatively set goals.

Feedback to students also can affect their performance in a positive manner. Goals and feedback increase performance, and both together are more effective in motivating high performance than either is alone (Locke & Latham, 1990).

Increasingly, attention is being devoted to motivation from a social and cultural context as our population continues to diversify. In their work with Latino children, Rueda and Moll (1994) suggested that motivation is socially negotiated and context specific. What a person finds motivating may depend on the culture in which he or she develops and the situation in which he or she acts and lives. Hawkins (1994) found that motivational factors in Asia — and the subsequent effect on learning — differ from those in Western society. Given Locke and Latham's (1994) findings regarding goal setting, it would appear that some aspects of motivation theory cross cultural lines.

However, given the work of Rueda and Moll (1994) and Hawkins (1994), perhaps other aspects of motivation theory do not.

The Expectancy Theory of Motivation, popularized by Vroom (1964), is based upon the premise that employees' motivation is affected by their confidence in that they will get what they want. Their confidence involves three beliefs: (a) they believe they can perform well enough to get what is offered, (b) they believe that they will get what is offered if they perform well, and (c) they believe that what is being offered will be satisfying. According to Green (1992), motivation and performance strategies that fail to address all three aspects do not work.

Intrinsic and Extrinsic Factors of Motivation

Motivation theory and research have often focused upon the intrinsic (internal) and extrinsic (external) aspects of motivation. Generally, intrinsic motivation deals with those aspects of motivation that seem to come from within an individual, and extrinsic motivation deals with those aspects that come from the individual's environment. For example, anxiety can be both intrinsic and extrinsic in that the individual first has a propensity to be anxious (intrinsic), but the anxiety may change, given the context of the situation (extrinsic). A good example of this is a student leader who is going to give a speech for a student government banquet. Some students will be more anxious in giving the same speech to the same group than other students. This may be due to their perceived ability to speak publicly (intrinsic), the conditions of the environment, such as the interest of the audience in the presentation (extrinsic), and their preparation for the speech (intrinsic and extrinsic).

Other intrinsic variables in motivation are commitment, curiosity, self-confidence, and psychological and emotional wants and needs. Intrinsic motivation implies that a person is internally motivated and works on his or her own force. Extrinsic factors could be resources to achieve a goal, incentives, work conditions, or punitive outcomes. Extrinsic motivation implies that people are motivated to perform a specific behavior due to the particular outcome that results from it. Intrinsic and extrinsic motivational variables are often perceived as being opposite to one another and more of one implies less of the other (Thierry, 1990).

The role of incentives (extrinsic motivation) in generating commitment to goals was found to be complex in research by Lee, Locke, and Phan (1992). They found that offering bonuses for trying to reach an impossible goal can actually lower performance. Offering incentives for pursuing easy goals can aid commitment, but the commitment is to low performance. Bonuses for moderate goals have been shown to be most likely to promote high performance.

From popular literature advisers often learn that they can motivate others in simple and easy ways. The research suggests, however, that motivation is a complex concept and that many variables may affect one's motivation, including culture, self-confidence, rewards or punishments related to a particular action, the level of ability the person has to complete a specific task, and resources available to accomplish the task. There is some evidence that intrinsic and extrinsic rewards are negatively related. Where there is already a high degree of intrinsic reward, such as a musician who composes jazz simply because he or she loves doing so, extrinsic rewards may actually reduce the effectiveness of the intrinsic rewards (Deci, 1975).

Kouzes and Posner (1987) found that effective leaders were skilled in using both intrinsic and extrinsic rewards in an additive way rather than an either/or manner. Thierry (1990) took issue with the very concept of intrinsic and extrinsic motivation as an either/or concept, preferring to consider motivation as affected by both personal and situational characteristics that interact with one another to cause a particular outcome.

This caution is helpful to advisers in that if one looks for simple solutions while working with students, then one will fail as an educator and facilitator of student development. Every student is unique, and what will motivate one student will not motivate another. This understanding is critical to an adviser's effectiveness.

Motivating Individuals

How can these key concepts be applied to the role of adviser with individual student government leaders? First of all, the complexity of the research on motivation supports what most advisers have known intuitively all along: no two persons are motivated in the same manner! Some students are highly motivated without much involvement from an adviser, and seem to excel in their roles with little or no help. Others seem to be intrinsically motivated but need an adviser's assistance to help sustain that motivation, especially if external forces, such as limited resources or organizational communication problems, interfere with the student leader's effectiveness, causing the student to become discouraged.

Much of an adviser's role is to assist students in developing skills that they can use effectively as student leaders. One area in which advisers can be of significant assistance is helping students set both individual and organizational goals. Based on Goal Setting Theory, the following points are worth noting as an adviser facilitates the development of student leaders.

Given sufficient ability and high commitment to the goal, the harder and more specific the goal, the better the performance. Advisers should encourage those students with the ability to do so to set specific and difficult — but not impossible — goals. Whether this goal be the accomplishment of a large, involved activity or event; the attainment of a significant goal for a fund-raiser; or the achievement of a particular award such as NACURH School of the Year, a difficult goal can serve as a strong motivating force for an individual. Being specific about the goal is a critical component in this process as researchers have found that the lack of specificity negatively affects the achievement of a goal.

Those people who thought most intensely about how to solve a particular problem were most likely to demonstrate their commitment to solving the problem. Advisers must encourage students to think critically and deeply about a particular problem they may be having as student leaders. The investment of time and effort into solving a problem can result in a viable solution. An adviser can assist students in recognizing the various nuances of a problem that may not be readily apparent, and give them some "food for thought" as they consider how to bring about a solution. The more students understand the various factors of a particular situation, the more likely they are to identify a solution that is sufficient to meet the complexities of that particular problem, and subsequently they are motivated to actively resolve the issue.

Goals that are assigned with a rationale are just as motivating as those set in a participative manner. Living in a country based upon democratic principles, leaders often assume the best way to reach a goal is to have everyone participate in setting the goal. However, sometimes this is not possible, either due to time constraints or the inability to bring together those people involved in achieving the goal. It is helpful for student leaders to know that they may be just as successful in achieving an organizational goal that is assigned, provided that the rationale for the goal is clearly understood by those who are responsible for achieving the goal.

Goals and feedback increase performance, and both together are even more effective in motivating high performance than either is alone. As students increase their skills in goal setting, they will be more likely to achieve those goals. If an adviser also provides them with supportive, yet honest, feedback on their progress toward the goal, the educational aspect of the process is enhanced, not only for achieving that particular goal, but also for subsequent performance.

The Expectancy Theory of Motivation also has some key concepts that can be used effectively by advisers in assisting student leaders to be highly motivated. The theory is based on the premise that a person must have three beliefs (listed below) to be highly motivated, and that motivation and performance strategies that fail to address all three aspects do not work.

They believe they can perform well enough to get what is offered. Advisers can assist students in accurately assessing the skill level for a particular task or activity and, if it is found wanting, can assist them in developing the skills necessary for the job. For instance, a student interested in becoming the RHA president must be able to establish confidence in others that he or she should be selected for the position. Advisers can assist a student in organizing a plan of skill development and service that will help him or her to believe that he or she has a reasonable chance to be elected president.

They believe that they will get what is offered if they perform well. If students do not believe that they have a reasonable chance to get whatever the goal offers (a successful event, a more responsible position of leadership, recognition, or an award), then it is unlikely that they will be highly motivated toward the goal. Advisers can assist students in assessing the likelihood of achieving a particular goal, and if reasonable, encourage the students to work toward the goal. It is also important for students to consider realistically the possibilities of not achieving the goal. For instance, not every institution wins the NACURH School of the Year award, in spite of the many wonderful programs that are developed each year on numerous campuses nationwide. This is a difficult and delicate balance to achieve as an adviser: encouraging the pursuit of the goal within a context of reality.

They believe that what is being offered will be satisfying. Advisers can assist students in assessing whether or not what they want to pursue is of real value to them. For instance, does the student understand the full responsibilities of a particular position and the impact it may have upon his or her other activities and obligations? Advisers can help students assess values that are pertinent to a particular goal.

As student populations continue to diversify, advisers must understand that what they view as motivating may not be motivating to another person due to variations in culture, gender, economic status, sexual orientation, religion, and so forth. Many current and previous theories have a strong bias toward an individualistic orientation, with little or no attention to context or culturally based influences. Sociocultural Theory argues for a reconceptualization of individual cognitive activity towards a perspective that highlights the interdependence of cognitive and sociocultural activities. In this view, motivation is not located solely within the individual, but also with reference to the social and cultural context within which individual actions take place (Rueda & Moll, 1994).

When working with individual students it is advisable to discuss these issues, not only for the learning that the adviser will experience, but also as an opportunity for the individual student to reflect upon the role of culture in his or her life. The following questions may be used as a guide when assessing what might effectively motivate a particular student.

1. What is the role of culturally based knowledge in the motivation of a particular student?

2. What cultural signs and symbols does the student see as motivating?

3. How does the student culturally interact with others (Rueda & Moll, 1994)? Does he or she like to work individually or in group situations? What conflicts might this student experience in working with other student leaders due to variations in culture, gender, religious belief, or sexual orientation?

4. How does the student's culture view obligations to the family, particularly as they relate to regular participation in activities on weekends and holidays?

5. What holidays does the student honor or celebrate? How can advisers assist students in celebrating their culture and honoring their cultural and religious holidays? How can advisers assist students in planning for these events in their lives in conjunction with their student government obligations and their roles as students?

6. How does the gender of a student relate to what he or she finds motivating? What styles of communication are gender related (Gilligan, 1982; Miller, 1976)? How does sexual harassment affect motivation (Mitchell, 1994)?

7. What symbols, biases, or stereotypical actions might negatively affect the motivation of a student (e.g., swastikas, burning crosses, or demonic symbols)?

8. What are the financial needs of a particular student? Does the student need to work to pay for expenses? How might the student's financial needs affect his or her ability to take on volunteer roles with no compensation (Mitchell, 1993)?

Motivating Groups

As advisers, much of one's advising takes place in the context of motivating student government groups to achieve goals. Advisers can assist students in the motivation of groups in at least five ways: (a) sharing expectations, (b) role modeling, (c) conflict management, (d) rewards and recognition, and (e) training and development.

Sharing Expectations

Effective leaders are skilled at letting others know what is expected of them. When group members do not know what is expected of them by the leader and/or adviser, they can react with confusion, frustration, and sometimes even anger if the project is an important one. Often the result is that they lose interest in the project because they believe they can spend their time in more productive ways. In other words, they lose their motivation for the project.

Effective advisers will stress the importance of establishing clear expectations within a group. Advisers must be clear about what they expect of individual student leaders as well as the larger group. If an adviser expects to have weekly meetings with student leaders, that should be made clear. If an adviser expects minutes to be distributed prior to the next meeting, then that expectation should be made clear as well. If students are expected to attend workshop sessions at leadership conferences, then the expectation should be stated before the conference begins.

It is equally important that students share their expectations of each other at the beginning of the formation of the group, whether that be each semester or quarter, or on an annual basis. It is a good idea to repeat the process whenever changes in personnel occur in a group. This gives the group a chance to rethink their expectations of each other and to mature as an organization. It is recommended that after an expectation session has occurred, everyone receive a written copy of the group expectations.

Role Modeling

Role modeling is one of the most powerful behaviors that advisers can use to motivate others. Students will look to advisers to "see" what leaders do. They will observe and reflect upon advisers' actions in their roles as leaders. If advisers are on time and prepared for meetings, then student leaders are more likely to be on time and prepared. If advisers clearly set goals and achieve them, then students are more likely to do the same. If advisers are enthusiastic and energetic, then student leaders are also more likely to be so. If advisers help clean up after events, then students are more likely to help take down the chairs, wash the dishes, and carry out the trash too.

Students will also observe advisers' actions from an ethical standpoint. Are an adviser's actions consistent with his or her words? Does the adviser admit mistakes and take responsibility for them? Does the adviser try to keep communication lines open even with "difficult" students and colleagues? Does the adviser treat students with dignity and respect? Students can learn how to be ethical adults and effective leaders by watching their advisers interact with students and colleagues.

Role modeling at leadership seminars and conferences is also important. Advisers should participate actively in the sessions and activities. If students are expected to be up early each day in order to attend all sessions, then advisers need to be up early for those sessions, too! If students are expected to participate in roll call, then advisers need to be out there too.

Conflict Management

As advisers know, conflict is a certainty when dealing with groups. As an adviser, it is critical to role model effective confrontation techniques when necessary. If inappropriate behavior is left unchallenged (missed meetings, lack of follow through, unethical behavior), then others in the group can become discouraged, resentful, and unmotivated as a result.

Sitting down with students to discuss problematic behavior within a context of their leadership development can be motivating in itself. Often students realize that a problem exists but they are unsure how to solve the problem. At other times they may sense that something is wrong but are not sure exactly what the problem is. Asking questions and finding out students' perspectives on the problem after identifying how they are being perceived by the adviser and others will assist students in developing a realistic picture of their effectiveness as leaders. Once the problem is identified, advisers and students can explore possible solutions.

Many times serious conflicts will develop within a group. It may be necessary for the adviser to step in and facilitate a mediation session between two or more parties. By establishing ground rules for the mediation (e.g., using "I" statements, listening without interrupting, etc.) an adviser can assist students in learning how to solve group conflicts in a mature and productive manner. The adviser also can help them to identify the true nature of the conflict, which often is not what it seemed to be at the beginning of the session. Advisers can assist group members in seeing the complexity of a situation. There are always at least two sides to an issue and, in a group, there may be several sides to the story. Then, after an understanding is established, the adviser can monitor the group's progress in resolving the issues at hand.

The adviser also can be alert to conflicts that may arise out of the diversity of the group. If group members come from a variety of cultural or ethnic groups, some conflicts may be due to a lack of understanding of different culturally based behaviors. Helping group members recognize these behaviors will increase cultural understanding and may reduce conflicts arising from cultural differences. This principle also can be applied to conflicts that may arise out of other human differences such as gender, sexual orientation, and physical ability.

Rewards and Recognition

People like to be recognized for their contributions and student government is a natural setting for noting the accomplishments and contributions of its members. There are many informal and formal ways to reward students for their participation. One easy practice is for the group to pick a "member of the week" to honor at the end of each meeting for contributions made since the last meeting. The student's name should be written into the minutes and could also be put in the residential newsletter.

When a student has done a particularly good job on a program or resolved a particularly difficult challenge, a note from the adviser is a nice way to mark the occasion. It is also wise to encourage student leaders to write notes that state their appreciation for a job well done or for making a specific contribution to the organization.

NACURH and the affiliated regional organizations sponsor a well-organized and regular system of awards and recognition through the "Of the Month" awards. The adviser should strongly encourage student leaders to nominate students, programs, and staff members for well-deserved recognition. Even if the nominee is not selected at the regional or national level, the sense of recognition at the local level will long be appreciated.

Check out the campus and local community for opportunities to recognize a group or individual members of the group. Many campuses have a student government organization that recognizes various campus clubs and organizations for contributions to the campus community. If not, perhaps the campus president or Dean of Students would be willing to acknowledge contributions with a note. Additionally, there may be local organizations that encourage community service with recognition for contributions made throughout the year.

End-of-the-semester or end-of-the-year celebrations can also be very motivating for students. Getting all the members together and giving out certificates of appreciation or awards can make for an exciting event that can be informal and inexpensive, or more formal, featuring a banquet or reception. It is important not to overlook anyone in the process, so it is wise to have a committee brainstorm the names of everyone who made contributions during the time period in question. If possible, put a program together with the honorees' names as a nice keepsake to take home or to share with family and friends.

Training and Development

One of the exciting aspects of working with university students is that they are immersed in learning and very willing to make the effort to develop skills that will help to enhance their effectiveness as leaders. One way to motivate students and keep them excited about their roles is to assist them in strengthening their skills and knowledge about leader effectiveness. This can be done in leadership seminars, role clarification sessions, and individual advising sessions, and through written sources such as newsletters, books, and magazines.

Training and development should be a regular part of an organization's plans. Retreats or workshops should be scheduled well in advance so that group members can arrange their schedules to attend. Written into the job descriptions of council members should be a strong expectation that they will attend development and training seminars and workshops in the normal course of their tenure.

Students should be offered the opportunity to learn how to be effective group members. Sessions should be planned featuring communication skill building, which includes learning about diversity issues, leadership concepts, effective time management, budgeting skills, and conflict management. Students love to take assessment tests, so if the budget permits, an adviser may want to offer the opportunity for group members to complete one or more of the many instruments available for individuals to gain insights into their communication or leadership styles.

As group members participate in these opportunities, they will clarify expectations of each other, learn how to communicate cross-culturally, and gain skills in leadership and management. Those skills and knowledge will enable them to be better group members and, if the group functions well, they will remain motivated and continue their participation in the group.

Practical Approaches

Advisers have the opportunity to motivate student leaders every day. There are hundreds of ways to motivate an individual student or groups of students. This section will (a) discuss public and private recognition, monetary rewards, honorary organizations, and honors and awards; and (b) provide numerous specific examples of ways to motivate students through recognition.

Public and Private Recognition

Student leaders like to be praised and acknowledged for doing something well. It is important to get to know the student leaders one works with as an adviser. This will allow an adviser to know what kind of acknowledgment each student prefers. Some students prefer to receive a note from their adviser and others would rather be told in person or be acknowledged publicly at a meeting for their hard work.

Public praise has many benefits and is often used to motivate others. An example of this is giving a weekly adviser award for doing "A Whale of a Job" that week. This inspires the students in the organization to do something to get the award as well as encouraging those students who have received the "Whale" to continue their quality work.

There are numerous awards that an organization, department, and university give every year to individual student leaders and student organizations. The adviser has the responsibility not only to make sure students are aware of these opportunities for recognition and reward but also to nominate students for such awards.

Private praise can be given in endless ways, such as in a personal note or during a one-on-one meeting. This kind of positive feedback should be specific and given as soon as possible after the behavior is observed. This kind of praise can include noting a person's positive attitude or good communication skills during a meeting.

Remuneration

There are several options for paying volunteer student leaders. There are advantages and disadvantages to paying or compensating student volunteers. Some of the clear advantages are that compensation can be a primary motivator for students to be in leadership positions and that the compensation validates the importance of the position. Some of the obvious disadvantages are whether students get involved primarily for the compensation and the availability of resources.

Mitchell (1993) identified five options for compensating students:

Conference costs. Compensate student leaders by covering the cost of attending leadership conferences in their state, region, and NACURH.

Salaries and stipends. Provide a stipend or salary for their involvement. Typically these are provided only to the executive officers of the RHA and not to hall council officers.

Summer jobs. Hire officers to work in the housing office in some capacity for the summer. This enables officers to make plans for the coming year for the RHA.

Room and board. Provide services in kind such as a room, or room and board. Some institutions provide single rooms or apartments to particular officers, such as the president.

Class credit. Provide one or two class credits per semester for various executive positions.

Students can be motivated by remuneration to get involved in an organization. They also may need the stipend or free room in order to be involved with RHA rather than work in another position to raise funds for school costs. Finally, receiving some type of compensation enables students to see their position as clearly valued and a significant responsibility.

Honorary Organizations and Honors and Awards

Every institution has various honorary organizations as well as honors and awards for student leaders. Advisers should recommend students for these organizations, honors, and awards. Also, it is important for advisers to keep students informed about their opportunities to be recognized individually and as an organization.

The National Residence Hall Honorary (NRHH) is an obvious opportunity for residence hall leaders to be recognized for their outstanding achievements as a leader and student. The NRHH chapter on a campus represents the top 1% of student leaders at that institution in the residence halls. Many NRHH chapters focus on recognizing hall leaders and developing new hall leaders. Institutions typically have some honorary to recognize campus-wide student leaders as well.

There are endless awards and honors through the community, hall, RHA, NRHH, and university, in addition to the state, regional, and national RHA organizations. NRHH has "Of The Month" awards (OTMs) for programs, advisers, RAs, student leaders, executive board officers, and National Communication Coordinators (NCCs) who have achieved excellence during a particular month.

Specific Examples

There are countless ways to motivate student leaders and to let them know about their successes. This in turn inspires them to continue working on their goals and to motivate other student leaders. Here is a list of practical suggestions that have been compiled from *96 Ways To Recognize* (National Residence Hall Honorary, 1996) and *100 Ways To Give Recognition To Volunteers* (Knasel & Kritzman, 1983).

1. Smile.
2. Send a letter of appreciation.
3. Say "We missed you."
4. Greet person by name.
5. Recognize personal needs and problems.
6. Write thank-you notes.
7. Distinguish between groups and individuals.
8. Seek input from students.
9. Be an advocate for students.
10. Review criteria for campus awards.
11. Be a mentor to a student.
12. Nominate for Hall of the Year Award.
13. Send letters to the families.
14. Create a special and fun award.
15. Make door decorations.
16. Distribute a publicity release.
17. Award buttons, T-shirts, and candy.
18. Send a letter to the president.

19. Say "Thank you."
20. Sponsor a day in honor of...
21. Post banners.
22. Award plaques and trophies.
23. Send notes.
24. Nominate for awards and honorary organization membership.
25. Share poems, quotes and words of wisdom.

There are numerous ways to motivate individual students and student groups. The best way for an adviser to motivate students is to get to know them as individuals and as a group. This will allow the adviser to determine what motivational techniques and tools will be most effective. The three case studies below can be used in training or for discussion with other advisers and students.

Case Study 1

The president and vice president of the RHA were elected together last spring. The organization was excited about their platform. The president and vice president had several new good ideas for the organization. They planned to attend hall council meetings every week, revise the election code, establish a hall council presidents' roundtable, and develop at least two new large RHA programs.

It is now the middle of November and only the president has been attending the hall council meetings regularly. The representatives who elected the president and vice president are beginning to question whether they will follow through with their commitments. The other executive board members are following through with their responsibilities but wonder when the rest of the president and vice president's platform will be initiated. The president and vice president both seem to think each is working very hard and that the other one needs to take some initiative to get things going.

1. What are the issues?
2. What motivational theory or theories apply to this situation?
3. What approach could be used to motivate the student(s)?

Case Study 2

A student organization at a large state university has initiated planning for the next school year. The organization is known for providing some outstanding programs for students on campus. The leaders are proud of the programs they have provided every year for the past 10 years. The organization has relied on students participating in their programs and getting involved in the organization because of the success of the programs. Over the past three years, the organization has experienced a gradual decline in membership and participation in their programs. It seems like the student interest in the organization's traditional programming for the past 10 years has declined also. The student leaders of the organization want to continue the traditional programming because they know how to do it well.

1. What are the issues?
2. What motivational theories apply to this situation?
3. What approach could be used to motivate the student(s)?

Case Study 3

The new executive board of the organization had a summer retreat in June. They developed goals, expectations, and tasks to be completed over the summer. They also worked on developing as a team and improving their communication skills. Over the remainder of the summer some of the executive members worked hard on their assigned tasks and some appeared to do nothing. The board returned early for the fall semester and reviewed their goals, expectations, and plans for the year. Some of them were motivated and excited about the upcoming year and plans. Other members were beginning to talk about how much they needed to get done and that they were unsure they could get everything done in time. Over the first month of the semester a few board members attended all the necessary meetings but did not follow through on their goals and the plans for the year. The remaining executive board members confront them but nothing changes. As a result, all of the executives are not following through with their goals and plans. Everyone on the executive board appears to be unmotivated.

1. What are the issues?
2. What motivational theories apply to this situation?
3. What approach could be used in this situation?

References

Deci, E. L. (1975). *Intrinsic motivation.* New York: Plenum.

Gilligan, C. (1982). *In a different voice: Psychological theory and women's development.* Cambridge, MA: Harvard University.

Gollwitzer, P. M., Heckhausen, H., & Ratajczak, K. (1990). From weighing to willing: Approaching a change decision through prior or postdecisional mentation. *Organizational Behavior and Human Decision Processes, 45,* 41-65.

Green, T. B. (1992). *Performance and motivation strategies for today's workforce: A guide to expectancy theory applications.* Westport, CT: Quorum Books.

Hawkins, J. N. (1994). Issues of motivation in Asian education. In H. F. O'Neil, Jr., & M. Drillings (Eds.), *Motivation: Theory and research* (pp. 101-115). Hillsdale, NJ: Lawrence Erlbaum Associates.

Hull, C. L. (1952). *A behavior system: An introduction to behavior theory concerning the individual organism.* New Haven, CT: Yale University.

Knasel, L., & Kritzman, M. (1983). *100 ways to give recognition to volunteers.* Kalamazoo, MI: Western Michigan University.

Kouzes, J. M., & Posner, B. Z. (1987). *The leadership challenge: How to get extraordinary things done in organizations.* San Francisco: Jossey-Bass.

Latham, G. P., Erez, M., & Locke, E. A. (1988). Resolving scientific disputes by the joint design of crucial experiments by the antagonists: Application to the Erez-Latham dispute regarding participation in goal setting (Monograph). *Journal of Applied Psychology, 73,* 753-772.

Lee, T. W., Locke, E. A., & Phan, S. H. (1992). *Explaining the assigned goals-incentive interaction: The role of self-efficacy, and personal goals.* Unpublished manuscript, University of Washington, Seattle, WA.

Locke, E. A., & Latham, G. P. (1990). *A theory of goal setting and task performance.* Englewood Cliffs, NJ: Prentice-Hall.

Locke, E. A., & Latham, G. P. (1994). Goal Setting theory. In H. F. O'Neil, Jr., & M. Drillings (Eds.), *Motivation: Theory and research* (pp. 13-29). Hillsdale, NJ: Lawrence Erlbaum Associates.

McClelland, D. C. (1961). *The achieving society.* New York: Van Nostrand.

Miller, J. (1976). *Toward a new psychology of women.* Boston: Beacon.

Mitchell, S. E. (1993). Motivation of paid and volunteer students. In N. W. Dunkel & C. L. Spencer (Eds.), *Advice for advisors: The development of an effective residence hall association* (pp. 55-62). Columbus, OH: Association of College and University Housing Officers-International.

Mitchell, S. E. (1994). *Creating campus climates that are free from sexual harassment: Implications for leaders in higher education.* Unpublished doctoral dissertation, University of San Diego, San Diego, CA.

National Residence Hall Honorary. (1996). *96 ways to recognize.* Macomb, IL: Author.

Rueda, R., & Moll, L. C. (1994). A sociocultural perspective on motivation. In H. F. O'Neil, Jr., & M. Drillings (Eds.), *Motivation: Theory and research* (pp. 117-137). Hillsdale, NJ: Lawrence Erlbaum Associates.

Skinner, B. F. (1953). *Science and human behavior.* New York: Macmillan.

Thierry, H. (1990). Intrinsic motivation reconsidered. In U. Kleinbeck, H. Quast, H. Thierry, & H. Hacker (Eds.), *Work motivation.* Hillsdale, NJ: Lawrence Erlbaum Associates.

Vroom, V. H. (1964). *Work and motivation.* New York: Wiley.

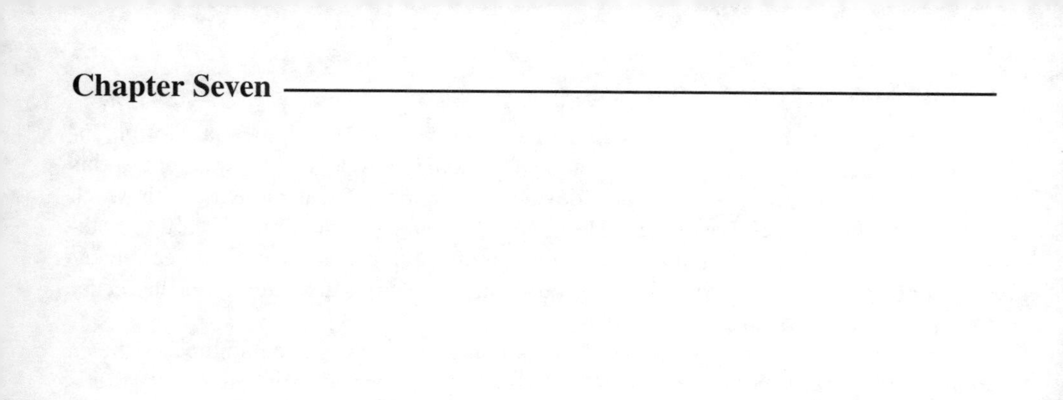

Chapter Seven

Group Development Concepts

Kent Sampson
Oklahoma State University

Group Development Concepts

This chapter reviews 13 conceptual models of group development and offers insight into group processes impacting student leaders in residence life. Inherent in this view is the philosophy that the student development approach is a guideline with which advisers should be well acquainted. The chapter concludes with brief overviews of ethical principles, decision making, and evaluation of group performance — three dimensions to be considered by the wise adviser. Finally, scenarios are offered for the reader to use as a discussion aid with others.

Someone once said that a camel was a horse designed by a committee. At times small group experiences do end in an unsatisfactory manner. Ideally, as the adviser utilizes concepts contained in this chapter, he or she will be less likely to work with groups that result in "camel" outcomes. The expression "none of us is as smart as all of us" underscores a belief in the ability of small groups to solve problems. If "two heads are better than one," then several heads must be best of all! We utilize groups to solve problems, and they are an aspect of nearly every dimension of existence. From birth individuals are shaped first by the family group and then by schools, churches, community groups, student committees, residence halls, Greek life, classes, work groups, political causes, friendship networks, and much more. Obviously the group has a significant impact upon the individual and upon the individual's ability to contribute to the environment in which he or she resides.

Indeed, in the postsecondary student's experience, it is likely that no one group is more influential than the one in which the student resides, particularly during the first two years. Thus, there is considerable implication for the development of community in the residence environment: floor, wing, hall, house, club, and so forth. This notion of community in residence life depends on a successful group and individual experience in order for such a community to exist. An outstanding example of individuals effectively working together in groups for a good cause has been the recent emergence of the national volunteer "Into The Streets" program which attracts college students into voluntary community service.

Residence life staff who advise groups must possess certain skills to be effective in bringing about group growth and productivity. Blimling and Miltenberger (1981) suggested eight such skills: (a) conceptual application skills, (b) counseling skills, (c) basic information skills, (d) administrative skills, (e) teaching skills, (f) leadership skills, (g) crisis management skills, and (h) good human relations skills. They posited that the degree to which residence life advisers possess these skills has a major impact on the degree to which groups are productive, positive, and achieve goals. They summarized the student development approach as follows:

1. An acceptance of a developmental philosophy characterized by the belief that individual growth toward maturation is universal, sequential, increasing in complexity, and quantitatively different.
2. Acceptance of students as determiners of their own destinies.
3. The belief that the role of student personnel professionals and, specifically, of residence hall staff as educators with definable skills, is to assist students in achieving goals that they have identified for themselves.
4. The belief that students are able to determine what is best for them.
5. Recognition that students are complex living organisms and the institution must deal with both their cognitive and affective development.

Accordingly the student development model can be viewed as including (a) self-assessment and goal setting, (b) assessment, (c) teaching and instruction, (d) evaluation, and (e) goal setting. This model views as critical the establishment of goals as a means of assessing where one is today and where one wants to be in the future. As goals are pursued the individual is able to identify his or her strengths and weaknesses. In the teaching stage the individual pursues skills that enables him or her to move closer to goal attainment. In the fourth stage, the student evaluates his or her competencies and readiness to achieve established goals and priorities. This stage then takes the successful individual to new goal setting. In the event goals are not realized, further teaching and instruction are necessary.

With the premise that group development concepts should be rooted in the student development approach, the next section of this chapter includes a review of 13 approaches to group development.

Coons' Five Stages of Development

In 1974, Frederick Coons, a psychiatrist who worked with the health center at Indiana University, identified five key aspects of the development of the individual: (a) resolution of the parent/child relationship, (b) solidifying a sexual identity, (c) formation of a personal value system, (d) development of the capacity for true intimacy, and (e) choosing a life's work (Blimling & Miltenberger, 1981).

These five stages must be negotiated by the college student in order for him or her to progress on to successful life ventures. The degree of achievement that the individual experiences in these varied stages influences his or her success and contribution to a group effort. For example, when participating in a group, the individual who doesn't have a solidly identified value system may be unreliable, or may not be able to contribute his or her own opinions or perspectives. Likewise, an individual who has not developed a solid sexual identity may participate in the group without an appropriate understanding of sex roles of group members and indeed may inhibit group progress.

Chickering's Seven Vectors of Development

In 1969, Arthur Chickering, a psychologist, researcher, administrator, and scholar, hypothesized seven developmental vectors for individuals between the ages of 18 and 25. Chickering suggested that many of these vectors develop simultaneously and represent key issues students face during the college years. Although vectors are integrated and may be tied together, the attainment of one was not contingent upon another. Chickering's seven vectors included: (a) achieving competence, (b) managing emotions, (c) becoming autonomous, (d) establishing identity, (e) freeing interpersonal relationships, (f) developing purpose, and (g) developing integrity.

The individual who successfully navigates and achieves integration of these vectors is more likely to become a strong group contributor. The less developed student would not likely become a full contributor to the group. Thus, it is helpful for the residence life adviser to be aware of these developmental issues in order to assist the individual where possible, as well as to recognize how that person functions within and impacts upon the group experience.

Carl Jung's Theory of Typology

Realizing that how individuals interpret information impacts both communication and effectiveness within groups, the focus now turns to Carl Jung's theory of typology. He believed that there are four distinct ways by which individuals observe and interpret information received from the environment. He then identified four psychological styles of observing experiences: analytical, feeling, intuitive, and sensate ("of the senses," such as hearing, seeing, etc.). Though Jung believed that nearly everyone possesses all four operating styles, each person prefers one type over the other three. Seeing the same phenomena through "differing lenses" serves as a source for unique interpretations. Certainly every adviser has observed these differing viewpoints as key issues in the group's development.

It may be helpful to examine the four styles more closely. The *analytical* individual considers how the pieces fit together. This cognitively oriented person wants to know the causes and effects of the situation. In contrast, the *feeling* type person operates based upon an "affect, not effect" mode. In other words, internal feelings drive this person's interactions and decision making. If the circumstance "feels" right, it has value.

The *intuitive* individual is one who trusts hunches. Such a person seems to operate instinctively, and often is unaware of how such insight came about. Intuitives are quick to comprehend the big picture and prefer not to "sweat" the details. A *sensate* person, however, is tuned to information acquired through the senses. The sensate prefers detail and desires closure. Operating in the "here and now" is important.

The above four types also differ in the degree of *introversion* and *extroversion*, or the degree to which they include others in processing the situation. Thus the introverted person processes the situation alone, while the extrovert desires to involve others in the experience. One final contrast to consider in looking at Jungian typology is that of *structure* and *flow*. The structured individual wants information in a logical, predictable form, while a flow-oriented person is content to deal with information as it comes.

Jung suggested then that each person possesses a combination of personality factors that, when summed up, becomes a frame of reference. The astute group adviser (and leader) then may best assess group progress (and group promise) based upon how individuals are "seeing" the issues. Differences within the group may be signals of how differing types are attempting to validate their frames of reference. An effective adviser will help to move groups away from the "I am right, you are wrong" mentality to one of looking for common ground from which to proceed.

Situational Leadership — Hersey and Blanchard

To better understand the group leader's role, Hersey and Blanchard (1982) offered a model of situational leadership. This model is based upon the contention that leaders are able to modify their style to fit the situation and that the primary situational factor the leader must respond to is the members' level of task maturity. They contend that there is no one best leadership style, only effective and ineffective ones. Style should be determined by the maturity of the group and its members in regard to a given task or situation. A group's maturity is based on the members' ability (high to low) to perform the task and their willingness and confidence to perform it. The authors contended that maturity is specific to a particular task and is not generalizable across different tasks. They identified four leadership styles: (a) telling, (b) selling, (c) participating, (d) delegating. Each style puts different emphases on the leader's relationship and task behaviors as they relate to the particular maturity level of the group. As the group becomes increasing mature to the task, the leader changes style.

The *telling* style of leadership is appropriate for groups with low maturity, that is, where members are unable to perform certain assigned tasks without detailed instructions. In the telling dimension, other appropriate words might be guiding, directing, or establishing.

The *selling* style is most appropriate for groups whose members are willing but unprepared to take responsibility for the task. This style involves both high relationships and high task behaviors. Here the leader is more directive and also reinforces members' enthusiasm and desire to perform. Alternative descriptions for selling would be explaining, verifying, or persuading.

The *participating* style is high on the relationship dimension and low on the task dimension, and is appropriate for groups with a moderately high level of maturity. In this case, the group has the knowledge and skill to accomplish a task but lacks the confidence and enthusiasm to carry it through. Here the leader provides a high level of support and encouragement, shares in the decision-making process, but provides little direction. The participating style could be described as encouraging, collaborating, or committing.

In contrast, the *delegating* style is for groups with a high level of maturity and the technical competence, knowledge, enthusiasm, motivation, and commitment needed to carry the task through. This style is low in task and relationship behaviors. Here the leader serves primarily as a consultant and supporter of the group's efforts. The leader in this situation offers the group a high degree of autonomy to resolve problems and make decisions. Alternate words for delegating would be observing, monitoring, or fulfilling.

Leaders, then, can facilitate the progression through the four styles by first providing directions, training, and instruction so members are able to successfully accomplish tasks. The leader next slowly withdraws directive behaviors to encourage members to assume increasing responsibility. Leaders then are able to increase support or relationship-oriented behaviors by giving praise and rewards for good performance. As group members gain confidence in their ability to perform without outside direction, the leader then slowly withdraws both relationship- and task-oriented behaviors and allows the group to assume full responsibility for itself. Hersey and Blanchard (1982) suggested that leadership is a process of influencing the activities of an individual or group in efforts towards goal achievement in a given situation. It follows then that the leadership process is the function of a leader, follower, and other situational variables, hence the formula L = (L, F, S).

Maslow's Theory of Motivation

Abraham Maslow (1954) advanced a summary regarding his long-standing concern for causation of human behavior when he attempted an organized presentation of the total spectrum of motivational factors. He identified seven basic needs: (a) physiological needs, (b) safety needs, (c) belongingness and love needs, (d) esteem needs, (e) self-actualization needs, (f) desire to know and understand, and (g) aesthetic needs.

Maslow posited that there is a hierarchy for needs satisfaction and suggested that some needs are more basic than others. Basic physiological needs such as food, water, and oxygen are seen as cornerstone needs. He contended that as these basic needs are satisfied the individual moves toward higher-level need behavior. Though there is no clear-cut consecutive pattern, and a certain amount of overlap, a logical progression from basic to more aesthetic needs tends to occur. From these key motivational needs of the individual come certain components that contribute to group strength and group development. These include belongingness or acceptance, esteem or value within the group, and status and relative rank within a group. Using Maslow's approach, it is interesting to realize that each group — and the individuals within each group — may go through some of these need levels in a slightly different way. Advisers can recognize students' places on the hierarchy ladder as they ascend toward maturity and reinforce their progress along the way.

Carl Rogers' Group Model

Often referred to as one of the founding fathers of counseling and psychology, Carl Rogers (1948) offered a comprehensive and discerning analysis of the process of learning and growth in groups. He noted several characteristics of groups that are relevant to today's adviser. He believed there are seven basic phases of the group process: (a) emotional release, (b) gradual exploration of attitudes, (c) growing conscious awareness of denied elements, (d) a changed perception of the problem in an altered frame of reference, (e) a changed concept of the group and the self, (f) a new course of consciously controlled action better adapted to the underlying reality of the situation, and (g) improvement in social and interpersonal relationships (Rogers, 1948).

Rogers pointed out the importance of affective as well as cognitive dimensions of the group experience. He recognized that group process is as important as content when attempting to solve problems or tackle tasks. Rogers' influence upon Benne, Bradford, and Lippitt (1951) was apparent as they described the step-by-step actions of most groups in discussion and group thinking. They believed the following nine stages were characteristic of most groups: (a) clarifying of group procedures, (b) building a feeling of permissiveness to discuss problems, (c) getting the problems out, (d) boiling the problems down and selecting a common problem, (e) developing and maintaining group direction, (f) maintaining realism in group discussion, (g) obtaining facts and data, (h) making group decisions, and (i) evaluating group progress. These components of the group process serve to remind the adviser of the importance of understanding and recognizing both content and process functions within a group.

Group Content and Process — Glanz and Hayes

Glanz and Hayes (1967) noted three distinct qualities that differentiate groups from other types of gatherings:

1. The members must be in face-to-face contact with one another.
2. It must be possible for them to have a high degree of interaction.

3. They must have some common goal for which they are willing to expend certain energies to reach.

The authors also recognized the importance of interaction, size, and function as being critical to the definition and use of the term "group." Most groups fall into one of three categories: those that attempt to accomplish a task, those that attempt to develop or change participants, or those that provide structure to learning situations.

Glanz and Hayes (1967) stressed the importance of the distinction between content and process of groups. *Content* is the "what" of a group discussion or the subject matter of the group deliberations or actions. *Process* is the "how" of a group discussion or the way the content is handled or discussed by the group. The content of a group is best viewed as its task or its purpose for being, while process refers to phenomena that clarify the dynamics of group behavior.

Group productivity tends to be superior to individual productivity when the task lends itself to a division of labor, when the presence of people tends to increase social rewards for productivity, and when members make contributions in their areas of expertise and do not continue to exert influence in areas where they do not have extensive knowledge (Glanz & Hayes, 1967). When the group approach is utilized to solve tasks, groups should be as small as possible, yet consistent with the task situation. It is important that persons with expert knowledge be included wherever possible to increase productivity. More time must be allotted for group task solutions than for individuals working alone. Provision should be made for social rewards for high group productivity.

Tuckman's Model — Forming, Storming, Norming and Performing

Tuckman (1965) reviewed 50 articles based on stages of group development with varying time periods. He distinguished between stages of social or interpersonal activities (social realm) and stages of group task activities (task realm), noting that some confusion in the literature existed because often this distinction was not clear.

For each realm he proposed four stages of group development. He indicated that in the *social realm* the stages are testing dependence, conflict, cohesion, and functional roles. In a *task realm* the stages are orientation, emotionality, relevant opinion exchange, and emergence of solutions. Tuckman believed that in any small cohesive group a task always exists, and that a task is accomplished through interpersonal relations.

At the conclusion of his review, Tuckman reduced his model to four words, "forming, storming, norming, and performing." He related each of the group stages to stages of child development. The *forming* stage is similar to the first year of an infant's life, including orientation, testing, and dependence. *Storming* is characterized by conflict, emotionality, and resistance to influence and task requirements, all characteristics of a rebellious young child. In the *norming* stage in-group feelings and cohesiveness develop, new standards evolve, and new roles are adopted. This sensitivity to others is mirrored in the development of a child and represents a central aspect of the socialization process. In the *performing* stage the group becomes a functional instrument for dealing with the task and present reality. This is more characteristic of the mature human being as well. In a 1977 review with Jensen, Tuckman added a fifth stage, *adjourning*.

This human developmental analogy might be appropriate for the adviser who sees a group in its immature, infantile stage as it begins to go through identification and focus upon the problem, and then brings it to an analysis and finally resolution. The adviser might observe these types of stages in the evolution of the group process.

Cartwright's Approach to Group Dynamics

Cartwright (1951) proposed eight principles of group dynamics that may be utilized to promote or encourage behavior or attitude change among group members. These eight principles are:

1. If the group is to be used effectively as a medium of change, those people who are to be changed and those who are to exert influence for change must have a strong sense of belonging to the same group.

2. The more attractive the group is to its members, the greater is the influence that the group can exert on its members.

3. In an attempt to change attitudes, values or behavior, the more relevant they are to the basis of attraction to the group, the greater will be the influence that the group could exert upon them.

4. The greater the prestige of a group member in the eyes of other members, the greater the influence he or she can exert.

5. Efforts to change individuals or subparts of a group will encounter strong resistance if deviation from group norms is the intended result.

6. Strong pressure for changes in the group may be established by creating a shared perception by members of the need for change, thus making the source of pressure for change lie within the group.

7. Information relating to the need for changes plus plans for change and consequences of change must be shared with all relevant people in the group if change is to be realized.

8. Changes in one part of a group produce strain in other related parts that can be reduced only by eliminating the change or by bringing about readjustment in the related parts (Cartwright, 1951).

Cartwright's approach critically underscores the issue of the dynamics and the process of what is occurring in the group experience. The group experience means there are interdependent issues, tasks, and concerns at work, and the wise leader and adviser must identify these early in the group experience. The ability to do so will enable him or her to be a more effective and respected adviser.

Sherif and Sherif Model — Results of Group Observations

No two social psychologists have had more influence from the standpoint of the observation of group behavior and the dynamics within it than Sherif and Sherif (1964). Their famous "Robbers' Cave" study was a masterpiece in observation of groups and provides advisers with insight into the way observers may be seen by group members. They concluded that observers gain acceptance and develop good rapport in the following ways:

1. To insure by word and deed that group members are aware of the observer's lack of authority in situations where the group needs to be together.

2. To appear in word and deed as a "bigger brother or sister" who is interested in them, wishes them well, and may be helpful on occasion.

3. To avoid any signs of dislike or disapproval of any member on the one hand or signs of favoritism on the other.

4. To avoid suggesting or initiating activities for the group, unless such activities are deliberately planned as a part of a research design.

5. To be helpful in activities initiated by group members without display of skills which put the observer in a rivalry situation for status with group members (Sherif & Sherif, 1964).

They found that the greatest difficulty for observers was to temper their efforts to be helpful, their efforts to be accepted, and their cautiousness in following instructions in a way that all three could be accomplished. Thus, advisers must be careful about being neither too aggressive — as though they are meddling or taking over — or too passive — as though they are indifferent or have little interest in projects and activities. The effective adviser knows how to show interest in activities by raising questions of concern, yet being careful not to compete with or "steal the show" from student leaders.

Gibbs and Gibbs Model — Group Roles

Gibbs and Gibbs established four types of roles into which groups enter (Bennis & Shepard, 1961): task roles, group maintenance roles, task and group roles, and individual roles. Their classification or taxonomy system enables the adviser to better see not only how groups grow and evolve but also the individual's contribution to the group as well as the group's impact upon the individual (Bennis & Shepard, 1961).

Task roles are primarily useful for contributing toward problem solution. Activities here include initiating, seeking information, seeking opinion, giving information, giving an opinion, elaborating, coordinating, summarizing, and testing feasibility.

Group maintenance roles are primarily useful for satisfying the needs of other members and contributing to group integration. Components here include encouraging, gatekeeping, standard setting, following, and expressing group feeling.

Task and group roles focus upon the activities being accomplished as well as the roles that the group may maintain. Components include evaluating, diagnosing, testing for consensus, mediating, and relieving tension.

Individual roles are expressions of personal, as opposed to group, needs. Elements here include being aggressive, blocking, self-confessing, competing, seeking sympathy, special pleading, horsing around, and seeking recognition or withdrawal.

Raths — Clarifying, "Show-How," and Security-Giving Operations in Groups

Raths approached the group model by observation of the teaching and learning process which individuals experience. He made reference to clarifying operations, "show-how" operations, and security-giving operations.

Group Development Concepts

Clarifying Operations

1. Clarifying through reflection.
2. Clarifying through use of a definition or illustration.
3. Clarifying by pointing out apparent inconsistencies.
4. Clarifying similarities and differences.
5. Clarifying through questioning underlying assumptions.
6. Clarifying through anticipation of consequences.
7. Clarifying through questioning meaning.
8. Clarifying by examining points of difficulty.
9. Clarifying if a personal statement was meant to show only a personal feeling or one that the individual feels all people must hold.
10. Clarifying by relating feelings to behavior.
11. Clarifying through a review of the steps in a person's logic.
12. Raising questions of purpose.
13. Seeking origins of an expression or idea.

"Show-How" Operations

1. Demonstrating.
2. Using resource persons and teaching aids.
3. Exploring alternate ways to solve the problem.

Security-Giving Operations

1. Meeting the need for belonging.
2. Meeting the need for achievement and personal growth.
3. Meeting the need for economic security.
4. Meeting the need to be free from fear.
5. Meeting the need for love and affection.
6. Meeting the need to be free from guilt.
7. Meeting the need for acceptance of the other person.
8. Controlling conflict situations (Raths, 1948).

Lifton — Approach To Group Member Roles

Lifton (1967) identified three roles which groups and individuals may adopt as they attempt to identify, select, and solve problems. The three are (a) group task roles, (b) group growing and vitalizing roles, and (c) antigroup roles.

Group Task Roles

Group members may facilitate and coordinate group problem-solving activities in at least a dozen different ways:

Initiator/contributor. Offers new ideas or changes ways of handling group problems or goals. Suggests solutions for handling group difficulties. Establishes new procedures and new organization for the group.

Information seeker. Seeks clarification of suggestions in terms of factual adequacy and/or authoritative information and pertinent facts.

Opinion seeker. Seeks clarification of values pertinent to what the group is undertaking or of values involved in suggestions made.

Information giver. Offers facts or generalizations which are authoritative or relates own experience pertinent to group problem.

Opinion giver. States belief or opinion pertinent to suggestions. Emphasis on proposal of what should become group's views of pertinent values.

Elaborator. Gives examples or develops meanings. Offers rationale for suggestions made before. Tries to deduce how ideas might work out.

Coordinator. Clarifies relationships among ideas and suggestions, pulls ideas and suggestions together, or tries to coordinate activities of members of subgroups.

Orienter. Defines position of group with respect to goals. Summarizes. Shows departures from agreed directions or goals. Questions direction of discussion.

Evaluator. Subjects accomplishment of group to standards of group functioning. May evaluate or question practicality, logic, facts, or procedure of a suggestion or of some unit of group discussion.

Energizer. Prods group to action or decision. Tries to stimulate group to greater or higher quality activity.

Procedural technician. Performs routine tasks (distributes materials, etc.) or manipulates objects for group (rearranging chairs, etc.)

Recorder. Writes down suggestions, group decision, or products of discussion. Provides "group memory."

Group Growing and Vitalizing Roles

Group members may also work toward building group-centered attitudes and orientation:

Encourager. Praises, agrees with, and accepts others' ideas. Indicates warmth and solidarity in his attitude toward members.

Harmonizer. Mediates intergroup scraps. Relieves tensions.

Compromiser. Operates from within a conflict in which his idea or position is involved. May yield status, admit error, discipline himself, and "come halfway."

Gatekeeper and expediter. Encourages and facilitates participation of others: "Let's hear." "Why not limit length of contributions so all can react to problem?"

Standard setter or ego ideal. Expresses standards for group to attempt to achieve in its functioning or applies standards in evaluating the quality of group process.

Group observer and commentator. Keeps records of group processes and contributes these data with proposed interpretations into group's evaluation of its own procedures.

Follower. Goes along somewhat passively. Is friendly audience.

Antigroup Roles

Group members may try to meet individual needs at the expense of group health rather than through cooperation with the group:

Aggressor. Deflates status of others. Expresses disapproval of values, acts, or feelings of others. Attacks group or problems. Jokes aggressively. Shows envy by trying to take credit for others' ideas.

Blocker. Negativistic. Stubbornly and unreasoningly resistant. Tries to bring back issues group intentionally rejected or bypassed.

Recognition-seeker. Tries to call attention to self. May boast, report on personal achievements, and in unusual ways, struggle to prevent being placed in "inferior" position, and so forth.

Self-confessor. Uses group to express personal, non-group oriented feeling, insight, ideology, etc.

Playboy. Displays lack of involvement in group's work. Actions may take form of cynicism, nonchalance, horseplay, or other more-or-less studied, "out-of-field" behavior.

Dominator. Tries to assert authority in manipulating group or some individuals in group. May use flattery, assert superior status or right to attention, give directions authoritatively, interrupt contributions of others, and so forth.

Help-seeker. Tries to get sympathy response from others through expressions of insecurity, personal confusion or self-deprecation beyond reason.

Special interest pleader. Verbally for "small business owner," "grassroots community," "homemaker," "labor," and so forth. Actually cloaking personal prejudices or biases with stereotypes that best fit individual need (Lifton, 1967).

No one can be a leader if he or she represents ideas or behaviors beyond the group's present knowledge or acceptance. The best leader is the one who helps the group achieve the desired goal. To do this the leader needs to help the group examine each of the following ideas or questions.

1. What common goal exists among group members?
2. What can they expect from the leader?
3. What roles does the group need?
4. What can group members expect from each other?
5. What limits do group members wish to set on their own behavior?
6. What limits exist which sets boundaries on group actions or goals? (Lifton, 1967).

It would be simple if the leader could just raise each question for discussion, conduct a vote, and record each decision. Unfortunately for those seeking simple solutions, this is not likely to be the case. Both individual and group behavior is much more complicated than simply the words being spoken. Thus, the effective leader from the very beginning describes to the group the leader's actual *desired* role within the group. This individual must be willing to let the group make its own mistakes.

Small Group Communication Theory — Burgoon, Heston, and McCroskey

In a functional approach to small group communication, Burgoon, Heston, and McCroskey (1974) identified seven unique characteristics of small groups: (a) frequent interaction, (b) development of a group personality, (c) the establishment of group norms, (d) coping behaviors, (e) role differentiation, (f) interdependent goals, and

(g) assembly effect bonus. The last category refers to the bonus in productivity that is gained by the combined effort of all group members working together versus the same individuals working independently.

Burgoon et al. (1974) also provided advice to advisers and groups that wish to avoid defensive behavior.

1. It is important that individuals avoid criticizing other group members who express different views.
2. Communication that is perceived as an attempt to control others will probably result in negative reactions.
3. People who bring "hidden agendas" to a group breed distrust.
4. If the group is to have a genuine relationship of trust it must learn to cope with deviance and signs of defensive behaviors by providing a supportive climate.
5. An appearance of lack of concern for the feelings of other members will likely produce defensiveness.
6. An attitude of superiority arouses defensive behavior.
7. The more dogmatic or close-minded people are in their beliefs about "truth" the more likely others are to react defensively (especially those who disagree).

Leadership and the Group

In his insightful and challenging book *Why Leaders Can't Lead,* Warren Bennis (1990) addressed the difficulty of being a leader and made reference to the "doppelganger" effect. A doppelganger is a ghostly double. One issue that Bennis raised was that often organizations tend to select others to work for and with them that are cut from the same mold. This, of course, lessens the opportunity for different points of view and diverse input into the process of decision making and group productivity.

Mintzberg (as cited in Bennis, 1990) named eight prime leadership skills including (a) peer skills, (b) leadership skills, (c) conflict-resolution skills, (d) information-processing skills, (e) skills in unstructured decision making, (f) resource-allocation skills, (g) entrepreneurial skills, and (h) skills of introspection.

Bennis also addressed the challenges and difficulties that groups and individuals face during times of disaster or major change. This might occur when a leader resigns or a group falls apart. He suggested 10 priorities that groups or organizations must pursue cooperatively if successful outcomes are to be achieved.

1. Recruit with scrupulous honesty!
2. Guard against the "crazies"! Though innovation is desirable, it may also be seductive and lead to massive failure.
3. Build support among like-minded people whether or not you recruited them.
4. Plan for change from a solid conceptual base.
5. Don't settle for rhetorical change. In other words actual change needs to take place versus writing or discussing without any action.
6. Don't allow those who are opposed to change to appropriate basic issues. Keep them involved and informed.
7. Know the territory!
8. Appreciate environmental factors! For example, a work environment that is too crowded or always too cold or hot will affect productivity and group morale.

9. Avoid future shock! In other words, ensure that as one projects and plans for the future, conclusions are based upon history as well as the current real situation. This will avoid trauma and lessen the anxiety of group participants.

10. Remember that change is most successful when those who are affected are involved in the planning. Nothing makes people resist new ideas more adamantly than their belief that change is being imposed on them.

Bennis (1990) distinguished between leaders and managers. Leaders are people who do the right thing while managers are people who do things right! Both roles are crucial, but they differ profoundly.

In a study of 60 corporate leaders over several years, Bennis (1990) defined four competencies evident in every member of the group: (a) management of attention, (b) management of meaning, (c) management of trust, and (d) management of self.

Regarding *management of attention,* many leaders have the ability to draw others to them because they have a vision, but also because of their extraordinary dedication to the work before them. *Management of meaning* basically reminds one that in order to solicit support and participation leaders must communicate a vision. Too much ambiguity or lack of direction is likely to lead to group failure.

Management of trust is essential to all groups and organizations. The primary determiner of trust is reliability or constancy. When a leader is effective in his or her management of trust, each individual always knows where he or she stands and the direction from which the leader is coming.

Management of self involves knowing one's own skills and deploying them effectively. This also refers to a leader's capability to assert discipline and self-control.

As Bennis spent time with these various leaders he collected synonyms for the word "failure." In his interviews he heard the words mistake, error, false start, bloop, flop, lose, miss, foul-up, stumble, botch, bungle, but never the word failure. One leader said that failure was just enabling her to get her mistakes out of the way as soon as possible so that she could proceed with success. Another indicated that failure simply is another way of doing things.

Without question, leadership (or the lack thereof) is keenly felt and seen in any group or organization. It provides the pace and an energy level to work, and it also empowers the work force. Empowerment then is the collective effort of leadership and group contributions. In an organization with effective leaders, empowerment is most evident in four themes:

1. People feel significant.
2. Learning and competence matter.
3. People are part of a community.
4. Work is exciting.

Thus, in his contemporary study of the challenges that leaders face today, Bennis (1990) reminded the reader of some of the inherent challenges and rewards for those who are most effective with groups and organizations.

Having considered major theories of student development which should offer insight for the adviser, the remainder of the chapter will focus upon three key dimensions of effectively advising and facilitating student groups: ethical principles, decision making, and evaluation of the group's performance.

Ethical Principles

For many years student affairs professionals have attempted to spell out ethical standards to ensure that professional staff and advisers to employ principles and practices that are just and responsible. Indeed to operate without such principles would suggest that student affairs employees have no profession! Canon and Brown (1985) emphasized the importance of Kitchner's five basic ethical principles: (a) act to benefit others, (b) promote justice, (c) respect autonomy, (d) be faithful, and (e) do no harm. While reviewing these five principles, it is imperative to give sound attention and consideration to the ethical duties and expectations of those who work with student groups.

Act to Benefit Others

Service to students is the basic principle underlying student affairs practice: the obligation to make a positive contribution to another's welfare. More specifically, student affairs professionals exist (a) to promote healthy social, physical, academic, moral, cognitive, career and development of students; (b) to bring a developmental perspective to the institution's total educational process and learning environment; (c) to contribute to the effective functioning of the institution; and (d) to provide programs and services consistent with this principle.

Promote Justice

Student affairs professionals are committed to assuring fundamental fairness for all individuals within the academic community. In pursuit of this goal, principles of impartiality, equity, and reciprocity are basic. When greater needs than resources are available or when interest of parties conflict, justice requires honest consideration of all claims and requests, and equitable (not necessarily equal) distribution of goods and services. A crucial aspect of promoting justice is demonstrating an appreciation for human differences and opposing intolerance and bigotry concerning these differences.

Respect Autonomy

Student affairs professionals respect and promote individual autonomy and privacy. Student affairs professionals also protect students' rights to act as a free agent, their right of self-determination, their right to confidentiality, and their right to informed consent. Thus, students' freedom of choice and action are not restricted unless their actions significantly interfere with the welfare of others or the goals of the college.

Be Faithful

Student affairs professionals are truthful, honor agreements, and are trustworthy and loyal in the performance of their duties.

Do No Harm

Student affairs professionals do not engage in activities that cause physical or psychological damage to others (intentional or unintentional). Student affairs professionals are especially vigilant to assure that the institution's policies do not (a) hinder students' opportunities to benefit from the learning experiences available; (b) threaten an individual's self-worth, dignity or safety; or (c) discriminate unjustly or illegally (Canon and Brown, 1985).

Criteria for Personal Ethical Choices

Student affairs professionals can ask themselves the following questions to reinforce their actions, decisions, or approach to practice.

1. Are you being responsible? Making a responsible choice?
2. What are the probable consequences of your choice?
3. If you were on the receiving end, would these consequences be acceptable?
4. Is this a special situation? Or are you pretending it is?
5. Can you discuss the problem with the affected parties before you make your decision?
6. Would you want your employees or colleagues to make the same decision?
7. Would you have any difficulty explaining it on "60 Minutes"?
8. Did you do what you said you would do?
9. Are you being honest with yourself about the real issue?
10. Do you "walk your talk"?
11. Do you obey the law?
12. Do you clarify organizational values and priorities?
13. Do you know and take care of your people?
14. Do you develop trust and respect with others?
15. Do you develop cohesiveness and teamwork vertically and horizontally?
16. Do you increase commitment of others by creating a sense of ownership?
17. Do you discuss ethical issues and dilemmas and encourage others to do the same?
18. Do you accept each other's differences and seek compromise?

Decision Making

An important element of the group experience is decision making. The manner in which groups and leaders reach decisions has much to do with the quality of the decision, but also the degree to which the group experiences cohesiveness. The group that selects an autocratic leader who may be more efficient in decision making may not feel as good about its representative input due to the tendency of that individual to decree what appears to be best from his or her perspective.

In a democratic society, *voting* in groups is well recognized. However, overdependence on voting is characteristic of groups and sometimes can be seen as an element of immaturity. For example, voting prematurely might be seen as a way to end discussion and debate rather than provide the opportunity to continue interacting and gain further growth and greater insight into the particular issue. Though voting is appropriate at times within certain groups, it shouldn't be an initial resort in most group processes. For example, the use of straw polls can gain perspective without formalizing a final vote. Since votes establish majorities and minorities, groups should avoid voting too early in the group process.

Another valuable tool in the group process is *compromise*. As complete agreement is seldom possible among all people on any issue, the desire in group decision making to move towards elements of agreement or to reach a compromise can be seen as a technique which values all input while at the same time moving toward a conclusion.

Another decision-making technique is that of reaching *consensus*. This is ideal for most problem-solving groups. Consensus is a decision agreed upon by all members, or action reflecting valid insights and values of all parties. It is a process in which the group attempts to isolate areas of conflict and disagreement through discussion. Through study, acquisition of facts, discussion, and other methods, the group agrees upon a common plan or decision. Consensus reflects the successful operation of group members and leaders. The size of the group may affect the achievement of consensus. Often the larger the group, the greater the difficulty in reaching consensus.

A final approach to decision making is that of *block-and-gap consensus*. In this approach the entire problem is surveyed and examined. Rather than isolating and highlighting areas of conflict, areas of agreement and common belief are selected from a common text. Though large gaps may exist between agreements, the focus is only on the blocks of agreement that exist. The thought here is that the early agreements can facilitate later successful efforts towards consensus. This block-and-gap treatment of the idea of consensus reflects the realistic appraisal of the nature of human beings to be different. Conflict divides; agreement breeds consensus!

Monitoring and Evaluating Group Performance

Evaluating the progress and success of the group includes monitoring group development. The following questions may be appropriate for the group adviser:

1. Are the participants the same group members for whom the program or event was designed?
2. If members with different needs or interests are participating, what changes in activities should be made?
3. To what extent is the behavior of group members consistent with the purposes of the group as well as theories of group development?
4. To what extent are group activities delivered as intended?
5. If attrition of group members occurs, when and why did it occur and who was lost?
6. How can the group's activities be modified to better meet the group's purposes or members' needs?
7. What things have happened or are happening that are unexpected?
8. How will my success as a group adviser be determined?

Evaluations are most useful when issues and activities are addressed that can help an adviser understand and design interventions to improve group functioning. Evaluations may be informal or formal. Informal efforts are often more useful and less expensive than comprehensive evaluations. They also are more easily obtained. On the down side, they are somewhat more subjective. In the informal evaluation, questions can provide data that will be of assistance in planning future events. For example, "Was this program helpful to you?" "How might this activity be improved to meet your needs?" "How many students attend this event?"

In the more formal planning process observations are made and information gathered during and not after the activity. This approach is intended to identify and correct potential problems prior to the conclusion of the activity. An example would be the use of a questionnaire to obtain objective data. Basic questions (e.g., "What do we as an organization want to do?") should be asked in varying ways throughout the program plan. The formal evaluation process allows for observation of who is involved and who is not. The following questions are intended to serve as an aid in evaluating the effectiveness of student groups. They should serve to illuminate concerns that are relevant to planning group activities. Additionally, some generic questions are offered which are useful for monitoring group performance.

1. What is the purpose of the group?
2. What do group members want from the group or from a particular activity?
3. What are the needs of group members?
4. What types of programs or events have proven useful for members of this group?
5. Do group members possess the skills, attitudes, and commitment to fulfill their responsibilities?
6. Are there any unusual or atypical environmental or group member characteristics that should be taken into account?
7. What kind and degree of outcomes can be expected given the purposes of the event and the group's purpose?
8. If changes in the behavior of group members are to be expected, when might these changes be exhibited?
9. What does the adviser need to know to determine whether a group has been effective?
10. How can a high-quality group experience be assured?

Hopefully these questions will assist the RHA adviser to better ascertain the growth of the group, the leadership capability of individuals within the group, and the potential for obtaining successful outcomes.

Scenarios for Discussion

The following scenarios are provided for use as discussion aids between students and advisers regarding how group performance and productivity may be enhanced.

1. Of four newly elected executive officers, only one, Paul, the vice president, is not "tight" with the others due to previous activities. What must be done to help Paul succeed as part of this executive team?
2. Gabe, an engineering student, has been elected hall president. Quite talented, he seems to operate on an "efficiency model" basis and appears "way too logical and analytical" for most of the other students. Can you help Gabe (and the group) to adapt and better work together?
3. The floor living unit has become divided over whether or not to allow residents to smoke. Floor leaders are in a quandary and are being criticized for doing nothing. Can you help them sort out this sensitive issue and reassess their leadership?

4. The housing department is considering a major policy change. Your group realizes the need for change on some issues. However, you suspect such may not be the case this time. How can you as the adviser aid here?

5. You have observed that the student government association you advise is no longer very productive. Attendance is declining and objectives have become blurred at best. Much business is incomplete. How does the adviser best intervene in this case?

6. You have inherited a group previously advised by a rather controlling individual. In fact, the group had become dependent on her for most things ranging from clerical support to paying bills. You believe it best to put more responsibility and initiative back in the hands of the group. How would you accomplish this?

7. Recent information has led you, the adviser, to conclude that the treasurer has been taking organization money and using it for personal needs. How do you approach this sensitive issue?

8. You are sitting with your RHA assembly when it becomes likely the group is about to make a decision which is heavily influenced by incorrect information presented earlier in the discussion. Do you intervene? If so, how?

9. Students in your group normally are able to make decisions in prompt fashion. However, this time they are indecisive and getting increasingly frustrated over their inability to reach closure. How can you as adviser help with this dilemma?

10. The Vice President of Student Affairs has requested your assistance in promoting the new room and board rates for next fall. Your RHA group has opposed these increases and feels that its opposition, questions, and concerns were ignored by the Vice President (and others). How do you proceed?

Conclusion

The complexities of human behavior, group work, and the significant roles and interactions between leader and group are not simple matters to facilitate, advise, or direct. This chapter on group development concepts has identified and affirmed certain basic components and successful ingredients of groups that may contribute to the achievement of desired results.

References

Benne, K. D., Bradford, L. P., & Lippitt, R. (1951). *Human relations and curriculum change.* New York: Holt, Rinehart & Winston.

Bennis, W. (1990). *Why leaders can't lead: The unconscious conspiracy continues.* San Francisco: Jossey-Bass.

Bennis, W., & Shepard, H. (1961). *The planning of change: Readings in the applied behavioral sciences.* New York: Holt, Rinehart & Winston.

Blimling, G. S., & Miltenberger, L. J. (1981). *The resident assistant: Working with college students in residence halls.* Dubuque, IA: Kendall/Hunt.

Group Development Concepts

Burgoon, M., Heston, J., & McCroskey, J. (1974). *Small group communication: A functional approach.* New York: Holt, Rinehart & Winston.

Canon, H., & Brown, R. (1985). *Applied ethics in student services.* San Francisco: Jossey-Bass.

Cartwright, D. (1951). Achieving change in people: Some applications of group dynamics theory. *Human Relations, 4,* 381, 392.

Chickering, A. W. (1969). *Education and identity.* San Francisco: Jossey-Bass.

Glanz, E. C., & Hayes, R. W. (1967). *Groups in guidance.* Boston: Allyn & Bacon.

Hersey, P., & Blanchard, K. (1982). *Management of organizational behavior: Utilizing human resources* (4th edition). Englewood Cliffs, NJ: Prentice Hall.

Lifton, W. (1967). *Working with groups: Group process and individual growth.* New York: Wiley.

Maslow, A. H. (1954). *Motivation and personality.* New York: Harper.

Raths, L. (1948). What is teaching? *Sociatry 2*(3, 4), 197-206.

Rogers, C. (1948). *Dealing with social tensions.* Danville, IL: Interstate Printers & Publishers.

Sherif, M., & Sherif, C. (1964). *Reference groups: Exploration into conformity and deviation of adolescents.* New York: Harper and Row.

Tuckman, B. W. (1965). Developmental sequence in small groups. *Psychological Bulletin, 63*, 384-399.

Tuckman, B. W., & Jensen, M. A. C. (1977). Stages in small group development revisited. *Group and Organizational Studies, 2,* 419-427.

Chapter Eight

The Role of the RHA in Developing Inclusive Communities

Ross Papish
University of Georgia

Vernon Wall
Consultant, New Visions

Introduction

The residence hall association (RHA) serves residents through a variety of functions. In many cases the RHA is successful at providing social and educational programs. At best, it becomes a unifying voice for the resident collective, a program board, and an opportunity for student involvement and leadership. The RHA may be the most significant opportunity for students to find a connection to the campus or to their community. It may be a chance to be heard; it may help some residents to feel that they belong, to feel that they matter. The essence of diversity within the RHA is to find the value and worth of all residents and to help create inclusive educational communities.

The first edition of *Advice to Advisers* challenged us to examine diversity through a personal lens, to look at ourselves as advisers as well as the RHA (Wall, 1993). Emphasis was placed on examining personal values to find a place for diversity in the philosophy of advising an RHA. The authors' goal in this edition is to challenge advisers to take the next necessary step: Action!

Implementing a process of inquiry, assessment, planning, change, and evaluation as it relates to diverse students and issues is a challenging task for which the adviser is responsible. This chapter will outline key areas where action is likely to impact on the perceptions and the reality of diversity within the RHA. Examination of the mission and values of the RHA, the process of diversification within the organization, the quality of campus life, and evaluation and assessment efforts can all contribute to an understanding of how the RHA, and specifically the RHA adviser, play a significant role in diversity education, representation, and inclusion.

Mission and Values

A clear mission statement is only useful if it is lived, not merely stated (Peters, 1987). It has become a part of housing practice to develop a mission statement for the department (ACUHO-I, 1991; Council for the Advancement of Standards for Student Services/Development Programs, 1997). While the RHA is a student-run organization, it is the responsibility of the RHA adviser to bring the mission and values of the housing department to the students' attention. The housing department and the RHA must explore the extent to which the mission has been embraced or complemented within the RHA, with special attention to initiatives related to diversity.

Has the RHA clearly stated a position regarding diversity? Many RHAs develop a constitution as the formal guide to organization purpose and practice (see Chapter 5 in this volume). Often included in the constitution is a statement of commitment to diversity education (Verry, 1993). It is the role of the adviser to assist student leaders in making the constitution and the diversity statement a way of acting, not just a way of thinking. Activities of self-examination, planning, programming, recruitment, and dialogue contribute to an action orientation related to diversity.

Advisers and RHA leaders should also be aware of regional and national RHA organization statements regarding diversity and, more specifically, whether there are any expectations that member institutions support the diversity statement. Institutions must recognize the extent to which their diversity statements are compatible with that of any organization with which they choose to affiliate. In some instances there may be complementary missions toward inclusivity, and in other cases (such as some religiously affiliated colleges and universities) the diversity statement may be a source of conflicting values or goals.

How has the RHA demonstrated a commitment to inclusivity? What role do RHA leaders see themselves and the RHA playing in the education of residential communities regarding diversity? An action orientation starts with the mission and values of the RHA and then is supported through intentional activities which indicate a commitment to diversity beyond thought or written statements. While many student leaders are sophisticated in their understanding of the developmental role of the RHA, it is the adviser's responsibility to make the group conscious of the value of an articulated commitment to inclusivity and diversity education. Modeling an action orientation will do more to create an organizational culture of proactivity, inclusion, and education than written intent alone.

The diversity statement of the University of Michigan RHA (1997) exemplifies this action orientation. It incorporates philosophical aims, specificity about inclusion, and statements of practical action and intent toward achieving inclusivity:

> The Residence Halls Association (RHA) — in order to represent all residents, and promote openness and the acceptance of all, despite differences — hereby pledges and affirms its support of the role of diversity on the University of Michigan campus and especially inside the residence halls.
>
> Through outreach and involvement with the Multicultural Councils and Minority Peer Advisers, the RHA will strive to create the best living-learning community for all, regardless of race, gender, ethnicity, religion, sexual orientation, lifestyle, or political beliefs.
>
> By supporting diverse groups and persons with funding and other requested support (that are within the RHA's means), the RHA will strive to understand diversity, expand diversity through the halls, and broaden diversity and its definition.
>
> With our work toward the goal of a truly diverse campus, we wish to create a tightly knit network of all the resources available for students in the halls; we desire that all can accept each other for who they are; and we hope to educate residents about their multicultural lounges, Multicultural Councils, and Minority Peer Advisers, and how they may fully use these resources.

"Mattering" within the RHA

The success of an RHA is dependent on many factors, yet the transcendent theme that may surpass all others in impact is that in residence halls, students matter and are highly valued (Komives & Tucker, 1993). Why do students get involved? Why do they want to hold leadership positions? In many cases students who get involved in RHAs find a home there, a place where they feel they belong, a place where their voices are heard and count. This is the essence of "mattering" within the RHA.

The challenge of diversification within colleges and universities has long been a central focus of student affairs work (Fenske & Hughes, 1989). Remaining in the forefront of diversity education, student affairs administrators have taken pride in the awareness and attention given to multiculturalism. Housing professionals in particular have had a strong impact on inclusivity through staff selection processes, staff development and training, and educational programs. To what degree has housing incorporated the RHA as an integral part of the diversification process?

In the latter context, diversification is used in the broadest sense as the infusion of consciousness regarding diversity. This approach to inclusion happens at all levels of an organization, from minority involvement, to having a voice within the organization, to educational programs, to the adviser level. Critical questions which reflect attention to an environment concerned with "mattering" include: Have diverse students historically been involved in and represented within the RHA? Why would minority students get involved (or not get involved) in the RHA? Why might a minority student want (or not want) to attain a leadership position within the RHA? Do diverse student populations feel welcome in the organization? What rewards are gained by ensuring diverse involvement and a commitment to diversity education?

Inclusivity Tug-of-War

Creating environments where students believe they matter is no easy task. Beyond the real issues addressed previously there is also the management of perceptions people hold, whether right or wrong (Schlossberg, Lynch, & Chickering, 1989). For many students perception is reality, and attention to (and especially the intentional inclusion of) minority voices and educational programs may be a unique challenge. The inclusivity "tug-of-war" is the perception that minority students may shift power from the majority student population. While diversification has little to do with power and more to do with equity and education, there will be varying perceptions. As more minority students become involved, majority students may resist or "flee." Some advisers may ignore this phenomenon. This issue is not unlike that which confronts our society as white residents flee neighborhoods when minority residents move in. Whether the separation or struggle between student groups is real is just as important as the perception of these barriers and differences. Advisers must take an active role in providing opportunities for dialogue on this issue. Whether through one-on-one advising, in-service training, public forums, or educational programs, advisers can offer crucial insights as to inaccurate perceptions and real struggles experienced by members of the organization and the community.

It is critical that student leaders be the driving force behind the process of education and inclusion while the adviser provides guidance and support. Beginning with philosophical questions and proceeding to assessment and then to action, RHA officers must lead and involve their constituency in this educational process. With intentional efforts balanced with an awareness of perceptions, the organization must take steps toward being a truly representative voice for all residents. It is easy to say that all students have the opportunity to take part, that all students can attend meetings, that all students can express their opinions, and that all students matter. However, how do advisers know that residents believe this? The adviser is in the fortunate position to help the student leaders, the RHA, and the community to examine the challenging issues of diversity with an objective eye and an action-oriented intent while managing issues of perception and equity. Activities which promote the exploration of community attitudes include sponsoring an open forum on diversity, conducting a community survey on peer and community relationships (some housing organizations conduct student satisfaction surveys which include questions from the RHA), interviewing past and current RHA leadership and members, and developing relationships with minority student organizations.

What is the RHA's Diversity Quotient?

Pascarella, Edison, Nora, Hagedorn, and Terenzini (1996) stated that perhaps the most intimidating questions posed to student affairs practitioners relate to assessment. "What evidence do you have that what you are doing is making a difference?" For many years, higher education has confronted challenges of diversity and inclusion. Smith, Wolf, and Levitan (1994) stated that studying diversity no longer means simply developing a demographic census of who is involved. The goal is to develop a process of change that can be sustained for the long term.

The challenge of knowing where to start on the journey toward creating inclusive educational communities may seem overwhelming to the RHA adviser. One strategy that may prove helpful is calculating the RHA's diversity quotient. This quotient is best represented through the equation:

Intent + Involvement + History = Outcomes

Intent includes the goals and objectives that have been developed in the area of inclusivity. What has the RHA done strategically to provide a plan of action for becoming an organization that values inclusivity? How is this value illustrated in action?

Involvement includes not only the diverse make-up of the membership but also the position or level involvement of its diverse members. What leadership positions do members of diverse groups hold? What efforts are being made to recruit and retain students who represent all residents?

The final component of the diversity quotient is *history*. This includes the history of involvement of diverse students in the organization and past incidents (both positive and negative) that have contributed to an image of the organization in the minds of students in relation to inclusion and diversity. These three components (intention, involvement and history) contribute to the *outcomes* of the RHA's efforts in the areas of diversity and inclusion.

Applying this diversity quotient to existing RHA issues is the next step. Two examples are listed below.

Issue: Retention of Minority Students in RHA

Intent

What goals have been established in this area by the organization?

What statements have been developed to illustrate commitment to the issue?

How will the organization know that the goals have been achieved?

Involvement

What opportunities for involvement are available for all students?

What support is in place for minority student member development?
What keeps minority students involved in the organization?

History

What trends can be seen related to retaining minority students in the organization?
How does the organization benefit from having diverse members?

Issue: Diversity Programming

Intent

What goals have been established in this area by the organization?
What support or training has been given to ensure programming success?
How will the organization know that the goals have been achieved?

Involvement

Are all students involved in providing and attending diversity programs?
Do nonminority students see the value of providing and attending diversity programs?

History

How have students supported diversity programming efforts?
What are the challenges to providing programming initiatives?

While this section has focused on the RHA and its culture, it is important to point out that the "diversity quotient" of the campus community and even the department of housing also must be assessed as strategies are developed. The RHA is a product of its environment. Issues and incidents occurring on campus affect the progress of the RHA in its attempts to move toward successes in this area.

The key to creating inclusive communities is asking the tough questions. The goal of this chapter was to provide advisers with a vehicle by which these tough questions can be framed. Through inquiry, planning, dialogue, and evaluation advisers can assist RHAs to provide safe places for all students to grow and contribute. It is crucial. It is important. It is what we should be about.

Typical Scenarios

The authors polled a few RHA advisers to find typical problems related to diversity and inclusivity. Each campus faces its own unique challenges related to diversity. Therefore, these scenarios are intended to provide proactive examination to help advisers address these and other issues with the student leadership.

Ask the following questions after each scenario:

1. What is the adviser's responsibility to the housing department regarding this issue?
2. What is the adviser's responsibility to or role in the RHA as a whole, and with RHA leaders specifically?
3. What is the historical context of this issue at the college or university?
4. Is the outcome more likely to be a temporary resolution or a long-term solution?
5. How might the adviser and the RHA include others who need to explore or understand this issue?

6. How do residents feel or what do residents want related to this issue?

Scenario 1: The Mission Statement Dilemma

The university does not support recognition of diversity or inclusion of specific minority groups, yet the RHA feels compelled to explicitly include these students. Some members of the RHA would like to do educational programs which may be considered controversial but necessary.

Scenario 2: Representation within the RHA

The RHA historically has lacked minority involvement. More specifically, there have been few or no minority leaders on the executive board. No one has complained, but some students (and the adviser) wonder why. There is occasional discussion among some members about whether or not this is a problem. Should anything be done?

Scenario 3: Preaching to the Choir

The RHA has conducted numerous educational programs on diversity and multicultural issues. Attendance at these programs continues to be residents who are already somewhat aware and enjoy these programs. There seems to be little success in reaching those residents who really need to learn about the issues. It is frustrating because some problems still persist even though specific programs have been targeted toward communities struggling with the issue. How does the RHA get through to these residents?

Scenario 4: The RHA and Resident Assistants

The RHA has attempted to recruit minority members and leaders. These efforts have been slightly successful. The problem is that many, if not most, of the minority students get recruited as resident assistants (RAs). The RHA serves as a stepping stone toward being an RA and thus struggles with recruiting new members all over again. Minority representation on the RA staff is much higher than in the RHA.

References

Association of College and University Housing Officers-International (ACUHO-I). (1991). *Ethical principles and standards for college and university housing professional: Standards for college and university student housing*. Columbus, OH: Author.

Council for the Advancement of Standards for Student Services/Development Programs. (1986). *Standards and guidelines for housing and residential life programs.* College Park, MD: Author.

Fenske, R. H., & Hughes, M. S. (1989). Current challenges: Maintaining quality and increasing student diversity. In U. Delworth & G. R. Hanson (Eds.), *Student services: A handbook for the profession* (pp. 555-589). San Francisco: Jossey-Bass.

Komives, S., & Tucker, G. (1993). Successful residence hall government: Themes from a national study of select hall government structures. In N. W. Dunkel & C. L. Spencer (Eds.), *Advice for advisors: The development of an effective residence hall association* (pp. 27-43). Columbus, OH: ACUHO-I.

Pascarella, E. T., Edison, M., Nora, A., Hagedorn, L. S., & Terenzini, P. T. (1996). Influences on students' openness to diversity and challenge in the first year of college. *Journal of Higher Education, 67*(2), 174-195.

Peters, T. (1987). *Thriving on chaos: Handbook for a management revolution.* New York: HarperCollins.

Schlossberg, N. K., Lynch, A. Q., & Chickering, A. W. (1989). *Improving higher education environments for adults: Responsive programs and services from entry to departure.* San Francisco: Jossey-Bass.

Smith, D. G., Wolf, L. E., & Levitan, T. (1994). *Studying diversity in higher education.* San Francisco: Jossey-Bass.

University of Michigan Residence Hall Association. (1997). *Diversity statement.* Available http://www.umich.edu/~rha/docs/diversity/diversity97.html

Verry, B. (1993). The organizational structures of RHAs. In N. W. Dunkel & C. L. Spencer (Eds.), *Advice for advisors: The development of an effective residence hall association* (pp. 45-54). Columbus, OH: ACUHO-I.

Wall, V. (1993). Diversity and the RHA. In N. W. Dunkel & C. L. Spencer (Eds.), *Advice for advisors: The development of an effective residence hall association* (pp. 89-98). Columbus, OH: ACUHO-I.

Relationships Residence Hall Associations Have with Their Institutions

Carolyn "Waz" Miller
East Carolina University

Allan Blattner
Allegheny College

Relationships RHAs Have

The purpose of this chapter is to illustrate why it is essential for residence hall associations (RHAs) to cultivate positive and mutually beneficial relationships with numerous campus constituents. Since an RHA represents a significant campus population, it serves as a natural conduit to a variety of campus groups. Due to the fact that an RHA is an integral part of the campus learning community, four essential principles which categorize learning communities will be discussed, and practical applications for developing relationships between RHAs and residence life offices in accordance with these principles will be shared. Additionally, since an RHA serves as a major leadership organization within the campus community, collaboration between RHAs and student government groups, programming councils, and other campus components will be examined.

Review of Background Literature

The Student Learning Imperative (American College Personnel Association, 1994) addressed many issues, needs, and reasons why student groups, such as RHAs, are practical avenues for student development. Student development provides advisers with a better understanding of student skills and knowledge (see also Chapter 7 on group development concepts). The hallmarks of a college-educated person include practical competence skills and a coherent integrated sense of identity, self-esteem, confidence, integrity, aesthetic sensibilities, and civic responsibilities (Astin, 1996). Skills such as decision making and resolving issues with others are commonly utilized within the RHA setting. Furthermore, the concepts of learning, personal development, and student development are inextricably intertwined. Higher education traditionally has organized its activities into academic affairs and student affairs. However, this dichotomy has little relevance to post-college life, where the quality of one's job performance, family life, and community activities are all highly dependent on cognitive and affective skills (Astin, 1996). Many adult skills are difficult to classify as there is overlap as well as growth which occur from both cognitive and affective development. It is a well-known fact that approximately three-fourths of student learning occurs outside of the classroom (Astin, 1996). This is why the residence hall community and the RHA are such successful conduits for student learning. The impact of an institution's academic program is mediated by what happens outside the classroom. Peer group relations, for example, appear to influence both affective and cognitive development (Astin, 1996). If a student is involved with a student organization, volunteer opportunity, or job setting, the student applies classroom knowledge within that environment. This practical application will substantiate the student's knowledge base, and understanding of the concepts and skill development will be enhanced.

Membership in an RHA as well as other purposeful organizations increases a student's learning. Exposure to governance, mission statements, and group goal setting increases one's awareness of civic responsibilities. Certain conditions promote learning more than others. For example, learning and personal development are enhanced when students participate in groups organized around common curricular issues (Astin, 1996).

When attending to conditions that support learning and personal development, synergy may result when students and institutional agents interact in ways that foster student interest and a feeling of belonging. The goal is to create environments where all students have opportunities to participate in ways that contribute something to, as well as take something from, an experience (Kuh, Schuh, & Whitt, 1991).

RHAs Focus on Learning Communities

Schroeder (1994) identified "the four I's" — involvement, investment, influence, and identity — as "principles *essential* to the development, implementation, and maintenance of learning communities" (p. 176). Schroeder further stated that "the principles are both sequential and cyclical — that is, increased student involvement leads to increased investment, which, in turn, leads to greater influence and eventual identity with the unit" (pp. 174-175). These principles provide a theoretical foundation for a discussion of practical suggestions aimed at building solid relationships between RHAs, residence life offices, and other campus groups.

Involvement

As an organization representing all students living in residence halls, the RHA is convenient to join, welcoming, non-threatening, and seeking active involvement by members. Since many RHAs establish executive board positions which require prior involvement within the organization, officers may bear the responsibility for recruitment of new members. The improvement of residence hall community living is the common goal that brings students together and promotes ongoing interaction. Most RHAs begin the year with leadership training which focuses on members getting to know one another on a personal basis. Members share individual goals, family information, hobbies, interests, etc., and begin to feel that they belong and matter to the organization. Many RHAs focus on building and maintaining close relationships among the members to prepare for the myriad of ups and downs experienced by any organization throughout the year. Many members become friends and provide ongoing support as well as healthy challenges to one another.

Once personal relationships are established and people begin to feel comfortable with the larger group, work on projects, policies, and programs can begin. Since RHAs represent the students living in the residence halls, it is natural for these organizations to work closely and continuously with housing or residence life offices. In order for this relationship to be supportive, contact must be regular and two-way. The RHA adviser serves as the liaison between the students and the staff. One way to insure that ongoing and open communication occurs is to include an RHA representative at weekly professional staff meetings. This individual can give a report on the most recent RHA meeting, answer questions, and request support as needed in a direct manner. It is beneficial for RHA members get to know the chief housing officer or director of the residence life department. These individuals should have good rapport and should be able to discuss openly key issues because they will pioneer new plans, policies, and programs and will often work together in order to benefit students. Hopefully, as a result of this positive and productive interaction, relationships will also develop between the entire RHA and the residence life staff.

Another important way for the residence life office to help involve an RHA is by assisting members with their personal, social, and career growth. Extracurricular involvement, particularly in leadership positions, has at least modest implications for students' career paths. This may stem from the fact that such involvements enhance self-confidence along with interpersonal and leadership skills (Pascarella & Terenzini, 1991). Additionally, research indicates that students are more likely to take advantage of educationally purposeful out-of-class learning opportunities when both the institution and the students devote time, effort, and resources toward this end (Kuh, Schuh, & Whitt, 1991).

Investment

Investment is a reflection of psychological ownership. It flows naturally from involvement. Investment is also a consequence of the ethic of care — students clearly care about one another and their group (Schroeder & Mable, 1994).

Students become comfortable with their roles and want to become more involved as they become invested in other RHA members as well as in the organization's goals. Organizational pride is prevalent and members want to utilize their leadership skills and potential to move the group forward. Expectations of members are clearly defined and responsibilities of officers and members are clarified in the RHA constitution.

Many times RHAs will institute a recognition program, such as Leader of the Week, to increase esprit de corps and reward individual efforts and contributions. This is especially meaningful when nominations are made by peers within the organization. This type of recognition also promotes a strong work ethic and encourages people to go above and beyond, as this is valued and appreciated. This feeling of being cared about, and being recognized as worthwhile, gives individuals a sense of purpose which carries over to other aspects of their lives.

One of the main ways that residence life offices invest in RHAs is by helping them obtain the funding necessary to realize their goals. It is highly advisable that a certain amount of money per residence hall student be allocated to the RHA budget. The residence life office can also be supportive as the RHA seeks to participate in fundraising opportunities such as carpet or refrigerator rental programs. Additionally, the residence life office should be receptive to other proposals for monetary support such as the sharing of vending machine revenue.

Depending on philosophy and availability, some residence life offices show investment in the goals of the RHA by providing some members (especially executive board members) an honorarium. This benefit can range from a credit on the college or university account to reduced room and meal costs to a cash stipend. Others are able to offer campus employment (either over the summer or during the academic year) that helps the student earn money; some of these positions directly relate to the office held by the student (e.g., employing the RHA treasurer over the summer to audit the hall government accounts).

Providing an office for the RHA is another way that a residence life office can show investment in the group. Many successful RHAs have office space which they use for meetings, storing files and equipment, as well as other important uses. Ideally the office should be located in a place that is central to campus and promotes awareness and accessibility. This may be an empty space in the same facility in which the residence life office is located or in a centrally-located residence hall.

There are many other ways that residence life offices can show investment in RHAs, including access to copy machines, telephones, and computers, plus helping to offset the costs of postage/mailing, long-distance calls, and printing/duplicating. Assisting the group to connect with other campus resources such as the food service and conference office may help them receive additional benefits from the institution.

Influence

Influence is essentially a consequence of an ethic of responsibility, where control is vested in group members and students exert maximum influence over their physical and social environments. This concept of principle influence is a cornerstone of student governance and a major characteristic of learning communities (Schroeder & Mable, 1994). RHA members come from individual residence halls and are entrusted by their hall constituents to represent accurately their perspectives and interests. Each hall must be represented appropriately in order to meet the needs of the residence hall population.

Since RHA members help establish expectations of one another and have the ability to change the constitution, they feel invested and, therefore, assist in holding members accountable to the organization. Members learn that it is permissible to disagree, just as long as this occurs in a diplomatic and acceptable manner. Through the RHA constitution, membership expectations are defined, including grade point average requirements, attendance policies, and membership role responsibilities.

Students need to understand that they are members of an educational community and that their actions influence how much they and others will benefit from the residence hall experience (Chickering & Reissner, 1993). When students become involved and express their needs through the appropriate channels, they can make a difference and promote change, just as they will have the opportunity to do later in life.

Students must be full participants in any effort to modify their residential environments, for they will ultimately determine the meaning and impact of any institutional policy (Kuh, 1996). As such, RHA members should be consulted on a continual basis regarding procedural changes and policy modifications recommended by the staff. For example, many colleges and universities will not change their residence hall handbooks without RHA approval. Additionally, changes or additions to residence hall policies should originate from the RHA. If students would like a policy implemented or changed, a resolution could be brought to the RHA, discussed and voted on by the members, and, if approved, forwarded to the appropriate administrators.

Depending upon policies and procedures within each institution, the involvement of the RHA can be solicited and integrated into the housing system. One example of student leader input in decision making is having an RHA member serve on the committee that makes recommendations regarding students who petition to break their residence hall contract. RHA members also gain a sense of involvement by serving on departmental committees, programming task forces, and staff search committees.

A critical time of the year for collaboration between the RHA and the residence life office is during the development of the housing budget. It is important to involve RHA members in this process from beginning to end. Fiscal control, such as managing large sums of money and contracting with outside agencies, helps students learn responsibility. In addition, the process of resource allocation provides many teachable moments if students have access to forums in which the trade-offs, conflicts, politics, and compromises that are part of institutional resource allocation are discussed (Kuh, Schuh, & Whitt, 1991). They will gain valuable knowledge regarding budget development within the department and the overall budget situation at the institution. This will enable the RHA members who participate in the process to help residence life professionals present and explain the budget to the whole RHA, hall governments, and individual students.

Identity

The RHA's mission is to provide residents with the best possible community experience. This includes making resolutions for policy recommendations and facility improvements as well as initiating fun, social, educational, and service opportunities and activities. All of the students within the RHA focus on improving the quality of the overall community through addressing student needs. This type of common focus is characteristic of a learning community.

Students who are RHA members also demonstrate their identity through wearing apparel that includes the RHA acronym or logo and the school name. This occurs both on campus as well as during local, state, regional, and national conferences. Some RHAs also denote members by placing name signs on their room doors. This actually serves a dual purpose: (a) to identify the RHA representative for hall residents, and (b) to provide special recognition for the individual member on an ongoing basis. Many RHAs do a lot of awareness promotion and public relations work, especially at the beginning of the school year. This helps to unite members toward the goals and also illustrates the importance of this organization to other campus constituents.

To summarize, residential communities that promote student learning and development are characterized by a high degree of student participation and involvement, control of bounded space, common interests and purposes, high degrees of social interaction and social stability, transcendent values, and student influence. In effective learning communities, students know they matter — their participation and involvement are central to their day-to-day experience.

Service Learning and RHAs

One of the most promising trends in American higher education is the rapidly growing campus interest in volunteerism and service learning. This interest is reflected not only in the establishment of President Clinton's Learn and Serve America: Higher Education program, but also in the burgeoning membership of the Campus Compact, a grassroots consortium of colleges and universities that is attempting to promote student involvement in community service activities (Astin, 1996).

During high school, many students actively volunteer their time toward community efforts, but this often does not carry over when they begin college careers. Since many institutions require freshmen to live on campus, and since the RHA is the largest residence hall student organization, it is a natural resource to tap in order to encourage continued volunteerism. Another reason the RHA is an excellent conduit to promote service learning has to do with its composition. Since peer influence is so powerful and students enjoy collaborating with one another, the RHA provides a vehicle for making this type of project work.

Many institutions have faculty interaction programs which provide teaching staff and residence hall students with opportunities to learn more about each other. Some institutions also have first-year-experience programs and residential college atmospheres which encourage faculty to live in the halls with the students. Service learning lends itself to collaboration between faculty and students in order to positively impact others. Service learning is a powerful pedagogical strategy that encourages students to make meaningful connections between classroom content and real-life experiences, with the potential to increase students' levels of civic responsibility and concern for social justice. Also, service learning provides exemplary, ongoing opportunities for collaborative activities between academic affairs and student affairs in which both parties can make significant contributions to the educational process (McHugh-Engstrom & Tinto, 1997). Many off-campus agencies offer rich opportunities for faculty and students to team up and give back to the greater community while also learning more about each other. Many institutions now require a certain number of service learning hours to be completed prior to graduation. Some faculty also have expectations for service learning as part of students' course work. Therefore it is imperative that both faculty and students connect and work together, as this cannot be a one-sided venture. RHAs have long been known to have philanthropic interests. Many assist with crisis situations and tragedies when they occur on campus, along with contributing regular volunteers for a myriad of service agencies within the community. RHA members are in key leadership positions which can really set the pace for an entire campus.

The RHA's Role in Campus Leadership

Since the RHA represents the entire residence hall student population, it can be highly effective in developing programs to address the needs of a variety of individuals or groups and in helping unite students on campus for a common cause. Depending on campus culture, this role can develop well beyond the residence halls. In partnership with other student organizations, RHAs have been able to realize their extraordinary potential in a variety of settings.

At the campus level, RHAs and student government associations have instituted programs such as an annual tree planting to recognize students who died throughout the year. Additionally, when incidents occur which trigger emotional reactions on campus, RHAs can work with programming boards and student affairs offices to help mend the campus climate and to focus energies in positive ways by hosting open forums, vigils, or memorial services.

In the local community, RHAs often assist community organizations by collecting items for canned food and clothing drives, by visiting with elderly or young people in residential care facilities, or by participating in "Make a Difference Day" or community clean-up projects.

At the state, national, or international levels, RHAs have worked with other RHAs and organizations to assist colleges and universities coping with the effects of a natural disaster or tragedy and to voice opinions on legislation affecting students and higher education.

Relationships RHAs Have

It is critical that RHA advisers encourage the members to seek connections with other student organizations and with offices besides residence life. This can be done in formal ways, such as sending RHA liaisons to meetings or programs held by these groups or including a variety of campus constituents on the distribution list for minutes of RHA meetings and/or organizational newsletters. This can also be accomplished informally by having members network with their student colleagues at campus leadership events or during community service functions. By ensuring that RHA representatives are integrated into the campus-wide leadership community, residential students can feel as if their needs as students and as residents can be addressed by the RHA.

Case Study One

You are the RHA adviser at a small liberal arts college that houses about 1500 students. The college's minimum cumulative grade point requirement for students involved in organizations is 2.0. For the past three years, the RHA's constitution has dictated that all executive officers must have a 2.4 cumulative grade point average (GPA). You just returned from the first RHA meeting of the year. During the meeting, a member unexpectedly brought up a motion to amend the constitution to change the 2.4 GPA requirement to 2.1. This occurred because the RHA vice president who had been elected during the previous spring did not return to the institution.

As the adviser, you find yourself in a quandary. You are torn because the executive board is fairly inexperienced and the individual many of the members support in becoming the new vice president has a lot of experience but his grade point average is 2.15. You also heard from the past RHA Adviser how much effort it took to increase the officer GPA from 2.0 to 2.4 as well as the role model rationale behind the decision. You have also worked closely with faculty in the residence halls who think the required GPA should be higher. You know what you think is best, but how do you assist students in exploring the issue? How do you let this be a student-driven organization while providing the "bigger-picture" perspective and being prepared to respond to your own supervisor?

Case Study Two

You are the RHA adviser at a mid-sized state university that houses roughly 4000 students on campus. It is late in the fall semester and your recent professional staff meetings have been dominated by discussions about next year's budget. There is disagreement about which halls are most in need of new furniture. Additionally, there is extra revenue forecasted for next year, so staff is debating whether the halls should be wired with data and cable connections or if the two vacant hall director positions should be filled. What role — consulting or decision making — is appropriate for RHA members in this situation? How can the members help share the final decision with the community at large?

References

American College Personnel Association. (1994). *The student learning imperative: Implications for student affairs.* Washington, DC: Author.

Astin, A. (1996). Involvement in learning revisited: Lessons we have learned. *Journal of College Student Development, 37*(2), 123-134.

Chickering, A. W., & Reissner, L. (1993). *Education and identity* (2nd ed.). San Francisco: Jossey-Bass.

Kuh, G. D. (1996). Guiding principles for creating seamless learning environments for undergraduates. *Journal of College Student Development, 37*(2), 135-148.

Kuh, G. D., Schuh, J. H., & Whitt, E. J. (1991). *Involving colleges.* San Francisco: Jossey-Bass.

McHugh-Engstrom, C., & Tinto, V. (1997 July-August). Working together for service learning. *About Campus,* 10-15.

Pascarella, E. T., & Terenzini, P. T., (1991). *How college affects students.* San Francisco: Jossey-Bass.

Schroeder, C. C. (1994). Developing learning communities. In C. C. Schroeder & P. Mable (Eds.), *Realizing the educational potential of residence halls* (pp. 165-189). San Francisco: Jossey-Bass.

Schroeder, C. C., & Mable, P. (1994). *Realizing the educational potential of residence halls.* San Francisco: Jossey-Bass.

Legal Issues

John H. Schuh
Iowa State University

Legal Issues

Few contingencies strike more fear in the hearts of advisers to residence hall student organizations (governance or special interest) than the potential for lawsuits. "Although administrators typically view student organizations as an important supplement to classroom learning, colleges may face liability for the actions of student organizations or for decisions to award or deny funding to these organizations" (Kaplin & Lee, 1997, p. 397). Fear of lawsuits, however, should not determine what makes educational sense for a residence hall government and its adviser. As Miller and Schuh pointed out over a decade ago, "[a] concern for potential litigation, however, should not dominate an innovative, educationally sound residence-hall administration program" (1981, p. 395).

By reading this chapter, the residence hall association (RHA) adviser will not become expert in all the exigencies related to student organizations and the law. Rather, the purpose of this chapter is to provide an introduction to several common problems related to advising the RHA and other student organizations in the residence hall setting. Very basic information will be provided and readers are encouraged to review the reference list if further questions arise about the legal aspects of working with student organizations. Two case studies are provided for discussion at the end of the chapter.

Readers are strongly advised not to assume on the basis of reading this chapter, or any other material, that they are expert in the law. That would be a tragic mistake. Perhaps the most important message of this chapter is that readers should realize that if they have any questions about the law, they should consult with their institution's legal counsel. If that resource is not available, a supervisor should be contacted. RHA advisers should not practice the law under any circumstances. As Gehring (1987) pointed out, "The office of institutional counsel can be a valuable asset to you, but only if you use it" (p. 116).

Constitutional Issues

In general, students attending institutions of higher education have the same rights as citizens who are not enrolled in colleges or universities. This means that they have the same rights and responsibilities as other citizens: freedom of speech, freedom to organize, freedom of the press, and so on. The U.S. Constitution, state constitutions, and contractual arrangements tend to govern the relationship that students have with their institution of higher education. One important element of the relationship that students have with public institutions is the influence of the Fourteenth Amendment of the U.S. Constitution. "The Fourteenth Amendment ... guarantees that the government may not deny anyone equal protection under the law. Obviously this does not mean that everyone is treated the same. The equal protection clause means that if an institution is engaged in state action, similarly situated individuals must be treated the same" (Gehring, 1993, p. 293). "In combination with civil rights legislation, the Fourteenth Amendment provides powerful protection to students and others" (Barr, 1996, p. 135).

RHA advisers at private institutions have a bit more latitude in dealing with student organizations under the law than do their counterparts at public institutions. "Public institutions and their officers are fully subject to the constraints of the federal constitution, whereas private institutions and their officers are not" (Kaplin & Lee, 1997, p. 38). However, certain legal theories do protect student rights at private institutions.

"Most prominent by far is the contract theory, under which students and faculty members are said to have a contractual relationship with the private school" (Kaplin & Lee, 1997, p. 47). Thus, the adviser at a private institution should not assume that students have no rights. It is highly likely that such students have a wide variety of rights, depending on the nature of the institution's contractual relationship with them, as Barr (1996) has pointed out: "Most private institutions have, however, adopted guarantees similar to constitutional protections as part of their contract of enrollment with students, even though they are not bound to do so" (p. 127).

Right to Organize

Students who attend public institutions enjoy a constitutionally protected right to organize. So, if they decide to organize, be it because of common interests or because they wish to govern themselves, they may do so and the college or university cannot stop them. Indeed, as Kaplin and Lee (1995) pointed out, "Students in public postsecondary institutions have a general right to organize; to be officially recognized whenever the school has a policy of recognizing student groups; and to use meeting rooms, bulletin boards, and similar facilities open to campus groups" (p. 516). As a result, if students in a residence hall decide to organize, they can. "Private institutions may prevent, limit, or refuse to authorize the peaceful assembly of any group, including student organizations" (Barr, 1996, p. 133).

This does not mean, however, that students who are organized into a group can do what they want, whenever they want. As a matter of course the institution can regulate how and when an organization may hold its meetings and other activities on the institution's property (see *Healy v. James,* 1972). What this means in practical terms is that the student government cannot hold a dance in the residence hall cafeteria in the middle of the dinner hour unless the organization has received permission. The organization may not spend the money it receives from its members for illegal purposes, such as buying controlled substances like alcoholic beverages for underage members.

Kaplin and Lee (1995) have identified three bases upon which student organizations can be regulated:

1. Student organizations seeking recognition may be required to abide by reasonable campus law.
2. Student organizations may not interrupt classes or reasonably interfere with the opportunities to obtain an education.
3. The organization may not be engaged in illegal activities or activities which may incite lawlessness (pp. 517-518).

If these criteria are satisfied, then the student organization can conduct its business. The reader is cautioned to note that what has been described above applies to public institutions and may not apply to private colleges and universities. Students who attend private institutions are not afforded the same constitutional rights as their peers who attend public institutions. "In general, the courts have ruled that private institutions are not constrained by the First Amendment of the Constitution in their dealings with students, as long as they follow the policies and procedures outlined in official institutional publications" (Correnti, 1988, p. 29). While private institutions may determine from a legal perspective that it would make the most sense not to allow students to organize, such decisions may not make the best educational sense for students or the best practice for the institution. Powerful developmental arguments exist to support students' participation in campus organizations and other leadership experiences which provide a lasting benefit to them (Pascarella & Terenzini, 1991; Schuh & Laverty, 1983). Generally speaking, the educational value attached to student organizations outweighs the legal risks taken by allowing students to form organizations.

Free Speech Issues

The First Amendment to the Constitution gives students not only the right to organize, but also the right to engage in free speech. As is the case with many other constitutionally guaranteed rights, free speech is not absolute. Students may not incite others to riot, nor defame others (see Gehring, 1991, pp. 403-404). They also may not disrupt activities on campus (such as making so much noise outside a classroom that instructors cannot be heard by their students).

Advisers can provide assistance when they point out to students that they may not slander (defame a person orally) or libel (defame in writing) others. If they work with students who print newsletters or other publications, advisers should point out that "[t]he First Amendment, however, does not mean that the student press has an absolute freedom to publish" (Gehring, 1986, p. 30). "The right to a free press protects student publications from virtually all encroachments on their editorial prerogatives by public institutions" (Kaplin & Lee, p. 539), but cavalier student editors need to realize that if they are not very careful, they may be held accountable in the courts for their publications, perhaps without institutional support (Schuh, 1988, p. 317).

Often, students will operate their own radio stations and free speech issues can arise related to that medium. The reader should review *Aldrich v. Knab* (1995) for details about the operation of a radio station.

Nondiscrimination

Generally speaking, student organizations may not discriminate against members of certain groups by denying them membership. This can be a function of federal law or, in some cases, state law. This principle can be true at both public and private institutions (see Kaplin & Lee, 1997, p. 407). Advisers would be well served to monitor the membership patterns of their organizations. If it appears that individuals from underrepresented groups are not members, it is time to ask pointed questions for educational as well as legal reasons (see also Chapter 8). "In light of such constitutional and regulatory requirements, it is clear that administrators cannot ignore alleged discrimination by student organizations" (Kaplin & Lee, 1997, p. 408).

Managing Risk

The concept of risk management includes financial management and human and physical engineering techniques (Hammond, 1984, p. 136). One of the challenges to organizational advisers is to use whatever tools are available to minimize risk. First, a brief introduction to the elements of negligence will be presented. Then, selected aspects of risk management will be introduced.

Negligence

Barr (1989) and Gehring (1991) have prepared excellent discussions of negligence on legal issues and student affairs work. They identified several elements that must be present in establishing negligence. Among these are:

1. Having a duty to another person, such as maintaining facilities in a safe condition.
2. Breaching that duty, such as not repairing a broken window pane for three months after the damage occurred.
3. As a result of the breach, causing damage to another person or that person's property, such as a student suffering a cut arm by reaching through the broken glass.

If any one of these elements is missing, then negligence has not been demonstrated. It seems intuitive that the prudent residence hall administrator, as a matter of practice, would always want to keep facilities in good repair and plan programs that are safe for the participants.

Gehring (1993) observed the following related to negligence: "The courts have recognized three general duties: (1) to provide proper supervision, (2) to furnish proper instructions, and (3) to maintain equipment in a reasonable state of repair" (p. 276). When planning programs or activities with students, therefore, the adviser should minimize the risk involved in the activity by heeding each of these elements. For example, programs should be planned for facilities that are designed for them. Ice skating races, for example, should not be planned for frozen city thoroughfares. Equipment problems that endanger the health or safety of participants should be addressed immediately, even if that means postponing or suspending the activity until the equipment or facility can be fixed. Students should be well versed in how to participate safely in the activity. If participants are in competition with one another, they should compete with individuals who are at approximately the same level of skill. Having the institution's touch football champions scrimmage with the defending Super Bowl champions would make no sense; similarly, all competitions sponsored by residence halls must be safe activities including people of similar skill levels.

Remember that in the eyes of the law people under age 18 are considered minors. That means, for example, that in working with campers and conferees, or enrolled students during the academic year who are under age 18, a much stricter level of supervision is necessary. "With minors, an entirely separate and more restrictive set of regulations may be imposed to meet the obligation of closer supervision (Gehring, 1993, p. 276, citing *Stone v. Cornell University*, 1987). It is a good idea to identify the minors among the resident population of each facility. If these students choose to participate in various activities, special planning will be necessary to meet their special legal circumstance.

It is not uncommon for students to threaten to file lawsuits and, from time to time, they do. In contemporary higher education, lawsuits abound, at times over issues that appear to be trivial (Stevens, 1992). The pain and anguish of being sued are very real, especially upon receiving the papers from the plaintiff. Nonetheless, being sued is very different from having lost a court case. Remembering the elements of negligence identified above will be helpful as advisers work with student groups and try to avoid circumstances with potentially adverse legal consequences.

Legal Issues

Risk-Reduction Strategies

As mentioned earlier in this chapter, elements of risk exist in almost any program or other circumstances related to the operation of residential facilities and programs. Rather than virtually eliminating risk by closing down the residence halls, the adviser, in concert with the RHA, has to develop a plan to reduce risk in the various activities and programs offered by the organization. Several strategies are identified in this portion of the chapter.

Position descriptions. If a residence hall staff member advises the RHA, it is important that this activity is part of the staff member's position description or is assigned to the person through a memorandum of understanding or other official university record. While it is logical for a residence hall staff member to advise the RHA, what happens if the same staff member is asked to advise the parachuting club on campus? Is that part of the staff member's official responsibilities? If it is not and a problem, such as an accident, should arise, the staff member may not be able to call on assistance from the university's legal staff, insurance policy, or other resources in case of litigation. Staff members need to make sure that their work as advisers is considered part of their official duties and that the institution will assist them in case of litigation. If not, they may have to secure their own legal counsel.

Risk transfer. One can transfer risk to other entities through the use of insurance. Insurance can be obtained in several ways. First, individual staff members can purchase their own liability policies, often through their professional associations, for a modest premium. Second, the institution may have secured insurance for all staff members to cover potential liability problems. Third, insurance can be purchased by individuals participating in specific activities. Some institutions have such insurance policies available to students and others participating in activities that will provide accident and death insurance for the duration of the activity. The premium for this kind of insurance is usually very inexpensive and will provide basic accident coverage.

The purchase of insurance will not solve all of the adviser's problems related to potential litigation, but it is an option that advisers ought to consider. In addition to insurance, some states claim governmental immunity from tort liability (see Miller & Schuh, 1981), which may provide something of a shield from liability for the adviser. Advisers ought to determine if their state makes such a claim. Obviously, governmental immunity would apply only to state institutions.

Another strategy that can be extremely useful is to hire professionals to provide services that students desire for their events. For example, if transportation to a recreational site is involved, the most desirable (although perhaps more expensive) approach is to hire a licensed carrier. The carrier then has the responsibility to provide a safe vehicle and a competent driver. Another example of hiring professionals is to have meals at restaurants or catered by licensed business people who know how to avoid food poisoning. Finally, for reasons that will be identified later in this chapter, if alcoholic beverages are part of an activity — and it the author's general position that they should not be — then alcohol should be provided in a licensed establishment rather than having several of the students "bring the beer."

Waivers. At times, participants are asked to sign "waivers" which claim to absolve program planners or the institution from liability in case of accidents which result in injury or death. These waivers generally do not protect the adviser, the organization, or the institution from losing a lawsuit. "The mere use of waivers intended to absolve program sponsors of liability does not necessarily preclude claims to recover damages" (Miller & Schuh, 1981, p. 394). In general, individuals cannot waive their rights in advance of the activity. For a more detailed discussion of waivers, see Kaplin and Lee (1997, pp. 141-142).

A more useful purpose of a waiver is to have individuals acknowledge that they have completed a training program prior to participating in an activity and that they understand specific risks attendant to a program, trip, athletic contest, or similar activity. "What a written release or waiver may do, and its real value, is demonstrate that the plaintiff assumes the obvious or ordinary risks incident to the activities in question" (Richmond, 1990, p. 329). The waiver will not eliminate the possibility of a lawsuit, but it will point out to each person signing it that there are risks associated with a specific activity.

More useful than a waiver form, an appropriate training program is important to ensure that students have developed a sufficient level of skill so that they may participate in a program with a limited degree of risk. Two cases are useful in this regard. *Regents of the University of California v. Superior Court* (1996) and *Loder v. State* (1994), both dealt with injuries students suffered in activities outside the typical classroom. In the first case the court determined that the question of liability "turns on the (student's) level of experience" (Regents of the University of California v. Superior Court, 1996, p. 1206), while in the second case the student prevailed because proper instruction in dealing with a horse was not provided. In the second case, it was determined that "field trips ... among others require proper instruction. Failure to provide proper instruction can result in a suit for negligence if an injury is caused by that failure" (1994, p. 1096).

Planning. Miyamoto (1988) provided an excellent framework for planning extracurricular programs: "The institution is often the center of the student's life ... it is not unreasonable for students to assume that institutions will regulate extracurricular activities so as to protect participants from unreasonable risk of harm" (p. 152). Program advisers, officers, and others associated with RHA activities would be well served if they adopt several principles designed to minimize the risk associated with certain events.

First, an industry standard for a particular activity or piece of equipment should be followed scrupulously. For example, the Red Cross (or similar organization) water safety recommendation for providing a certain number of lifeguards trained at an expressed standard should be met or exceeded. No compromise should be made with industry standards or the program planners risk exposure.

Second, events that involve transportation are inherently risky, given the number of automobile accidents that occur in this country every day. If the event involves transportation of program participants and a common carrier is not hired, vehicles from the institution's motor pool should be used rather than student cars. One can assume with a greater level of confidence that institutional vehicles undergo more frequent inspections for safety than student vehicles. Additionally, if student drivers are utilized, all of them should have valid, current driver's licenses. This also means that if vans or other large vehicles are used, appropriate levels of licensure should be held by each driver.

The state may require a chauffeur's license rather than a standard license to operate such vehicles. This detail should be checked well in advance of the activity.

Finally, some activities have a high degree of risk. Amateur boxing matches, tugs-of-war, eating contests, and so on are risky endeavors. Risk can be minimized by identifying substitute activities. None of these are so inherently valuable that a substitute activity cannot be employed without affecting the quality of the program. If the activity involves a certain degree of risk, "institutions should have procedures detailing the safety measures that organizers of an extracurricular activity must take given the nature of a particular event" (Miyamoto, 1988, p. 176).

Special Situations

While other circumstances may raise concerns for RHA advisers because of potential legal implications, four special situations, common to most campuses, are fraught with danger and merit further discussion: contractual obligations, money handling, alcoholic beverage possession and consumption, and copyright law.

Contracts

At times student organizations will need to engage in contractual agreements with vendors, suppliers of good and services, and so on. Nothing can be worse for an organization than for an uninformed member or officer to sign a binding contract that obligates the organization to a commitment it cannot keep. So, a few steps need to be taken to make sure that such does not happen.

First, officer orientation should include a discussion of who is authorized to sign contracts on behalf of the organization. The best way to arrange for this is to have two officers sign a contract. That way, no single individual can make a mistake that all will regret. Additionally, to bind the organization contractually to an obligation over a certain amount (perhaps $50.00 or more, depending on the nature of the organization), the bylaws should require that a motion be passed authorizing the contract.

Second, members should be instructed that they are never authorized to make an agreement, sign a contract, or engage in some other activity that obligates the organization financially. They need to realize that they may face personal exposure if they make such arrangement.

Third, depending on the complexity of the contract, before anyone signs it on behalf of the organization, legal counsel should be consulted. A review of the document by the campus attorney may save a great deal of grief in the long run.

Handling Money

Chapters 11, 12, and 13 deal with issues relating to raising and managing money. Nonetheless, it is important to emphasize that the adviser may very well have a fiduciary responsibility for handling funds, including overseeing the development of a budget and handling funds (Maloney, 1988). Depending on an institution's arrangement for managing student funds, this responsibility could extend to making sure that (a) funds are handled (i.e., deposited and expended) in ways consistent with institutional policies and state law, (b) all funds can be accounted for by an external audit, and, most importantly, (c) the trust of the members of the organization is sustained.

Advisers need to realize that handling money is a very serious responsibility and, if they co-sign purchase requests or other authorizations to expend funds, they need to be absolutely certain that each expenditure is completely consistent with institutional requirements. Simply turning the organization's funds over to the student treasurer and assuming that everything will be fine is myopic at best and, at worst, may subject the adviser to legal action. If the adviser has limited or no experience working with students who manage organizational accounts, it is advisable to have an orientation session with the institution's purchasing agent and comptroller, or their representatives.

Alcoholic Beverage Possession and Consumption

Few problems are more difficult for the RHA adviser than those attendant to the possession and use of alcoholic beverages. "Unintentional injury is often associated with alcohol, and even when there was no intent to harm, both the institution and its agent may be found liable" (Barr, 1996, p. 140). Probably the place to start this discussion is to reiterate the obvious: It is against the law for persons under the age of 21 to drink alcoholic beverages. Penalties for violating this law vary widely from state to state (Gehring, 1991), but the point is that the activity is illegal everywhere.

What is the adviser to do? Students want to drink in many circumstances, often see institutional alumni/ae and friends doing so on campus (at a pregame tailgate party, for example), and very well may have been doing so before they enrolled in college (Myrick & Gonzalez, 1990). This is a dilemma of a major order, without easy solutions, because it is quite difficult to explain why benefactors can drink on campus but students, even if they are of legal age, cannot do so in the residence halls or at residence hall events.

Three legal decisions are instructive to the RHA adviser. Excellent summaries of these cases were provided by Gregory (1985) and the reader is encouraged to review them in detail; other cases were identified by Gehring (1991).

One of the most notable legal decisions regarding drinking is *Bradshaw v. Rawlings* (1979). In this case, a passenger was injured in a car operated by a person who had consumed alcoholic beverages at a college picnic. Subsequent litigation resulted in the college and the adviser, who attended the picnic, not being held negligent.

A second noteworthy case involves *Baldwin v. Zoradi* (1981), in which a person was injured in an off-campus drag racing incident. The driver of the car had been drinking in an on-campus residence hall prior to the accident. Again, the institution was not found to be negligent by the courts.

Finally, in *Zavala v. the Regents of the University of California* (1981), the plaintiff suffered injuries from a fall in a residence hall after attending an event where alcoholic beverages were served. Residence hall staff members supervised the activity. California is a comparative negligence state, and the decision in this case was to find the university 20% liable for the plaintiff's injuries.

Several guidelines are offered to the organization adviser related to the possession and consumption of alcoholic beverages. First, "the use of institutional funds to purchase alcoholic beverages should be avoided" (Schuh, 1984, p. 68). Not only may this kind of purchase be illegal, but it also potentially places the organization as a direct sponsor of the event, whether it wishes to be a sponsor or not. If the organization is going to have an event where alcoholic beverages can be consumed legally (such as a dinner for residents of an over-21-year-old residence hall), the event should be held at a licensed establishment, such as a bar or restaurant, where the bartender, server, or other trained employee can monitor the consumption of alcohol. If the student organization is going to charge a fee to attend an event, none of it should be dedicated to purchasing alcohol.

Advisers should make it clear to the student group that they will not attend the event if illegal consumption is going to occur. Moreover, they are best advised to leave the event if underage drinking occurs. Finally, advisers should explain that they are not going to help organize or supervise an event if underage drinking is planned.

These positions are not easy to take. Students need to realize that the possession and consumption of alcoholic beverages is a serious matter with significant legal consequences and that advisers have a responsibility to their institutions not to be a party to the legal problems, injuries, or worse that so often result from drinking by minors.

Copyright Law

Legal questions often accompany the development of technology. In the case of the development of videocassette players to record and telecast movies and other entertainment events, the law governs what can and cannot be done in the residence hall setting. On the surface, renting a videocassette at the local convenience store for a modest fee and showing it in the residence hall lounge to a group of students seems like a wonderful way to offer entertainment at a very low cost. The only problem with this activity, unfortunately, is that it is probably illegal.

Shuh (1989) discussed how the copyright law applied to the use of videocassettes and concluded that showing a copyrighted videocassette of a movie or other material in a residence hall lounge is an infringement of the copyright law. The adviser needs to make sure that students do not engage in this activity, and warn them that if they do, they run the risk of the penalties identified above.

The copyright law indicates that the owner of an article retains exclusive rights to display the work publicly (Smith & Fossey, 1995). If a copyright is violated, the violator may be liable for actual damages and lost profits. The court also may grant legal fees and court costs (Scheuermann, 1989). So, the penalties for violating the law can be substantial (Burgoyne, 1992).

Holders of copyrights can sell a license to parties who wish to display works publicly. This is a common practice in the music industry. If copyrighted material is to be shown as a residence hall activity, a license should be procured. The institution's business office or purchasing department can be helpful in securing the license.

A Final Word

Several basic principles of law address problems common to advising a student organization. While RHA advisers have a professional responsibility to understand the legal rights of students and student organizations, it is not necessary for them to become experts on the law. RHA advisers should never attempt to practice law, but instead, they should utilize the office of institutional counsel regarding legal questions and concerns.

RHA advisers should avoid being preoccupied with the potential for lawsuits; even the most cautious face the possibility of being sued. Generally, the law requires one to behave as a "reasonable person" would under similar circumstances. A basic understanding of legal principles and the use of legal counsel, accompanied by common sense, should reduce the adviser's exposure to unpleasant legal entanglements and, more importantly, reduce the risk students face in participating in residence hall activities.

References

Aldrich v. Knab (1995, March). *The college student and the courts, 22*(2), 1122-1123. Asheville, NC: College Administration Publications.

Baldwin v. Zoradi, 123 Cal. App. 3d 275; 176 Cal. Rptr. 809 (1981).

Barr, M. J. (1989). Legal issues confronting student affairs practice. In U. Delworth & G. R. Hanson (Eds.), *Student services: A handbook for the profession* (2nd ed., pp. 80-111). San Francisco: Jossey-Bass.

Barr, M. J. (1996). Legal foundations of student affairs practice. In S. R. Komives & D. B. Woodard, Jr. (Eds.), *Student services: A handbook for the profession* (3rd ed., pp. 126-144). San Francisco: Jossey-Bass.

Bradshaw v. Rawlings, 612 F.2d 135 (3rd Cir., 1979).

Burgoyne, R. A. (1992). The copyright remedy clarification act of 1990: State educational institutions now face significant monetary exposure for copyright infringement. *Journal of College and University Law, 18,* 367-379.

Correnti, R. J. (1988). How public and private institutions differ under the law. In M. J. Barr (Ed.), *Student services and the law* (pp. 25-43). San Francisco: Jossey-Bass.

Gehring, D. D. (1986). The student press: A legal perspective. In J. H. Schuh (Ed.), *Enhancing relationships with the student press* (pp. 29-43). San Francisco: Jossey-Bass.

Gehring, D. D. (1987). Legal rights and responsibilities of campus student groups and advisors. In J. H. Schuh (Ed.), *Handbook for student group advisors* (pp. 115-149). American College Personnel Association Media Publication No. 43. Alexandria, VA: American Association for Counseling and Development.

Legal Issues

Gehring, D. D. (1991). Legal issues in the administration of student affairs. In T. K. Miller & R. B. Winston, Jr. (Eds.), *Administration and leadership in student affairs* (2nd ed., pp. 379-413). Muncie, IN: Accelerated Development.

Gehring, D. D. (1993). Understanding legal constraints on practice. In M. J. Barr and Associates, *The handbook of student affairs administration* (pp. 274-299). San Francisco: Jossey-Bass.

Gregory, D. E. (1985). Alcohol consumption by college students and related liability issues. *Journal of Law & Education, 14,* 43-53.

Hammond, E. H. (1984). To risk or not to risk: That is the question. In H. F. Owens (Ed.), *Risk management and the student affairs professional* (pp. 135-146). NASPA Monograph Series Volume 2. NP: National Association for Student Personnel Administrators.

Healy v. James, 92 S.Ct. 2338 (1972).

Kaplin, W. A., & Lee, B. A. (1995). *The law of higher education* (3rd ed.). San Francisco: Jossey-Bass.

Kaplin, W. A., & Lee, B. A. (1997). *A legal guide for student affairs professionals.* San Francisco: Jossey-Bass.

Loder v. State (1994, Sept.). *The college student and the courts, 21*(4), 1096. Asheville, NC: College Administration Publications.

Maloney, G. W. (1988). Student organizations and student activities. In M. J. Barr (Ed.), *Student services and the law* (pp. 284-307). San Francisco: Jossey-Bass.

Miller, T. E., & Schuh, J. H. (1981). Managing the liability risks of residence hall administrators. *Journal of College Student Personnel, 22,* 392-395.

Miyamoto, T. (1988). Liability of colleges and universities for injuries during extracurricular activities. *Journal of College and University Law, 15,* 149-176.

Myrick, R. D., & Gonzalez, G. M. (1990). *Alcohol and other drug prevention through teacher advisors (middle school unit): Teacher's manual* (U.S. D.O.E. Alcohol and Drug Prevention Grant [S 184A90089]). Gainesville, FL: University of Florida Counselor Education Department.

Pascarella, E. T., & Terenzini, P. T. (1991). *How college affects students.* San Francisco: Jossey-Bass.

Regents of the University of California v. Superior Court (1996, Sept.). *The college student and the courts, 23*(3), 1206. Asheville, NC: College Administration Publications.

Richmond, D. R. (1990). Institutional liability for student activities and organizations. *Journal of Law & Education, 19*(3), 309-344.

Scheuermann, T. (1989). Some basic concepts of copyright law. *Synthesis — Law and Policy in Higher Education, 1*(4), 33, 39.

Schuh, J. H. (1984). The residential campus: High risk territory! In H. F. Owens (Ed.), *Risk management and the student affairs professional* (pp. 57-82). NP: National Association for Student Personnel Administrators.

Schuh, J. H. (1988). The student press. In M. J. Barr (Ed.), *Student services and the law* (pp. 308-322). San Francisco: Jossey-Bass.

Schuh, J. H. (1989). Developing a policy for the use of videocassettes on campus. *Synthesis — Law and Policy in Higher Education, 1*(4), 37-38.

Schuh, J. H., & Laverty, M. (1983). The perceived long term effect of holding a significant student leadership position. *Journal of College Student Personnel, 24,* 28-32.

Smith, M. C., & Fossey, R. (1995). *Crime on campus.* Phoenix, AZ: Oryx.

Stevens, A. (1992, November 18). Personal injury lawsuits by students are endangering university budgets. *The Wall Street Journal,* pp. B1, B6.

Zavala v. Regents of the University of California, 125 Cal. App.3d 648,178 Cal. Rptr. 185 (1981).

Case One

You are the adviser of a residence hall group at a private college that is located 15 miles from a picturesque recreational area, complete with camping, golfing, tennis facilities, and a lake used for swimming and boating activities. Typically at the end of the spring term your student group and their guests spend a weekend at the lake and they have a wonderful time.

A number of the students who are part of your group have little or no experience in handling a boat. You are concerned about the risks involved in having novices out on the water handling their own boats. The student leaders tell you that in the past this has never been a problem, and that the weekend of activities has been an annual event for ten years.

Legal Issues

What are the liability risks involved in this weekend? What steps could you take to minimize the risks? With whom might you consult to put various safeguards in place to insure that adequate protections are in place for you, the organization, and your college?

Case Two

As the adviser of the RHA you have significant responsibility, particularly since the association receives an annual fee of $10 for every student who lives in the residence halls. This amounts to quite a bit of money and, over the years, the students have augmented their resources with a variety of fundraising activities. All funds are supposed to be handled through a campus student organization banking system operated by the bursar's office.

You have begun to hear rumors about off-campus bank accounts the RHA has established to purchase items not quickly or legally acquired using the bursar's system. Moreover, you are concerned about the sloppy mistakes that the past several treasurers have made. As a consequence of all this, you'd like to have a thorough review of the financial transactions of the RHA. Is this your responsibility? How might you accomplish this? With whom would you consult? How would you work with the officers? What if irregularities were uncovered?

The Money Management of Residence Hall Associations

Mark Hudson
Donna Turner Hudson
University of North Dakota

Bob Tattershall
Washington State University

Introduction

Money makes the world go 'round. While making and keeping track of money is not the primary pursuit of a residence hall association (RHA), a good financial base gives an RHA the resources to make student participation worthwhile. Practicing some fundamentals of sound money management can also keep an organization and its adviser out of serious trouble.

In order to learn about financial practices of RHAs, the authors administered a survey to 25 RHAs, both public and private, during the winter of 1992-1993. The results can be found in the first edition of this book (Hudson & Hudson, 1993). This chapter has been revised to include the results of a survey administered in 1997 to 20 participating institutions utilizing diverse financial arrangements. No significant differences were found among the financial practices of public and private institutions, regardless of size. The variations in practices appeared to be due more to philosophical differences than to differences in size or structure.

This chapter will cover the following five topic areas: (a) sources of funding, (b) assessing and collecting funds, (c) tracking funds, (d) RHAs and taxes, and (e) planning for the unexpected. The chapter is designed to assist RHA advisers in the following ways:

1. The chapter provides information on various aspects of an organization's funding structure, pointing out issues for consideration, and offering new ideas based on the survey results.
2. As a review of funding practices, the chapter may assist those considering establishing a new RHA, revising the financial structure of an existing organization, or reviewing an organization's financial health. The chapter provides ideas on what works — and what does not — at a variety of institutions around the country.
3. A list of questions is provided near the end of the chapter. These questions are intended to be conversation starters for advisers and students who may wish to consider making changes to their RHA's financial structure.
4. Three case studies have been provided as learning tools for skill building in money management.

The method by which an adviser assists students with managing the financial aspects of their organization will be very similar in tone and philosophy to the way an adviser performs many of her or his other duties for the organization. Developing an overall philosophy of advising is not something that will be addressed in this chapter; however, it is important to consider one's own attitudes toward advisement and how they apply to financial management.

Advisers operate in many different ways regarding an organization's finances. Some serve as de facto accountants for organizations, assuming responsibility for alerting the officers to any potential problems, and offering well-informed solutions when they arise. Others believe it is best to play the role of observer, offering timely questions for consideration, but generally allowing students to make their own decisions.

How an adviser chooses to serve may depend on several factors. One of these factors is the expectations that the institution has of its student organization advisers. Intertwined with institutional expectations is the degree of personal liability to which an adviser may be held. According to the opinion of the National Association of College and University Residence Halls' (NACURH) Certified Public Accountant, the more closely the organization resembles a nonprofit corporation with a board of directors, the less an adviser will have personal liability for the financial decisions of the organization unless, of course, the adviser is negligent in some manner. Because this is an era in which one must think about protecting oneself from legal liability in any activity, it would behoove an adviser to determine to what extent the institution would support her or him in case of financial mishap.

The adviser's role may change from one year to the next, as do the students and their needs. Depending on the maturity level or organizational experience of the group, an adviser may be more or less active in contributing food for thought, providing "reality checks," and/or making suggestions.

Sources of Funding

One of the most important aspects of managing funds is the initial acquisition of the money. A generalization drawn from RHA advisers responding to the survey is that RHAs with a stable base of funding are the most consistently successful organizations. This stability may be achieved in a variety of ways.

Seventy-eight percent of survey respondents require that students pay a fee to support the activities and programs of the RHA (Table 1). More about required fees can be found later in this section.

Alternatively, or in addition to mandatory fees, many institutions rely heavily on predictable revenues generated from service programs. It is very common for institutions to collect funds from a variety of these sources, such as linen or refrigerator rental, storage of belongings, and so forth. Money from these programs is often designated for the RHA.

The institutions which reported less consistent success in meeting organizational goals are those whose income is derived solely from optional sources, that is, from the sale of activity cards or from collecting or charging fees for events or services in which students may or may not choose to participate.

Many of the institutions responding to this survey have recognized the wisdom of obtaining funds from diverse sources and/or through creative means. Some RHAs combine a required fee with money collected from the sale of services, programs, and/or activity cards. One institution reported that a $5,000 contribution of food and services to their RHA was a part of the institution's contract with an outside food service provider. (See Chapters 12 and 13 for more ideas on raising funds.)

Diversity in funding sources can be very helpful to an RHA. Many RHAs recognize that relying on a single resource for all funds can be financially dangerous, depending on the source's year-to-year stability. This is particularly true if the sole (or substantial) source of funds is another organization. For example, on some campuses, RHA funds are obtained through the annual allocation process of the institution's student government. Unfortunately, the campus political climate can adversely affect the process and outcome.

According to our survey, many advisers advocate the establishment of a required RHA fee for at least three reasons, in addition to the benefit of providing a stable funding base.

1. It gives the RHA credibility as a permanent entity within the institution. Because residents pay for it, they assume their RHA will continue to exist and be a part of their lives. Residents are also more likely to take advantage of services and programs (and potentially participate in its leadership) if they believe the organization is there to stay.

2. There is an assumption of accountability toward something for which students are required to pay. While no one likes to hear complaints, knowing that people will complain if dissatisfied makes the organization stronger and more responsive to student needs.

3. A required fee means that the organization is able to budget from year to year with a good indication of how much money it expects to collect. This allows the organization to develop and execute programming each year that meets a standard of quality that students can expect. If financial resources vary greatly from year to year, the possibility of maintaining a consistent level of quality programming may not be possible. A dependable funding source means that precious time can be spent on developing services and programs which benefit students (and their leaders) rather than on fund-raising.

Assessing and Collecting Funds

There are many ways of assessing and collecting a required fee. Some housing organizations build the RHA fee into the overall housing cost, so that the students never see a separate billing. Other institutions bill the fee with the housing charges, but list it on the bill as a separate item. Another option is to collect the fee from residents upon check-in.

An organization which allows each hall to collect fees from students as they check in may be unintentionally creating an unstable funding situation. This can occur if the relationship between the halls and the RHA is not a mutually supportive one. On one campus responding to our survey, the RHA receives its allocation of funds from the individual residence halls. On 39% of the campuses responding to this survey, the central RHA collects the funds and allocates them to the halls. Either scenario can work both for the halls and for the RHA, as long as there exists a cooperative arrangement between the two. Whichever entity collects and disburses the funds is typically viewed as the more financially stable. Along with this financial stability often comes an image of status or power. If it is the goal of the institution to build the strength of the central RHA, it may be useful to consider this point.

It may not be necessary to allow either entity to collect all the funds and disburse them to the other if a power imbalance is hurting the overall organization. In fact, at 57% of the institutions we surveyed, the RHAs receive their financial support in ways other than through a hall government allocation process. For example, the residence life office may decide how much of the fees collected from students should be allocated to both the RHA and to the hall governments. Or perhaps a required fee could be added for whichever group needs the increased support.

Tracking Funds

Accounting for RHA funds in a responsible manner is an important part of the students' learning process, and is critical to the success of the organization.

Where are funds kept?

Ninety-four percent of those institutions reporting indicated that they keep RHA funds on campus, utilizing their college or university accounting system. Advisers cited the security of institutional accounts and procedures as the reason for this choice, despite the perception that following campus regulations is often a cumbersome process. Very few institutions indicated that funds are kept in off-campus checking accounts. For many years this was a common practice, as it offered instant access to dollars. However, because very little accountability is provided through this practice, many institutions have discontinued this option. One institution did report, though, that its business office now allows (and even encourages) student organizations to take their money "off campus." The reason for this change in policy was to lessen the strain on the institution's accounting system during a time of shrinking resources.

A few institutions reported that their RHAs keep some funds in off-campus interest-bearing accounts to provide resources for scholarships. Most institutions are able to use their alumni associations or development offices for this purpose, which affords the security of an on-campus account. There is also enhanced investment potential, as organization funds are pooled with the larger institutional investment portfolio. Resources used for scholarships typically are derived from fund-raising events, rather than from collected fees. This is because RHA leaders often feel an obligation to spend the money they collect each year from current residents on those same residents, rather than saving the money for use by future students who receive scholarships.

How are expenditures made?

Eighty-nine percent of institutions responding to the survey indicated that their RHA guidelines require the development of a budget prior to spending money. Those respondents felt that a budgeting process forced the organization's members to plan their expenditures for the entire year to ensure that resources were spent in responsible ways.

Individual financial decisions are made solely by a vote of the RHA, according to 83% of institutions. However, several respondents indicated that some small amount ($25-$200) is made available to the chair of the organization for discretionary spending, while others give some flexibility to the chair in consultation with the adviser.

Actual expenditures are made through a variety of means. Most RHAs either utilize their institution's pre-approval purchase order process or they reimburse the individual making the purchase by issuing a check based on the receipt. One practice that seems to be declining in popularity involves pre-established charge accounts with various off-campus vendors and retailers. Our most recent survey indicated that one institution uses a major credit card company which automatically deducts costs for purchases from their off-campus checking account. This system provides ready access to goods and services, but can be abused easily by individuals making unauthorized charges.

To authorize expenditures after RHA approval has been given, most organizations require the signatures of both an officer and the adviser.

How are funds monitored?

Eighty-three percent of institutions responding indicated that their RHAs use a centralized accounting system to monitor funds through their housing office and/or the institution. Many of these organizations also keep track of funds using their own system as a check and balance. The organization's system is often more detailed and provides useful information which better correlates to the organization's expenditures. Seventeen percent of institutions surveyed indicated that they are using a paper-ledger tracking system while 83% use a computer-based program for tracking funds. The computer spreadsheet program mentioned most often was Excel. This is a significant shift from the 1992-1993 survey in which only 48% reported using a computer to track expenses. Auditing RHA accounts is accomplished in a variety of ways by the survey respondents. Approximately one third indicated that the RHA is self-audited by the students in the organization. Another third reported that the adviser conducts the auditing. The final third utilize their institution's formal auditing process.

The institution's regulations for all student organizations often determine the manner in which RHA funds are tracked, and the students may have little input in the decisions to keep funds on or off campus, or how expenditures are processed. Likewise, many advisers cite their own personal responsibility for maintaining a solid grasp on financial matters, and feel more comfortable being very involved in this process. However, most advisers recognize the need to balance this concern with an interest in helping the students to gain valuable skills in money management. Therefore, a close partnership is most often cited as the relationship between the organization and its adviser.

RHAs and Taxes

Every RHA should investigate the issue of taxes. Increasingly, institutions are choosing to make a distinction between the activities of the institution and the activities of its student accounts. Some institutions have made the case that they merely hold the money of student groups in campus accounts but have no control or responsibility for the activity of the student group or its finances. The principal effect of this stance is that the IRS may determine that the financial activities of student groups, specifically RHAs, are not covered under the institution's employer identification number. Thus, the university may rightfully claim to be exempt from various federal, state, and local taxes, but student groups may not. Should the IRS come calling, it would be best if the adviser and the students were aware of the taxable status of the RHA.

If the RHA is eligible to use the institution's employer identification number, the financial officers should be knowledgeable of accounting changes that would alter the RHA's relationship with the institution. However, if the RHA is not eligible to use the institution's employer identification number, the advice of a local accountant should be sought immediately as the RHA could be liable for back taxes.

NACURH received tax-exempt status in December 1996 following a long and arduous process. Any RHA that is not covered by its institution's employer identification number should consider following a similar process. At the time NACURH received tax-exempt status, the process involved completing an application and submitting a $500 tax-exempt application fee. The organization must also ensure that specific language is included in its constitution that verifies the intent to follow the requirements pertaining to organizations under 501(c)(3) of the U.S. Tax Code. The IRS can offer specific advice as to what should be written. It can be assumed, however, that unless the RHA has a letter of determination from the IRS verifying its tax-exempt status, the organization does not have such status.

Critical to NACURH's success in obtaining tax-exempt status was a willingness to pay back taxes and interest on unpaid back taxes. The RHA must be ready financially to do the same, as the IRS may determine that the RHA should have been paying taxes all along. Moreover, the IRS may decide that the RHA does not meet the criteria for tax-exempt groups, requiring not only back taxes and interest, but payment in the present and future for taxes owed annually. One of the primary considerations regarding whether or not the RHA will meet the IRS criteria concerns payment of officers. Any payment to officers over $100 that resembles a salary conflicts with the IRS definition of nonprofit. The organization is then liable for taxes under the Federal Insurance Contributions Act (Social Security taxes). In addition, money given to outside organizations must meet the same standard as money kept by the RHA, that is, funds must remain dedicated to the same purposes which allowed the RHA to receive tax-exempt status under 501(c)(3).

It should be noted that organizations are liable for tax returns for three years after filing. The statute of limitations is three years on auditing an organization's tax returns and this statute of limitations never starts to run until the organization has begun to file returns.

NACURH did receive tax-exempt status, but this did not eliminate the need to file tax returns or to pay taxes. Income that NACURH receives that is not considered essential to the primary purposes of NACURH is considered taxable by the IRS, and is thus considered unrelated business income. The prime example of unrelated business income for NACURH is the payment of endorsement fees to NACURH by corporate sponsors. On such money, NACURH is taxed beyond its enumerated business expense deductions as determined by an outside accountant. NACURH must file Form 990 annually because its annual gross receipts exceed $25,000. Determining whether or not an RHA's gross receipts exceed $25,000 should be a simple matter.

RHA advisers should ask for outside assistance in determining what income may or may not be considered essential to the primary purpose of the organization. NACURH pays a CPA to develop compilations of 11 bank accounts providing some measure of accountability to member institutions regarding how money is spent. However, a compilation is not an audit. NACURH cannot perform an audit economically due to distance; however, it may well be in an RHA's best interest to seek an annual audit by an accounting firm, particularly if larger sums of money are being considered.

Planning for the Unexpected

Good financial management includes planning for unexpected situations in which the organization's finances take a sudden downturn. For example, an RHA may plan a large-scale event which is very costly, expecting to make up the expended dollars in ticket sales. But, despite careful planning and flawless preparation, the event is a bust and much money is lost. On some campuses, the residence life organization, or the larger institution, would assume responsibility for underwriting the RHA. It is a good idea to investigate whether or not an institution is prepared to accept responsibility — and to what extent — before the need arises. If the institution is not willing or able to assist the RHA in time of need, it is best to set up a contingency fund.

How much money should be in a contingency fund? This depends somewhat on the availability of funds that could be acquired outside the organization to cover losses in time of need. It may be helpful to consider setting aside for contingencies an amount such as 5% or 10% of the total RHA budget. This can be an item figured into the development of the annual budget. The obvious question to be answered is: Would these amounts be sufficient to cover the losses of the RHA if a major event completely fails?

NACURH keeps approximately 10% of its conference income in contingency funds. Since NACURH is liable for half of a loss on any given conference, it is reasonable to keep enough funds to assist in losses over several years. Taxation of contingency funds may also be a consideration. Investment income derived from conference contingency funds has been deemed to be essential to the primary purpose of NACURH (see the section on RHA and taxes). This will remain the case until such time as the investment income exceeds the income from dues and conference fees, when it will then become taxable. In NACURH's case, such a problem will be a long time coming. RHA advisers may wish to be aware of the change in taxability of investment income for future reference.

Some organizations set aside a fund and let the fund roll over to the next year's budget; however, many feel it is important to spend all the money to the benefit of those who provided the money. In this case, the organization could certainly plan a special end-of-the-year event to utilize the unused contingency funds. This would be a great way to recognize the fiscal responsibility which allowed those funds to remain in the account.

More often than not, organizations react to unexpected losses by significantly restructuring their budgets. This is not an inappropriate process but it may result in the organization's inability to fulfill some of its goals. If a major loss happens near the end of the year, restructuring may not be an option and a contingency fund may be the only way to cover the loss.

Unfortunately, many RHA treasurers or presidents (or advisers) have been taken by surprise near the end of the semester by finding that a smaller account balance exists than had been assumed. It is always wise to check account balances periodically, and to double check the organization's own records against those that may be kept by the institution's accounting office. Discovering early that less money exists than had been assumed can allow an RHA to reevaluate its upcoming activities and reduce the expected outlay of resources.

What about bad debt?

An often-overlooked potential drain on resources is the reality of bad debt. An organization is most at risk of this occurrence if it collects annual or semester fees from individual students and a check is returned for insufficient funds. The organization may have an opportunity to recollect that fee from the resident if the problem is discovered early. However, when the fees are collected by the institution as part of room and board costs, bad debt is not always realized in a timely fashion. Institutional policies vary, but often institutions do not write off on accounts-receivable bills for over a year. In the past, many institutions were able to absorb this type of bad debt; however, during this era of shrinking budgets, more of it is getting charged back to organizations. Putting away a small amount that would be equal to the amount of bad debt that the institution typically incurs would be prudent. If the RHA budget is $10,000 and the institutional debt is 2%, the RHA should set aside 2% of that $10,000 for a bad-debt fund. This amount should roll over from year to year because in all likelihood, bad debt will not be realized in the same year in which it is incurred.

Reviewing the Money Management System

The following questions will provide a checklist for new advisers or those who are interested in making changes to their RHA's financial organization system. When planning changes in the system of managing funds, it is important to consider the view-points and wishes of the student leaders of the organization, the students whose money is in the trust of the organization, and the institution of which the organization is a part.

Sources of Funding

1. From how many and what sources are RHA funds derived on your campus?
2. Are at least part of the funds derived from a required fee?
3. How much control does the RHA have acquiring its funds?
4. How stable is the primary source of funds? To what extent is there a danger that funding from this source could be cut?
5. What untapped funding sources may exist for the RHA? How might the RHA pursue those options? (See Chapter 12 on local funding sources and Chapter 13 on corporate fund-raising.)
6. Which entity (halls or central RHA) collects fees? Or is another system used? Is the current system meeting the organization's goals?

Assessing and Collecting Funds

1. Is there a comfortable balance between the RHA and the individual hall governments regarding access to financial resources? If not, what adjustments could be made to help both groups?

Tracking Funds

1. Are RHA funds kept in a location which allows for easy access but provides for appropriate review?
2. Where can funds earn the best interest rate (if a choice is allowed) and still be accessible for expenditures?
3. Should — or can — some of the RHA's money be invested in longer-term, higher-interest-bearing accounts?

4. Who should be allowed to make purchases for the organization?
5. By what process should purchases be made?
6. Who should authorize purchases?
7. By what process should the larger residence hall student body be informed of how the RHA spends its money?
8. Who should monitor the funds of the RHA?
9. Should RHA accounts be routinely audited? By whom? How often?

RHAs and Taxes

1. Does your RHA fall under the tax-exempt status of your institution?
2. Does your expenditure-tracking system identify expenses that may not be considered tax exempt?

Planning for the Unexpected

1. What is the contingency plan for an unexpected loss of resources?
2. Are the organization's members and adviser aware of the bad-debt situation on their campus, and its ramifications to the RHA?

Summary

Money management is certainly not the most exciting aspect of advising an RHA. Managing money in a responsible way, however, is not only essential to the life of the organization, but can be an opportunity for student leaders to build valuable life-long skills.

Acquiring funds through a stable source is essential to a successful RHA. Requiring residence hall students to pay a fee to support the activities of their RHA is one way to ensure stable funding. Additionally, the experience of many advisers is that multiple income sources is the best insurance for funding stability.

In the development of processes for tracking and expending funds, accountability should be a major goal. Periodic reviews of these processes ensures that they remain compatible with current student needs and institutional agendas.

Tax liability is becoming more prevalent in some organizations. Making sure the adviser asks the right questions to safeguard the RHA would be prudent.

Planning for the unexpected is an important key to financial security. Decisions on how best to do this should be made in consultation with officials at the institution. Managing funds well is an important function within the life of the RHA because it allows the organization to concentrate on the activities that are most important to residence hall students. Putting in sufficient time up front to develop and monitor financial processes will ensure that very little time needs to be spent later in managing problems.

Case One

An RHA member comes to a meeting with information from a local bank offering an interest rate on checking accounts which is better than all others in your community. She has checked into the institution's policy for student organizations and has learned that while the institution recommends funds be kept on campus, organizations are not required to do so. And, there is *no* interest-earning potential offered through the institution! She encourages members of the RHA to vote for removing funds from the institutional account and putting them in the local bank. What's your opinion? What would you do?

Case Two

The vice president of this year's RHA is the son of a local grocery store owner. Twice during the first few months of the school year, items for RHA events have been purchased from this grocery store. The RHA vice president tells the group his dad will allow the organization to set up an account at the store, as long as his son signs off on the purchases, and the RHA agrees to shop only at this store for its grocery items. The vice president pushes for this idea and implies that his dad will discount most of the items the group purchases. Do you see any reasons why the group should not enter into such an agreement?

Case Three

The campus-wide student government wants to sponsor an all-campus dance with a popular regional band. The band is expensive, and the student government asks the RHA to share in half the cost and to co-sponsor the event. What points should be considered before responding to the request?

Reference

Hudson, M., & Hudson, D. T. (1993). The money management of residence hall associations. In N. W. Dunkel & C. L. Spencer (Eds.), *Advice for advisors: The development of an effective residence hall association* (pp. 123-132). Columbus, OH: Association of College and University Housing Officers-International.

Table 1
Institutional Comparison Of Required Fees

Hall Capacity	LARGE PUBLIC >1,500	LARGE PRIVATE >1,500	SMALL PUBLIC <1,500	SMALL PRIVATE <1,500
Number of Institutions	9	3	3	3
Average Required Fee	$19.67	$16.25	$24.75	$12.50
Range of Required Fees	$6-$38	$8-$23	$10-$45	$10-$15

Chapter Twelve

An Introduction to Raising Money

Edward Grandpré
Mississippi State University

Gary Kimble
University of Southern Mississippi

An Introduction to Raising Money

Inherent in most campus residence hall associations (RHAs) is the need for financial resources. With financial resources from the regular budgetary process stretched to the limit today, there is an ever-increasing need for external promotion and fund-raising activities to augment RHA budgets. Regardless of whether the RHA is financed through voluntary membership fees, through an allocation from the housing or residence life departmental budget, or from their own fund-raising efforts, the one constant among RHAs seems to be the need for additional funding. As noted in Chapter 13 on corporate fund-raising programs, a number of companies exist which offer the RHA a variety of revenue sources through packaged fund-raising programs. Much of this revenue is seasonal in that programs are offered either at the beginning or at the end of each term. These programs are an excellent source of revenue for the RHA.

This chapter will focus on two major approaches to generate revenue throughout the year: (a) fund-raising through the use of campaigns, and (b) raising money from institutional and revenue-generating projects at the campus and community levels. The second section includes the results of two surveys, a 1992 survey of RHAs to determine the types of institutional fund-raising and revenue-generating projects utilized at the campus and community level, and a 1997 study of RHAs to determine how much money was being raised from various sources. The examples discussed throughout the chapter are actual projects used by campus organizations, and each has been utilized to generate funds and enhance the image of the organization. A third section provides exercises for advisers to conduct with their RHAs to enhance their fund-raising abilities.

This chapter offers readers a basic understanding of the components necessary for making any fund-raising project a success. Many of the ideas can be implemented with little or no alteration. They can serve as a starting point from which to develop institution-wide or need-specific projects to meet the organization's goals. With this knowledge, coupled with ideas generated from students and an understanding of the institution's needs, advisers will be able to guide the planning and implementation of fund-raising activities.

For many RHAs, without the added financial support generated from fund-raising activities, the level of service and programs would decrease. Effective fund-raising techniques have become a universally necessary skill for advisers of today's organizations. The ability to secure adequate funding is becoming an increasingly indispensable skill in the operation of an organization. The leader or adviser who is a competent fund-raiser is viewed as a highly valuable asset to any organization.

Finally, a brief note. The terms "funds" and "money" are used in a broad sense which includes not only cash but also donated goods and services which can be used to offset the cost of RHA programs or operations. Keeping a broad perspective on fund-raising can help RHA members to be creative, to increase their self-sufficiency, and to present an excellent calendar of programs to their constituency.

Successful Fund-Raising Campaigns

According to Stein (1994), a successful fund-raising activity is one that satisfies four major objectives. First, it is financially successful; it makes money that can utilized to support the association's goals. Second, the event generates enthusiasm for the fund-raising activity. Third, the activity fosters and reinforces a positive image of the association and its members through the exposure, publicity, and public relations associated with the activity itself. Fourth, the activity generates genuine support for the overall efforts and goals of the sponsoring organization.

It is important to remember that it is generally easier to raise funds for concrete projects than for abstract ideas. A well-planned project strategy, complete with a defined purpose, an established budget, and an outlined approach will generally be supported by a receiving agency. Whether seeking support from businesses, community, or campus constituents, potential donors, sponsors, or contributors will generally be more receptive to a detailed and purposeful idea.

Successful fund-raising campaigns do not just happen. They are the result of planning and hard work. As in any fund-raising campaign, there are models which, in themselves, cannot guarantee successful results, but improve the chances for success. RHAs can utilize a practical model (Pendleton, 1981) which includes the following seven steps.

Determine the Needs

In determining the needs, two questions must be addressed: Why are we seeking funds? How much do we need? Once these questions have been answered, the group must proceed with a positive attitude. Each member must be enthusiastic and keep in mind that there is no need to apologize for seeking support for a worthy cause. It should also be remembered that causes do not need workers as much as they need informed and dedicated advocates.

Put Needs in Writing

This is the design-and-define stage of the fund-raising campaign. The statement can be brief, but it must be clear and concise. The statement must reflect relevance, importance, and urgency. It should also reflect that the needs are marketable and that the targeted population can be persuaded to support the project. In many cases, solicitation of money is only part of the campaign. Many businesses or agencies support RHA efforts through special discounts or donation of goods or services which the RHA can use or raffle off for capital. The fund-raising campaign often will be more successful if the group can set forth goals that embrace humanitarian concerns. The group should outline the project's benefit to the students, the donor, the university, and/or the community.

Develop a Schedule

Unless plans are made in advance, the early phases of a fund-raising campaign often will take too much time. A calendar may be used to divide duties among the volunteers and offers a check on progress. The fund-raising campaign should have definite starting and ending dates. The RHA should consider the timing of the campaign. Make sure that the campaign does not compete with other projects and that the campaign fits in with the time of the year. Do not attempt to generate revenue in exactly the same fashion each year. Although annual drives can be effective, the group can enhance its chances for success with creative revisions in programs or advertisements. The group may want to stage a special event to advertise the campaign. This is an excellent method to kick off the campaign and enhance the publicity and support. Utilize other campus events already planned to complement the campaign.

Define a Target Population

Who is the targeted population? Funds cannot be raised without asking. Whom do you ask? How long is the list of potential sources of revenue or support? Are individuals, organizations, and/or businesses being targeted? Compile lists, with addresses, of area businesses and campus organizations. Update the lists often. Maintain records of previous donors or supporters and the extent of their support. This is essential for generating thank-you letters and for providing publicity for the supporters.

Establish Committees and Train Volunteers

Volunteers are the image makers. They give credibility to the organization. The use of volunteers implies shared decision making. As mentioned previously, causes do not need workers as much as they need informed and dedicated advocates. Two key points to remember are: (a) always respect the volunteers' time, and (b) people respond to rewards and recognition. Many RHA fund-raising activities or projects involve selling. These direct-sales efforts involve the association's volunteers.

Prior to sending volunteers out to sell, training is highly recommended. In training, be sure to discuss the requirements or expectations of the volunteers related to time. Teaching volunteers how to sell means teaching how to (a) identify potential customers, (b) approach customers, (c) explain the product, (d) emphasize the benefits to the purchaser, (e) explain the nature of the sponsoring organization, (f) clarify how the money will benefit the organization, (g) handle objections, (h) appropriately thank the prospect whether or not a purchase is made, and (i) maintain accurate records. Discourage overly aggressive or hard-sell tactics. Training efforts should also emphasize the purpose of the fund-raising campaign to the volunteer; the timing of the campaign; the campaign budget; the procedures that will be followed; and the types of gifts, revenue, or services which will be sought from businesses.

Establish a Budget and Maintain Quality Records

It is important to keep in mind the cost of the fund-raising idea. Every effective campaign involves mailings, the initial investment, printing costs, and possible shipping costs. A common mistake is to set fund-raising costs too low. Successful fund-raising is not possible without accurate record keeping, such as the documentation recommended below.

1. Records of prospects
2. Former donors
3. Former customers
4. Inventory
5. Budgets
6. Income and expenses
7. Taxes

8. Permits, licenses, required forms
9. Minutes or summaries of planning meetings
10. Copies of letters received and sent
11. Evaluations of current and past fund-raising projects

One of the most critical components of fund-raising involves the money collected. Where money is concerned, two key words are accountability and security. Many institutions require all income from fund-raising activities to be deposited in a special activity account. Many also require periodic audits. Typically, institutions require two or three signatures on checks issued from the account. Advisers need to pay special attention to financial record keeping to prevent errors which could be embarrassing to the organization or detrimental to the institution.

Evaluate the Campaign

As with any effective program, an evaluation is essential. Based upon the evaluation, decisions regarding future campaigns will be simplified. During the evaluation, checks can be made to insure that recognition has been given to volunteers and campaigns supporters.

In addition to following the procedures outlined for a fund-raising campaign, attention must be given to avoiding common errors or, as Seymour (1966) described them, the "seven deadly sins" of fund-raising:

Ad-libbing. No study, no planning, no preparation, no consultation, no concurrence, and hence no organized and unified agreement.

Panhandling. Asking for support merely because you need the money. No explanation; hence no motivation for thoughtful and proportionate giving. "Any amount will be welcome" cheapens the cause and beggars the giver by putting fund-raising ahead of the program.

Automation. The human equation gives way to mechanics, with the voluntary mission abdicated to the postman and publicist.

Groupism. The opposite of universality — undemocratic, divisive, and sterile. No single group can organize a community.

Averaging. An accent on averages leads to lower standards in leadership, volunteer participation, and levels of giving.

Pessimism. Only genuine emergencies can make fund-raising assets out of gloom and despair. More often than not the aim is too low and it becomes necessary to plead rather than challenge. Whenever the volunteer lets the organization know that the campaign is not going well, the chances are that everything will stop right there.

Parsimony. The good omelet needs enough broken eggs. More often than not, fund-raising costs are set too low.

As indicated earlier, development of a strategic plan, active involvement of each member, training, and awareness of common errors contribute to a successful fund-raising campaign. The following examples and suggestions will enhance the RHA's chances for conducting an effective and successful campaign.

Institutional and Self-Generated Funds

To gain more insight into what RHAs are doing to raise money from their institutions, through their own programs, and from outside sources, two different surveys were distributed by the authors. The first, in 1992, focused on different ways to raise funds. The second, distributed in 1997, focused on how much funds were being raised from various sources.

For the first survey, ideas were solicited by sending requests for information to three different computer-based list servers, RHA-List, NCC-List, and DISCUSS @ Housing (Texas A & M University, 1991). A survey was also distributed at the 1992 South Atlantic Affiliate of College and University Residence Halls Conference at Knoxville, TN, and at the 1992 Southern Association for College Student Affairs Conference at Atlanta, GA. The information was reviewed and categorized by the authors using qualitative techniques (Lincoln & Guba, 1985).

Many RHAs which responded to the surveys used a variety of funding methods to raise money. Seven different types of local funding are described below, including advantages, disadvantages, and examples. Finally, programming ideas submitted by participating institutions are included.

Institutional/Departmental Funding Support

Institutions and housing departments supported a majority of the institutions participating in this study. Support often came in the form of a direct allocation of funds from the institution or department. Some institutions provided support through a centralized allocation system managed by an institution-wide student government organization. Other RHAs were funded by a per-student fee, such as an activity fee, added to the housing bill.

Advantages. Such funding is a direct representation of the commitment by the department and/or the institution to the mission of the RHA. Such support can be as valuable as the money itself. Further, this kind of funding can be more stable than rental or sales revenue, car washes, or other such market-driven funding sources. In the case of a student activity fee, if residence hall students are allowed to set or to have input in setting fees, there is more control over income than with other sources. When RHA officers must justify the fees to their constituencies, a measure of accountability is built into the system.

Disadvantages. One disadvantage of such funding can be a loss, or perceived loss, of autonomy. If the institution or department determines the level of funding, the RHA may feel under administrative control, creating the potential for conflicts. If the institution has financial problems, direct funding may be subject to budget cuts or even elimination in favor of other institutional priorities. A specified activity fee may be safer from such cuts, although setting the fee may not be completely under the RHA's or students' control, especially at state-supported institutions where a single state governing board controls all fees. Adding such a fee, if one does not currently exist, may take several years and, in the case of state-supported institutions, could require coordination with other state-system colleges and universities.

Vending and Other Contract Services

Many institutions contract for a variety of services with private companies. Such deals are often quite lucrative for both the institution and the company. Several institutions reported adding a fee to contracts under the control of the housing department, designated for the RHA. Others designated a percentage of the institution's share of the profit to be distributed to the RHA and other student groups. Examples included contracts for food services; book stores; convenience stores; laundry services; video and other amusement games; soda, snack, and other vending machines; and so forth. Food delivery companies may provide incentives by donating a percentage of their sales in residence halls to the RHA. The RHA can publicize their relationships with vendors in the halls, providing a low-cost way to make money for both the RHA and the companies. Companies may require specific considerations for the contract, such as advertising or "Official Sponsor" status. Such sponsorships may have legal ramifications for the institution, requiring consultation with advisers and other university officials.

Advantages. This seems to be a fairly stable, low-risk source of funding. The RHA assumes little, if any risk, and can gain a considerable amount of money. RHAs could publicize the relationship, especially when they receive a percentage of the income, to make students aware that they support RHA programs by soliciting certain vendors. RHAs also can get involved in the contracting process, both as an advocate for students and for the educational benefit of the individual students involved.

Disadvantages. Such funding is very market driven. When money is tight and students are spending less, RHA income can drop if it is based on a percentage. Flat fees are a little more stable, but offer no increases if income goes up. In a poor economy, additional fees and splitting of income may be less desirable to both the institution and the company. Both increase the company's costs, and could keep some companies from bidding with the institution if the profit margin is already small. There may also be a great deal of competition for a share of the institution's profits, requiring the RHA and housing department to spend time dealing with institutional politics.

Sales, Rentals, and Services

Another common form of fund-raising involved selling, renting, or providing services to students. RHAs reported being involved in the sale or rental of various products in two ways, either directly, by buying and then reselling or renting the items, or indirectly, by acting as an agent for a separate company. Many institutions reported serving as an agent for On-Campus Marketing (OCM) and Campus Fund Raisers (CFR) to sell exam kits, welcome kits, carpeting, linens, and other items. One institution, Georgia College, also reported selling baskets for Secretary's Day. Regulations at some institutions prohibit private companies from using space on campus unless they are sponsored by a campus organization, creating a wonderful opportunity for additional fund-raising.

Some institutions also reported renting and/or selling refrigerators, Microfridges, lofts, furniture, used textbooks, school paraphernalia, telephones (if they are not provided in the room), and so forth. Another idea is to rent space to other student groups. If the institution or the housing department has some unused space which can be renovated, other organizations may be interested in renting it for dances or other socials.

An Introduction to Raising Money

RHAs often provide services to on-campus students as part of their mission. Some services can be made self-supporting, or even make a profit, providing financial resources for other worthy, but unprofitable projects. Institutions reported providing a variety of services as fund-raisers, including copier services, typewriter rentals, birthday cake or Valentine's Day candy and flower deliveries, movie rentals, vacuum cleaner rentals, luggage carts for moving in and out, and so forth. The profits were small, but could be used to expand services in the future.

Several institutions (Mississippi State University, Texas A & M University, University of Arizona, University of Florida, and University of New Hampshire) reported selling an activity or membership card which, for one price, enabled the student to use all of the RHA's or hall council's services. Students not purchasing a card paid for each service as it was used. Pricing was set to encourage the purchase of the activity or membership card. In most cases, the activity card was sold by the individual hall council, not the RHA. Other service ideas included a sidewalk sale where groups or individuals paid for booth space at a campus flea market (Gardner-Webb College and James Madison University).

Special events on campus may provide a golden opportunity to make money. Parking at concerts and sporting events is often at a premium and, with permission from the institution, space could be sold to visitors. Booths to sell school paraphernalia or food at homecoming, a campus spring carnival, and Freshmen Day were just some of the examples (Gardner-Webb College, Santa Rosa Junior College, and University of Arizona).

RHAs should be careful to ensure that any items with their institution's name or logo are officially licensed by the institution. Such items are registered trademarks and/or copyrighted, and using them without advance permission is illegal. Wholesalers should be able to provide adequate documentation. If items are being custom made to the RHA's specifications, and include the institution's name or logo, contact the campus licensing office for information on obtaining permission to use the desired items.

Equipment an RHA may need for their functions, such as sound and light systems, tables, casino party equipment, helium tanks, large-volume popcorn machines, and so forth, can be rented to other organizations when not in use by the RHA or individual residence halls.

Interest in recycling seems to be increasing at many institutions. Since residence hall students create a certain amount of recyclable waste, one institution (Mississippi State University), reported recycling of waste paper and aluminum cans to raise money. The amount generated was small, but the project also generated favorable publicity and environmental benefits. Research in a local area may be necessary to determine if other campus agencies manage campus recycling, or if the market for a specific type of recyclable product, such as paper, is saturated.

Advantages. Sales, rentals, and services can be a big money maker, as well as providing an important service to students. The student body is, to some extent, a captive market.

There are a number of options to simply buying and renting high cost items such as Microfridges. Some RHAs reported renting units from a supplier and re-renting them to students. Responsibility for repairs and replacements remained in the hands of the supplier. Another option is a rent-to-own plan. These kinds of plans, which avoid making a large one-time purchase of equipment, allowed RHAs to enter a rental program without having to raise large amounts of start-up capital.

Disadvantages. Extreme care should be take in selecting a company to sponsor on-campus (see Chapter 13). Poor products or services will reflect not only on the company but on the RHA as well. Some products may create ethical problems, such as credit card applications designed to offer easy credit, at high cost, for inexperienced students. Sales and rental projects taken on solely by the RHA may have high start-up costs, such as refrigerator rentals, which may limit profits for several years. As mentioned earlier, rental plans may be a solution.

Such projects also require consistent leadership and may entail hiring someone, possibly a graduate assistant, to manage the program. Adding employees, however, cuts down on profits unless the individual's expertise can increase sales or rentals. Another issue is storage space. Large rental items, such as refrigerators, require summer storage, and space is often at a premium on many campuses.

Raffles and Games

Raffles and other games of chance are a common way of raising money by RHAs, as well as many campus and community groups. In some states, a raffle may be legal only if the profit is to be donated or used for educational purposes. In other areas it may be completely legal or illegal. It is critical to consult with the institution's legal counsel before undertaking such a project. Several institutions reported raffling off free housing fees, a prize which could be pure profit if the housing department donated the prize. Other institutions mentioned raffles for bicycles, shopping sprees, clothes, stereo equipment, tuition and other fees, trips (especially to football bowl games), athletic tickets, concert tickets, televisions, video recorders, home video game machines, and cash. The more creative and attractive the prize, the better the chance of increasing ticket sales. Another idea is to sponsor a joint raffle with other student organizations. This could increase potential sales by providing additional ticket sellers and access to new markets. Knowing what students want and would be willing to take a chance on will determine the success of any raffle.

Other games of chance were not mentioned often but, depending on the institution and local law, should not be overlooked. Bingo is often a profitable venture for many civic groups and can be a lot of fun. While casino parties are popular, gambling for real money is illegal in many areas and should be avoided.

Another type of fund-raising game is a "penny drop," where various groups compete to raise the most money for a cause from loose change (University of Southern Mississippi). Residents could compete between halls, with a prize for the hall raising the most money. Students drop their change in a jar to support their hall, vote for their favorite campus leader or sports team, and so forth. An interesting idea is to dress up student leaders or resident assistants in disgusting make-up and costumes. Students vote for the "ugliest" student leader or resident assistant. One variation is for pennies to count as a positive vote and silver coins and bills as negative votes which can be used to offset pennies used to vote for an opposing candidate.

Advantages. If sales are strong and the prize worthy, raffles have the potential to raise a considerable amount of money. The two most critical components are having dynamic salespeople and a great prize.

Disadvantages. Raffles involve a considerable amount of work. Selling sufficient tickets requires a number of dedicated workers willing to get out and sell. If the RHA published a drawing date and sufficient tickets have not sold by that time, the RHA can easily lose money. If prizes are not donated, the high purchase price of an attractive prize can also create a problem.

Program Fees

Some RHA activities are so popular that students may pay to attend or participate. This can help defray the cost of the event and, if the function is popular enough, raise money for other projects. This was perhaps the most varied area of fund-raising. A few institutions reported having dances and other social events as fund-raisers (Indiana University of Pennsylvania and Santa Rosa Junior College). Mississippi State University reported charging only students who did not purchase a voluntary activity card. Other institutions which charged a voluntary social fee or hall dues did not mention if students who did not pay that fee could participate in activities on a charge-per-activity basis or if they were simply restricted from the events. Some examples included Halloween balls, Valentines Day dances, hay rides and country dances, small concerts, comedians, movie nights, trips to sporting events, and so forth. With the consent of the promoter, bulk purchasing and reselling of concert tickets possibly with transportation or some other special extra can also raise funds. In fact, almost any popular, quality program can raise money to help defray the costs of the event.

Another idea is an Activity Fair or Freshmen Fair where student organizations and local vendors gather in a central location to recruit members and customers (Mississippi State University and University of New Hampshire). Vendors and non-residence-hall organizations can be charged a fee for their booth.

One area of expertise for many RHAs is leadership development. The RHA can sponsor a campus leadership conference and charge a small fee to non-residence-life leaders. This would require offering more general sessions of interest to all student leaders, in addition to specialized sessions for specific residence hall offices.

Advantages. Program fees can limit the cost of an event even if the event does not make a profit. A small fee can help an RHA put on an expensive program without going bankrupt.

Disadvantages. Charging fees can reduce attendance, especially if the fee is too high. Some institutions stated that charging a fee was in contradiction to their RHA's purpose of providing activities to students. Programs must be entertaining and creative if students are expected to pay to participate. Many students are on a tight budget and entertainment is a luxury they may not be able to afford. If an RHA is partially funded by an activity fee or departmental allocation, students may respond negatively to paying what they perceive as more money for events.

Interest Income

Interest income can be generated in a number of ways. The most common method is to deposit a percentage of funds in certificates of deposit, a savings account, or some other interest-bearing account. If an RHA receives large allocations once or twice a year and can afford to tie up some funds for a few months, this kind of income is very attractive. A small number of institutions reported considering setting up some kind of trust fund (North Carolina State University and Mississippi State University). Money is deposited into the account and only the interest is spent. Depending on how the trust fund is established, some of the principal could be removed in an emergency. One possibility is that contributors could donate money to the RHA through the institution's development office, allowing the contributor a tax deduction, and eliminating the RHA's need to maintain a foundation of its own (University of Florida).

Advantages. Interest income can be a low-maintenance source of revenue. The institutional development office or a local bank can help manage the account. A trust-fund-style account can be very stable. Making interest income part of an RHA financial package requires a long-term view and adequate planning.

Disadvantages. Interest rates may fluctuate and the returns can be small, especially if the RHA does not have much money to invest. An RHA without much spare cash may find interest income more trouble than it is worth. A trust-fund-style arrangement may take considerable time to raise sufficient principal to generate enough interest income to be useful. When a large sum of money is maintained in a trust fund, other departments may find it attractive and attempt to secure it for purposes other than the RHA. Please consult with the institution's legal counsel when arranging any long-term financial packages (see also Chapter 10).

Campus Practices

The second survey was mailed to all Association of College and University Housing Officers-International (ACUHO-I) member institutions. Addresses were obtained from the ACUHO-I Central Services Office in Columbus, OH. The surveys were addressed to either the chief housing officer or the person designated as the "educational" officer on the ACUHO-I database.

One hundred and fifty institutions returned surveys. The mean number of residence hall students at the institutions returning surveys was 2,730. The number of residence hall students ranged from 140 to 11,000. Sixty percent of the institutions returning surveys were public institutions, 37% were private, and the rest did not respond to the question. Over 95% of the institutions were four-year schools, 1% were two-year schools, and the rest did not respond to the question. Almost 70% of the responding institutions were members of the National Association of College and University Residence Halls, Inc. (NACURH). Regional affiliations are shown in Table 1.

The survey contained questions to determine how much money was raised through various fund-raising practices. Those practices included corporate fund-raising programs from CFR and OCM. Overall, the largest amount of funds is coming from housing department allocations, followed by OCM's carpet sales program, and then a tie between CFR's Exam Kits program and local fund-raising events (Table 2).

Since many institutions also have individual residence hall building governments in addition to the campus RHA, additional questions were included on the survey about funds raised by those groups. When asked the total budget for all individual hall governing groups, in addition to any campus-wide RHA funds already reported, 49% of the responding institutions indicated a mean total budget of $22,874.11 for the individual hall groups, or $8.38 per resident.

The survey also contained questions to determine how much money was raised through various fund-raising practices by individual residence hall governing groups. The largest source of funding for individual residence hall governing groups was housing department allocations, followed by allocations from the campus wide RHA (Table 3).

In the 1992 survey, a majority of the institutions listed direct allocations from their institution or the housing department as a source of funding. In the 1997 survey, the largest source of funding, in terms of dollars, for campus-wide RHAs and for individual residence hall governing groups was housing department allocations. Often, the adviser and RHA executives are the primary liaisons between residence hall student organizations and the housing department. Therefore, it is critical for advisers and RHA leaders to maintain a strong working relationship with the senior housing staff, especially those involved in budgeting funds. If the adviser is an entry-level staff member, or in a large department with many mid-level managers, he or she must ensure a strong line of communication to those responsible for budget. This line may be through supervisory channels, as part of the department's formal organizational structure, or on an informal basis directly to the chief housing officer or other senior staff responsible for budgets.

Exercises

1. Have students prepare a mock presentation and give it to the other RHA officers and/or individual building governing group officers prior to soliciting money from donors. Let the officers provide a critique to the presenters. The chief housing officer and other senior staff may be another source of meaningful feedback.
2. Ask the group to discuss what they would do if this year's fund-raising efforts produced an additional 25% above the budgeted amount. What would they do if the results are 25% below the budgeted amounts?
3. Create a wish list of items needed by RHA. Have it available to persons soliciting funds from different groups in case someone wants to give more than what they are being asked for.
4. Meet with the institution's development officers. They may have wonderful ideas for student-group fund-raising. Some institutions provide development accounts for student groups so that donors get the tax benefits of donating to a charitable organization.
5. Ask the RHA's officers what they would do if someone proposed a "Slave Sale" as a fund-raiser? How about a date auction? How do their values play into fund-raising?
6. Construct a list of former officers and ask them to make donations to the RHA. A letter from the current president to past officers may spark pleasant memories

and the desire to see the RHA program continue. Have an alumni reception during homecoming.

7. Determine the considerations the RHA is willing to make for donors. This may include listing their names in newsletters, flyers, and so forth, or other forms of public recognition. What will the RHA do if donors want to have a program carry their names?

8. Which donors are unacceptable to the RHA or to the institution because of their products or business practices?

Conclusion

In this chapter, the focus has been on raising money at the local level. Responses from RHAs participating in two national surveys showed a broad range of fund-raising packages designed to support their operations. RHA officers and committee members must remember, however, that while having money is important, fund-raising should never become an end unto itself. It should always be a means to an end, with the end being services and programs for residence hall students.

References

Lincoln, Y. S., & Guba, E. G. (1985). *Naturalistic inquiry.* Beverly Hills, CA: Sage.

Mississippi State University (1991). *Discuss@Housing.msstate.edu* (Computer Network). Starkville, MS: Housing and Residence Life, Mississippi State University.

Pendleton, N. (1981). *Fund raising: A guide for non-profit organizations.* Englewood Cliffs, NJ: Prentice-Hall.

Seymour, H. J. (1966). *Designs for fund raising, principles-patterns-techniques.* New York: McGraw-Hill.

Stein, W. F. (1994). *Fundraising for sport and recreation.* Champaign, IL: Human Kinetics.

Texas A & M University (1991). *NCC-List* (Computer Network). College Station, TX: Texas A & M University. listserv@listserv.tamu.edu (subscribe NCC-L).

Texas A & M University (1991). *RHA-List* (Computer Network). College Station, TX: Texas A & M University. listserv@listserv.tamu.edu (subscribe RHA-L).

Table 1
NACURH Regional Affiliations

Region	No.	%*
Central Atlantic	7	6.7
South Atlantic	23	21.9
Middle-America	17	16.1
Pacific	13	12.4
Great Lakes	15	14.3
Inter-Mountain	9	8.6
Northeast	12	11.4
Southwest	4	3.8
No region listed	5	4.8
Total	105	

*Does not equal 100% dues to rounding.

Table 2
Mean Funds Raised by Campus-Wide RHAs

Source	No. of Institutions	Total Mean Amount Raised	Mean Amount per Resident*
Campus Fund Raisers			
Exam Kits	63	$2,461.89	$0.90
Welcome Kits	40	1,451.68	0.53
On-Campus Marketing			
Carpet Sales	17	2,705.00	0.99
Diploma Case Sales	2	412.50	0.15
Linen Sales	51	1,819.96	0.76
Donations**	14	1,910.71	0.70
Local Fund-Raisers	46	2,647.17	0.90
Endowments	4	1,737.50	0.64
Interest Income	6	327.50	0.12
Housing Allocation***	101	14,491.35	5.31

*Based on a mean of 2730 residents among those schools reporting total residence hall population.

**Includes cash donations and the cash value of goods and services donated.

***Housing and residence life departmental allocation from the department budget, or collected by the department on behalf of the RHA.

Table 3
Mean Funds Raised by Individual Hall Governing Groups

Source	No. of Institutions	Total Mean Amount Raised	Mean Amount per Resident*
Local Fund-raisers	27	$5,146.37	1.89
RHA Allocation**	17	5,631.53	2.06
Housing Allocation***	26	15,290.00	5.60

*Based on a mean of 2,730 residents among those schools reporting total residence hall population.

**Allocations from the campus-wide RHA, which may have been raised in a variety of ways (as reported in Table 2).

***Housing and residence life departmental allocation from the department budget, or collected by the department on behalf of the individual governing group.

Corporate Fund-Raising

Part I

Howie Dumhart
Campus Fund Raisers

Corporate Fund-Raising - Part I

As housing staff look at the overall program designed by residence life offices, they are generally faced with a very critical dilemma — how to fully fund residence hall associations (RHAs). What is truly needed by residence populations must be balanced with students' dreams and aspirations. When examining this dilemma, a possible solution to the problem could be derived by looking outside the campus realm to companies that exist to service the residence student market. In looking beyond the university setting, several new factors arise that must be considered.

The first portion of this chapter will explore factors which exist in the relationship between an RHA and an outside vendor. Then, the purposes of fund-raising efforts will be discussed, especially in relation to interaction with outside vendors. What are the benefits of choosing to work with an outside vendor, and what are the disadvantages? Subsequently, factors contributing to successful RHA-vendor relationships will be considered. Finally, ideas for sending delegations to regional and national conferences will be shared.

What to Look for in an Outside Company

Whether the purpose is only to purchase a particular product, or to offer one service of a larger program provided by the RHA, *price* should solely dictate decision making. Remember that the quality of the product or service must be equal when comparing price (compare apples to apples). Once the relationship is expanded beyond a single component, there are multitudes of issues to explore prior to making a decision to work with an off-campus company or vendor. Although the following information might not often appear directly on the surface or be addressed in a company's brochure, there are several ways that the adviser can find the answers to the following questions: Does the company have some grounding in student development? Does the company understand what the RHA is attempting to accomplish through its program? How can the company service the organization through other portions or parts of its structure? Who are the key players within the company's organizational structure, and what is their motivation and involvement with the product or service that they will provide for the group? What are the corporate values exhibited by the company, and are they congruent with the values that the RHA wishes to promote? Does the service or product that the company provides truly meet a need of the RHA's constituency?

When considering whether to enter into a relationship with a company, the RHA must assess the company's motivation for existence. Obviously, the company exists to make a profit; no company can survive without making money. However, does the company understand that the purpose of the RHA is to provide a friendly, warm, and fostering environment for the residence students? Does the company recognize that the RHA is attempting to enhance the growth of individuals within the organization, as well as that of the residence hall population? Does the company support and understand the overall value of the RHA's entire program versus the individual aspect of this particular program? Succinctly, the company should have some type of understanding of why an RHA exists and of its purpose. Without this basic understanding, there may be many stumbling blocks in the relationship. There could be many ethical fine lines to cross as the RHA's relationship with this company progresses.

The Purpose of the Fund-Raising Effort

One of the first things the RHA must accomplish is to clearly define its purpose for existence. Is the mission to improve the overall quality of life within the residence halls, while adding to the personal development of group members, or does the group exist solely to function as a group? Hopefully, the former is the answer most groups and advisers would give to this question. The premise on which most fund-raising companies are built is that cutting out a middle person is not truly to a group's advantage, although in most cases the group could make more money. The time and energies needed to accomplish one particular project are much better spent working on other more encompassing goals than attempting to maximize the group's profit. When group members analyze whether it is more appropriate to utilize an outside company or to attempt to do a project themselves, there are several key questions to which the adviser must respond. Will the success of a program be borne by one person or a small group of individuals? How much supervisory time and energy will be funneled into this project? Does the outlay of funds restrict the group's efforts until the payoff (return of capital)? What will be the consequences if the project does not succeed at all? After the project has been completed for the first time, does it become turnkey, or does it continue to need a lot of attention?

If the project will be borne by one individual or by a small group, several negative aspects could disrupt the positive energies of the group. If this group does not accomplish its specific goals, the entire organization will suffer. Working with students, advisers know how fragile the environment is in which the group functions. Students have many other aspects of their lives that carry more weight than the success of the organization. Fortunately, this is not the general rule. Most advisers have found wonderful students to work on committees; however, the danger is always there. Should advisers risk the overall success of the group on the added margins that may be gained by not using a professional company?

Unless advisers are part of a very progressive, forward-thinking organization, advisement of an RHA is only one aspect of their overall job responsibilities. Advisers must weigh the impact of time commitment to a specific project. The overall development of the group must outweigh the commitment to any one project. Once a certain level of hands-on involvement is established, there will be an expectation for that level to continue in future executions of a similar project. The management and commitment necessary to support a profit-worthy fund-raiser will almost always be in addition to an adviser's job description or assigned responsibilities. Is the time better spent on the overall development of the group?

Often groups feel that they can complete a project themselves and make larger net profits. However, they fail to recognize that the money they invest in a project restricts their accomplishment of other goals. The loss of the use of the monies actually eats into those larger net margins, and the risk of failure is always present when doing any project. The larger corporate company spreads that risk over a number of groups, allowing the failure of any one group to be borne by the whole. Groups often fail to calculate into their profit formulas the added person-hours needed to accomplish a specific project, or the monies that come from their budget or the residence life budget. The group and the adviser must look carefully at the big picture before investing the group's money, time, and energies for only the possibility of increasing the bottom-line profit.

Advisers are responsible for keeping success moving on a steady course. It is important not to let a group get too excited about the success of one project, nor to allow the demise of one project to paralyze the group. Should a group decide to take on a fund-raising project as its entire focus for a semester or a year, and should that project not reap the success the group had anticipated, the group's goals may not be achieved. Would it not be better for the group to achieve a moderate, guaranteed level of success through a varied program versus a potential for greater financial reward?

The danger of developing a great fund-raiser that has many facets to its success is that it will continue to need attention to remain successful. If a project will be used to complement the overall program, then it should be as low maintenance as possible. The less time given to that project, the more energies can be targeted toward creative growth-inducing activities. There are very few projects which will generate high-profit potentials that will not also be high maintenance. Isn't the adviser's time better spent moving the group along in other aspects of group development?

With any project, the RHA should consider how it will maximize involvement of group members while minimizing financial risks. Let the bulk of the capital investment be borne by the selected company. Focus the group's energies on the interactional aspects of servicing the student population. Make sure to maximize the opportunity for positive public relations within the residence population and the campus community at large. Remember that the development of the group, the leadership opportunities, and the service of the residence population are key elements of the purpose of the RHA's existence.

Advantages of Working with an Outside Company

Professionalism

The foremost advantage of choosing to allow an outside fund-raising company to provide a service or product for the RHA is the professionalism that the company would bring to the project. The adviser should assist students to look for a company whose sole purpose is existing to accomplish the program or to provide the service or product needed by the group. Once the decision is made to use an outside vendor, critically analyze whether the company being considered truly has the expertise and ability to make the group look good. Look at their written and published materials. Do they have form and function? In other words, are they clearly organized and do they define the relationship between the group and the company? Most important, are the responsibilities of the group directly outlined, leaving very little to interpretation?

Does the company have the proper support personnel to ensure that the group will receive the guidance needed to make the program a success? Does the company answer questions promptly, supporting any discussions with written materials to prevent miscommunication? Are advisers able to reach those people in control of decision-making responsibilities when confronted with a critical issue, or are they forced to work through a middle person? Can the adviser develop a relationship that will enhance the group's experience? The answers to these questions should be very positive in order to assure that experience with this vendor will accomplish the group's goals.

Capitalization

The next advantage of working with an outside vendor is the capitalization of a project. Obviously, there are ethical and institutional issues to address when the RHA considers funding a project for which the primary purpose is to raise additional monies. Is it permissible by institutional rules, and more important, is it fair to use the funds collected from students through dues or given to residence life offices from activities fees to do a project the purpose of which is to increase the group's treasury? There is always the chance for failure; therefore, it also involves a risk of funds that really should be used to provide educational programming. The professional fund-raising company should minimize the group's risk by assuming all the burden of funding the project. All aspects of the project that involve investment of capital before being assured income should be borne by the company. Remember that there are no easy ways to make money; group members will still have to invest their efforts and time to accomplish tasks associated with the fund-raising project.

Quality of a Project or Service

The outside vendor should provide a product that will exceed anything that the group could provide by itself. The product should set high standards and have a consistency that does not waiver. The group should be proud to represent itself as the agent of the company or as the ultimate supplier of the service or product. When considering a product, examine its true value relative to the difficulty the group might have in providing the product by itself. The finished product should exhibit a professional standard that is uncompromised.

Thoroughness of Service

An outside vendor should be available to the adviser throughout the completion of the project, especially during the execution or delivery of the product or service. Will the company be available to assist in a crisis situation? Does the company have a sufficient number of personnel to ensure that they can provide support to the group? What does the company do from its end to make sure that the final execution of the program is successful?

The adviser should examine the support materials provided by the company to the group. Those support materials should provide the group with constant coaching throughout the process. In all cases, the materials should be clear and concise, enabling the students assigned to the project to complete their tasks while gaining a degree of self-esteem and satisfaction.

Make sure that the company has a positive track record and will continue to be available to the group for follow-up. The successful completion of one project should lead to potential long-range relationships and many successful programs. Make sure that the company is going to be there for the group well beyond the completion of the initial project.

Disadvantages of Working with an Outside Company

Control of the Project

The foremost disadvantage when working with an off-campus company is that control of the execution of the project is transferred to that company. It is extremely important that the track record of the company be examined thoroughly to ensure that the project components and completion will meet the group's needs and expectations. If possible, do not invest any monies in a project and try to control the financial aspects of the program until the company has executed all of its contracted responsibilities. Once the control of a project is given to an outside company, the group's reputation and public relations image will suffer if any elements of the program or product do not meet consumers' expectations.

Any time that the group does not control the financial aspects of a program, the risk of a potential problem exists. Make sure that the institution is guaranteed a minimal safety valve to ensure that the consumer has the opportunity for a refund. If the group controls the monies collected for a project until the consumer has received their goods or services, very little risk exists. In the worst scenario, the group would simply need to refund the monies to the appropriate parties.

When giving control of a program to an outside vendor, make sure that several checks and balances exist which will enable the group to monitor the company's progress. Have some type of alternative plan should the company not meet expectations. Challenge the company to be congruent with the group's principles and values. Do not allow the group's image to tainted by its association with an inferior product or by a lack of execution on the part of the contracted company.

Review the questions in the previous section entitled "what to look for in an outside company." Monitor the company's work. If the adviser ensures that the responsibilities of the company and the group have been clearly outlined, there will be no need to worry about giving up control of the program.

Ongoing Trust Must Exist

Once an outside company is selected for a project, the group must continue to develop a working relationship. Successful execution of one project should not erase all doubts completely. Do not fail to continue to challenge the vendor to reach for a level of excellence. Look for a company that has a long-standing track record. This will help to alleviate some concerns. However, it is important to give notice that the company cannot rest on its laurels. How does the company respond to a problem or mistake? No company can be error-proof, but the response to a shortcoming should exceed the group's needs or expectations. At that point, the group can begin to be assured that the relationship is a sound one and a correct one for the group.

As time goes on and the relationship continues with a company, it is important not to become complacent. Make sure that the adviser role is maintained and critically analyze the vendor. Advisers certainly do not want to have a hostile relationship; however, it is good for companies to know that their actions are being monitored.

Loss of Revenue

Members need to realize that there is a trade-off when working with an outside company. Most of the time, as previously discussed, there are many reasons for working with an outside company. Advisers must be aware of the profit differential and be satisfied that net incomes are sufficient.

Most important, if the organization has given the start-up financial risks to the outside company, the difference in fewer profits may be greatly outweighed by the opportunities. Advisers never want to risk the financial stability of the group for increased profit margins.

Loss of Program Integrity

It is extremely important to realize that the company is representing the group. The company should also demonstrate an awareness that its product, service, and interactions will reflect back to the group. As previously discussed, it is important to know the company and its employees, for their failures could tarnish the group's image. The company has an ethical responsibility to represent the group in a manner that is consistent with its expressed and implied values.

Advisers must monitor the project on a consistent basis. Are tasks and other aspects of the project being fulfilled in a timely fashion? Is the delivered product the same as that which was promised or shown in a sample? Always have a sample from the original discussion to compare to the final product. Did the company meet all the clearly defined expectations outlined at the beginning of the relationship? If not, advisers should have some channel for expressing feedback and having concerns addressed and corrected.

If advisers have clearly defined the role of the company, actively monitored its work, and remained involved through the completion of the project, this should not be a concern. However, if advisers do not play an active role, there will be room for the project to lose its integrity, therefore jeopardizing the public image of the group.

Loss of Group Identity

When a project is given to an outside vendor, the group risks losing any identity with its outcome. The group could possibly feel like a pawn in the process instead of a vital link to its success. It is important for the adviser to find a linking mechanism which will enable the group to feel responsible to and for the project. Any project should enhance the group dynamics which advisers and students work so hard to perpetuate. If there is little or no need for effort on the group's part, this may initially seem attractive. Over time, however, the group's self-confidence, and the self-esteem of the individual members, will dwindle. How many advisers are aware of groups that have balance sheets that are very positive, yet the group seems to flounder and go nowhere?

It is important that RHAs realize that they are a vital source and that the project could not be accomplished without them. By maintaining this posture, the adviser will avoid the pitfall of a group losing its self-respect. It is important to make things as easy as possible for group members, but remember that valuable lessons come from being part of the process.

Once the RHA has contracted for the performance of a service or project with an outside company, have at least one RHA member interface with the organization. Make sure to reinforce the importance of that individual's role and the group as a whole to the success of the project. An involved adviser will help the group avoid the chance of losing its identity.

Ensuring the Success of Projects

Have a Plan

Often groups and individuals fail to follow these three simple words. The most important thing that the group can do is to develop a comprehensive step-by-step action plan for the year. Advisers would profess that people and groups that are the most successful in life have had a very defined set of goals and a planned strategy to reach those goals. Other portions of this book are dedicated to helping advisers improve those skills which are necessary to emphasize this concept of developing a plan for the group.

Without belaboring the point, at the earliest stages of the group's leadership, the adviser should work with the group to formulate goals for the upcoming year. Now that the adviser knows where the group is going, how does he or she guide members in that direction? What financial resources are needed in order to ensure the success of the group? Hopefully, the group already has some funding sources. However, regardless of the balance in the treasury, what amount must be raised through fund-raising efforts? Advisers and group members should define the needs of the group, along with the path the group must take in order to be successful. In essence, the adviser must facilitate the formulation of an action plan with the group.

Advisers should have a clearly defined financial picture, which should help greatly in determining the fund-raisers the group will need to do. Hopefully, some of those fund-raisers will provide the opportunity to accomplish other secondary goals of the group. An example would be that the delivery of a product or service would also provide an opportunity for a positive public relationship. The plan enables examination of the potential for a relationship with an outside vendor with a clear picture in mind — does what the company has to offer fit into the plan? One can easily say no to a company if it does not meet the goals and expectations of the group. Most important, the group now has developed a clear picture of where it would like to go. It can now make decisions based on that plan and should have a benchmark to determine the value of goods or services offered by outside vendors.

How to Determine if a Program will be Successful

When considering a product or service for the RHA, thoroughly test the program by examining each of the following six aspects which are critical for successful fund-raisers and programs: Who is the target audience? When is the best time to reach the target population? What setting offers the greatest visibility? What is the budget for the program? What publicity is needed? What new and unique ideas will improve the chances for success? The more systematic members are in examining each of the following points, the less chance for failure. These basic principles work very well with individual programs and also are effective when examining an outside vendor's products or services. Put their programs to these tests or questions before committing to utilizing their services.

First, *who is the target audience?* There are a multitude of subgroups within the campus environment that can be identified for fund-raising efforts. Obviously, there exists the residence population, but there are also many subsets of the general population. Know the market and determine whether a need or desire exists for the product or service that will be offered. If there is a natural need or desire, or if one can artificially create that need or desire, the program will be on its way to success. Make sure that whatever is provided is not being met through some other means, for if the target audience has had the need fulfilled through some other means, then there exists the risk of failure.

The second point to consider is *when is the best time* to reach the target population? Many different timing opportunities will enhance abilities to reach the target population. Once the audience is established, examine all the different timing patterns which will expose the group to that target population. The annual calendar provides holidays. The academic calendar provides unique time frames to use for the group; the time of week, community calendar, sports calendar, alumni calendar, and so forth are all time frames which could provide a vehicle to reach that group for whom the program is designed.

Third, *what setting* will afford the group the greatest visibility to that target population? A multitude of locations exist on and surrounding the campus that will afford the group an opportunity to reach the targeted population. Examine the population being addressed and then determine where and how the group can make itself most visible to that audience. Utilize natural and predetermined locations which will afford exposure to the targeted population. Many campus locations, such as student centers, quads, cafeterias, events, classes, and programs, have physical properties that naturally provide exposure to certain groups. These will give members access to groups of people that may not always be available.

Another part of the puzzle which the group is responsible for analyzing is whether the location selected to execute the program will enhance or distract from the project. Many fund-raisers have failed because the setting actually sabotaged the efforts of the group that planned the program. Make sure that the location is critically analyzed to determine that it will support and enhance the program.

Fourth, a strong *budget* or financial plan must exist to execute the program. Although this is addressed elsewhere (see Chapter 11), the key points to keep in mind are as follows: Is there a less-expensive way with the same level of quality to execute the program? It is only common sense that the less something costs, the greater the profit potential. Determine that the financial resources exist to accomplish the program. Finally, assure that the profit potential is worth the person-hours the group will invest in the execution of the program.

Fifth, and most important, excellent *publicity* and/or promotional materials must be present to enhance the program. Using the most effective means of publicity will get people excited about the product or service. If people are excited and talking about the program, then there is positive movement toward a successful program. If the group is lackadaisical about its publicity efforts, utilizing the norm for getting the word out, it is playing into the trap of ineffective publicity, which causes the failure of most programming efforts. When the group creates new, exciting, and unique means to spread the word to the target audience, there is a better chance of ensuring success.

Finally, look for *new and unique ideas.* Encourage the group to dare to be different. Break the mold and start all over. Look for programs that are unique while still adhering to the above-mentioned steps. Most groups and businesses today are caught in the trap of not wanting to take too great a risk. If one can alleviate as much of the potential risk as possible by putting the program through the previously mentioned steps, the group has the opportunity for the greatest financial success.

Tap into the creative power of the group. Test programs thoroughly. Know exactly how the group will execute the program. Proceed with the plan, monitor its progress, generate enthusiasm, and be assured of an increased potential for a successful program.

Reasonable and Thorough Planning

With an established plan that can be executed without constant guidance and attention, the RHA will be successful as long as the plan enhances its true purpose and does not distract from the overall college experience. The plan should not rely on one individual to execute it. The plan must include as many members of the group as possible and seek to have more members come to the group. The RHA should have reasonable goals to accomplish. Make sure that accomplishments are celebrated and say thank you to everyone who has been involved. Most important, make sure that every possible part of the plan is thoroughly examined. Finally, remain positive, enthusiastic, supportive, and set on a predetermined path, with the flexibility to move around obstacles while always returning to that predetermined course. Follow these simple rules and the RHA will thrive and flourish.

How to Get a Delegation to Regional and National Conferences

If the RHA's plan is complete, it will include how to generate the funds to send delegates to conferences. The plan should include a phase that makes individuals directly responsible for their portion of the cost of attending a conference. This could be accomplished through two methods.

The first method is that an individual could be directly accountable for time spent on the group's fund-raisers. In other words, if a project takes 10 person-hours to accomplish and generate $100 profit, the $10 per person-hour accrued by the project would be placed in an account for that person. This should help with many facets of the program; hopefully better publicity will be generated because group members who feel vested in what the group is attempting to accomplish will be selling the idea or concept. Keep a record of group members who really give of their time. They will be rewarded through reduction in costs to attend conferences.

The second method is similar in nature, but has an added financial incentive for group members. It works exactly as above, but the individual is rewarded with matching funding by the group from fund-raising or other sources of revenue (i.e., the amount of revenue a person generates is the amount of credit earned towards conference costs). Again, the member is being vested in the activities of the group, and at a the same time, rewarded for giving of his or her time. This is particularly effective when some type of sale of an individual item is incorporated (candy sales are an excellent example). If planned and executed throughout the year, this method of fund-raising can be a very effective means of getting group members to conferences.

Plan sales in the spring prior to the academic year, spreading them out over the entire year. Take advantage of the different moods and times of the year to capitalize on the target population. Any type of sales are most successful at the beginning of the school year when people have more money to spend, and budgets have not yet become a major issue. Next, holidays are a time frame of which to take advantage. The more thought that is put into the group's efforts, the more benefits will be derived.

Most important, have the group instill the concept that it is the individual's responsibility to help raise the funds to get to conferences. Plan ahead and execute those plans. Make sure that a variety of fund-raisers exists to ensure the overall success of the effort, but do not burn out the group members. Most important, do not fund-raise because of a crisis situation; many times, this type of effort will only get the RHA further in debt.

Conclusion

This chapter should be helpful in gaining a perspective on working with corporate fund-raisers. The most important tool of all advising techniques will be common sense. If it seems too good to be true, it probably is. If advisers sense that companies are trying to pull the wool over their eyes, they probably are. Be very pessimistic until companies have proven that they deserve trust and respect. Then, continue to monitor their performance and challenge them through feedback to become better. Many companies can help the RHA become more financially sound while at the same time enhancing the program and public relations efforts. The challenge is to seek out those companies, utilize the recommendations in this portion of the chapter, and make the RHA the most fiscally sound group on campus.

Corporate Fund-Raising

Part II

Michael Schoen
On Campus Marketing

Corporate Fund-Raising - Part II

The role that a residence hall association (RHA) plays on campus is vital to the adjustment of new students as well as the quality of living for all. For an RHA to function properly, however, it must be adequately funded. Budget cutbacks in recent years at many institutions have made funding an RHA an even greater challenge than in years past. To help increase and improve fund-raising, many RHAs have opted to use outside corporations for assistance. Although corporations can be an excellent resource for fund-raisers, the RHA must still accomplish several tasks before utilizing a fund-raising partner. First and foremost, an RHA must understand why it wants to raise funds and what it hopes to accomplish with the funds raised. Only after that has been determined should an RHA start the process of identifying an outside corporation as a fund-raising partner.

The first step in fund-raising is for the students to decide what they hope to accomplish. Much like a business must create a business plan and formulate a mission statement, students must decide on their fund-raising goals. These goals should be congruent with the organization's overall goals and mission. Defining goals before getting too involved in the fund-raising process will help students stay focused as they look at the myriad of opportunities available to them. It will also ensure that the RHA does not lose direction. Often groups will find themselves consumed with the thought of simply making money instead of realizing that raising money is simply the means to another end.

Goals can vary dramatically from institution to institution. Some institutions will view fund-raisers as simply another way to provide valuable services to their students and that will be their primary goal in working with fund-raising companies. Other institutions will work to raise enough money to help defray conference travel costs as well as fund various programs. Quite often, the RHA's vision will be a combination of these goals, and the RHA must determine the importance of each.

Once an RHA has formulated its goals and vision, members must determine the best way to raise the necessary money or to provide the needed services. It is extremely helpful for an RHA to think like a business. In deciding how to proceed, RHAs must look at their own strengths and weaknesses. RHAs need to utilize the strengths they possess as a group and minimize the weaknesses inherent in any student group. Some assets that most RHAs possess are access to the incoming first-year students, access to the residence hall areas, and a large word-of-mouth advertising network. By properly using these assets, RHAs can develop fund-raisers that will help them accomplish their goals. Fund-raisers that use an organization's strengths have a much better chance for success.

Equally important is to make sure that students realize that an RHA has weaknesses. Some of these weaknesses will be a result of simply being a student group, while others may relate to the particular student group in charge at that time. It is vitally important that students understand their weaknesses and look for fund-raisers that will not accentuate them. Most student groups have limited time during certain parts of the year. In addition, student groups often do not have much capital to invest in big fund-raising projects. It is essential that students realize the limitations they have when it comes to access to capital — the money needed to make a fund-raiser work. Any fund-raiser that requires the RHA to invest some of its own money in order to make more money is dangerous. Even though the fund-raiser might seem to be a guaranteed money maker, it is extremely risky using the organization's money up front. In business anything can happen and the organization should never take the chance of losing money on a fund-raiser. An RHA's money is earmarked for programming, conferences, and other student activities — not for making more money. Using a corporate partner is one of the best ways to minimize weaknesses the organization may have. Identifying these weaknesses and planning to combat them will go a long way toward making sure that fund-raisers are successful.

With the organization's goals in mind and a working knowledge of its strengths and weaknesses, it is time to focus on the fund-raising marketplace — the students — to assess what they need and want. Discovering the right products and services to offer students can be a very delicate process. Although it is true that one must take care not to turn the RHA or campus into a retail store, it is also true that one goal is to provide services that will assist students and their parents. Saving students money or making their move to campus easier are both extremely worthwhile services. Products offered should generally fall into at least one of the following categories: products that are difficult to transport to the institution, products that are difficult to find, or products that can be offered at a substantial discount from what a student would normally have to pay.

There are two great things about fund-raising on a campus. First, most students have homogenous needs. Although the student body might be incredibly diverse, there are things that most students need to purchase. The adviser is on campus and knows better than anyone else what the students need. Another advantage of the student market is that every year there are new potential customers. The influx of first-year students every fall guarantees a new audience for fund-raisers. Once again the challenge is to make sure that fund-raisers offer products and services to assist the student body. Many "win-win" fund-raisers are available that will earn a substantial amount of money for the organization while also providing great services to students.

Many student groups that go through this exercise find that the biggest obstacles they face in operating successful fund-raising programs are access to sufficient money, time, and expertise to operate the fund-raiser year to year. Partnering with an outside company can help overcome these challenges.

There are many reasons to work with outside companies on fund-raising programs. It is important to remember that many of these companies were developed with the explicit purpose of assisting student groups to raise money. The companies understand the special situations in which RHAs often find themselves. These companies work with institutions across the country so they know what works and what does not work. They can use experience gained over the years and improve the program every year because they do not have the same transition that is inevitable with student groups. Potentially the biggest advantage of using an outside company is that the financial risk and logistical headaches can be transferred from the student group to the outside company. A student group never wants to take the chance of losing money while operating a fund-raiser. Losing money is a very real possibility, so involving an outside company and asking them to take the risk will decrease this problem.

Working with an outside company also has some very real potential problems. If the company does not make a good impression, this could reflect unfavorably on the student group. The quality of the product; the level of service provided before, during, and after the sale; and the professionalism displayed throughout the program all will be evaluated and judged by the students. It is important to realize that in the minds of students and their parents, the company selected is effectively a part of the organization. If the company fails to provide the high level of customer care and service that is expected of the group, it will have a negative impact on the RHA. Another issue to consider is the uniqueness of an academic year. Many of the organization's fund-raisers can be conducted only once a year. If the outside company does not do a good job running the program, that program is effectively lost and the group will not be able to recoup the lost revenue. The outside company must understand the importance to the RHA of every fund-raiser. Gaining an understanding may be accomplished by frequently visiting with students and asking them questions, by maintaining a lengthy relationship with the organization; or by recognizing the amount of money raised may be a large percentage of the organization's total budget.

Clearly, there are many reasons to work with an outside company. The challenge is to find the right companies to partner with so that the organization can take advantage of all the benefits and reduce concerns about potential pitfalls. The best sources for finding good companies to partner with are other institutions. The adviser can obtain not only the names of potential partners, but also good references. Internet discussion groups and list services are often good ways of obtaining feedback from colleagues in a very short time period. Another excellent way to find the names of good companies is to go through national associations. The National Association of College and University Residence Halls, Inc. (NACURH), the Association of College and University Housing Officers-International (ACUHO-I), and most of the other national and regional housing and student development associations have worked with certain corporations for many years. Talking to companies currently contracted with the RHA can also prove to be a good source of information. The student market is a relatively small one, and there is an excellent chance that a vendor that has been trusted for one fund-raising project can refer another vendor for another project. The advantage of this is that the vendor knows the RHA and its goals and can recommend another vendor with a similar focus. The organization can also contact local vendors. Giving them a chance to work with the RHA on a fund-raising event can be an excellent way for them to get exposure on campus. Be careful, however, if they have not previously overseen a fund-raising event. The work involved in providing a properly run program can often be much greater than originally anticipated.

After identifying the right fund-raising companies, or having been contacted by them, the RHA must determine which company best meets its needs. If members have gone through the process of defining goals and objectives as a group, this process is much easier. It is also important to remember that sometimes the right choice is to select no one at all and to wait until members feel more comfortable with potential vendors who are interested in the RHA's business. The organization does not want to work with anyone who might take advantage of the students or who might not be in business six months down the road.

Often the decision-making process for choosing which company to work with comes down to two factors: price of product or service and commission percentage. Although they can be very important, decision making based solely on these two factors is extremely shortsighted. When looking at the price students are going to pay for the product or service, be sure to thoroughly evaluate the offer. The company offering the lowest price to students is not always offering the best value. Thoroughly reviewing the entire fund-raiser in terms of quality of product, return policy, and customer service is essential to judge which company is offering the students the best value. The other factor that usually influences the decision-making process is the commission percentage. When an RHA partners with an outside company, the amount of money paid in commission to the RHA is usually a percentage of the total sales generated. Commission percentage can be a red herring. Ultimately, the money earned through a fund-raiser is a combination of commission percentage and gross sales. A higher commission percentage offered by one company does not guarantee a higher commission. Understanding the difference and making sure that the RHA does well can make a big difference in the decision-making process.

A proper evaluation of potential fund-raising partners also takes into account the company's experience, goals, vision, staff, service, and flexibility. Working with a company that has experience with the institution, or institutions of similar size, can make a difference in the way the fund-raising program is administered. Operating a successful fund-raiser is similar to operating a successful RHA. Just as most programming sessions get better after a couple of attempts, so too does fund-raising. Every institution is unique, but a company with experience at the institution, or an institution with similar demographics, will have the advantage of knowing what to expect and how to react. Always make sure to get a reference list and client list (this is a list of all of the company's clients) from any potential vendor. Contact a minimum of two to three references as well as two to three clients not listed as references. The RHA must assume that the references will be positive, but contacting an institution that they work with but do not list as a reference is a good way to get a more objective idea of the company's level of performance.

In addition to experience, the RHA should make sure that its partners have a vision of the future. Review how the fund-raising program has evolved over the past three to four years and investigate where they see it going in the future. Also, try to examine the goals and mission statements of all the companies being investigated. Make sure their mission statements are congruent with that of the RHA.

The people that make up the company are also a valuable source of information. Talk to them at length and find out who will be working with the RHA on a day-to-day basis. (Sometimes this is not the same person as the salesperson.) Ask to speak to someone in customer service and find out what policies the company employs. If the fund-raiser is a product that can be ordered any time of the year, try to order the product and return it. Evaluate the service you receive and whether it measures up to what is promised. It is very easy to promise outstanding customer service, but quite another thing to actually deliver it.

Two other areas to evaluate in selecting an outside company are flexibility and stability. Each institution has its own unique characteristics so no two fund-raisers will ever be the same. It is important that outside companies realize that they must work with the institution in certain situations in order to make the fund-raiser work. Discover examples of how each company has tailored programs for institutions with special circumstances. The stability of the company is also important. In some instances, students will send money to the company before they receive their products. If the company were to fold or declare bankruptcy, the RHA would be in an extremely difficult position. To make sure that a company has a sound financial base, the RHA can request a Dunn and Bradstreet rating, which gives a cursory financial assessment of the company. If the company cannot provide that, make sure that it is a registered corporation in good standing with the local Better Business Bureau. Contact the local Chamber of Commerce for information on grievances filed against companies.

Sometimes the RHA will not have the sole authority to choose a preferred vendor without going through a bid process. Every state and every institution has specific rules and regulations pertaining to when and if something needs to go to bid. Some pointers that might be helpful when required to use the bid process:

Get input into the process. Usually the institutional purchasing office welcomes involvement from a student group in this process. Try to make the bid as specific as possible so that the RHA is ensured of getting the type of company desired. If experience is very important to the RHA, make experience one of the prerequisites in the bid. The same is true for any of the other traits that the RHA believes the company must possess. The more detailed the initial bid, the better chance that the company selected will be the one that is desired. If the RHA wants to differentiate companies, they should know what to compare from vendor to vendor. When comparing companies, the questions asked by the RHA will provide direction in choosing the company that best suits its needs. Make checklists of services that each company provides. These are helpful in determining a successful fit.

Long term agreements. These can be very beneficial to the RHA and the companies that are contracted for fund-raisers. Successful fund-raisers are enhanced when tests are used to find the best program for students and when vendors recognize the personality of the school. Long-term agreements grant vendors the relationships and the time to refine programs. Make sure, however, that any long-term agreement has an escape clause if the company is not performing the promised services. The RHA does not want to be tied to a company that is not meeting the group's expectations.

Exclusivity. Vendors may add a clause to an agreement to ensure prosperity on both ends. An exclusive agreement can usually produce a better deal for the RHA through negotiations. In turn, the vendor can provide quality services with possible incentives, such as keeping prices low.

Request for proposal. Often the type of company the RHA is seeking is a unique company with no real competition. In such situations, the RHA can sometimes avoid the bid process and instead use a request for a proposal. Take the time to talk to the people within the institution's purchasing office to learn all of the options.

To truly maximize the relationship between outside companies and RHAs, both groups need to look to each other as partners. Both groups must understand each other's goals and objectives and work closely together to continue to improve the relationship. The company can add a level of stability that the student group will not have because of the inherent transience of student groups. Many companies are frustrated with the student market because the constant transition results in companies having to resell themselves every year to a new group of student leaders. The program can never really move forward because the company is so busy reselling itself instead of improving the fund-raiser. This is an issue that will always surface because of the nature of student groups, but student groups can do several things to ensure the best possible relationship with their corporate partners:

Communication is the foundation for a good relationship. Good communication can guarantee that corporate partners are aware of what they are doing well and where they need improvement. The same type of communication and feedback provided to student leaders should be given to corporate partners. Fund-raisers will not be able to grow and improve without clear, objective, two-way communication. One common error among student groups is the fear of alerting a corporate partner that they have been contacted by a competitor. Competition is natural in the business world, and it is only fair to alert the contracted partner that the RHA is considering another vendor.

Meeting deadlines is essential to companies. Companies realize that students and student groups have tremendous demands on their time. In turn, student groups need to realize that working together is a true partnership and that if an agreement is signed, the student group needs to make sure to hold up its end of the schedule.

Proper transitions can make fund-raisers much more effective over time. If the outside company is forced to "reinvent the wheel" every year, the fund-raiser probably will remain stagnant. If a student group transitions the fund-raiser properly, the program can grow and improve every year. From detailed documentation, new RHA members can learn about previous fund-raisers and later add new information for future members. A fund-raiser can be successfully and painlessly passed on from year to year by taking thorough notes on phone calls, contacts, and important dates.

Fund-raising in partnership with an outside company can be a rewarding and profitable experience for an RHA. The key to success is finding the right fund-raisers and finding the right companies with whom to partner. Once this is accomplished, the stability and innovation that outside companies can provide should result in profitable and stable fund-raisers for the RHA for many years to come.

Projects

1. Discuss the process that is necessary in deciding between two vendors of the same type of fund-raising program.
2. Outline a good plan to transition a fund-raiser from year to year. Specify one of the programs the RHA currently offers.

History and Services of the National Association of College and University Residence Halls, Inc. (NACURH)

Ken Stoner, Former NACURH Adviser
University of Kansas

Krista Berry, Former Chair, NACURH Board of Directors
University of Nebraska, Kearney

Laura (Christianson) Boever, Former Chair,
NACURH Board of Directors
EBI Medical Systems, Tempe, AZ

Bob Tattershall, NACURH Adviser
Washington State University

History and Services of NACURH

This chapter will review the organizational purpose, structure, and strengths of NACURH; outline the development of the Association of Alumni and Friends of NACURH (AAFN); discuss the relationship between ACUHO-I and NACURH; and trace the history of NACURH from 1954 through 1998. An article by Wyatt and Stoner (1984; see Chapter 1 of this volume) is considered a companion piece to this chapter, providing insights into the historical significance and tremendous growth of NACURH as a student organization.

Organizational Purpose

As stated in NACURH's governing documents, the purpose of the organization is "to design and facilitate programs and informational services to promote the educational goals of residence hall students through discussion groups, seminars, and speakers at the annual conferences and other means of information exchange throughout the year" (NACURH, 1997, p. 2).

NACURH fulfills these goals in two ways. First, the organization stimulates the generation of new programs and fresh approaches for all college and university campuses by providing an environment conducive to exchanging ideas. This environment takes the form of annual national and regional conferences that are attended by member school delegations. These conferences provide opportunities for enhancing leadership skills, developing new program ideas, and motivating delegates.

Second, NACURH maintains a viable communication network among all member institutions. This is best accomplished through the effective utilization of the National Information Center (NIC) and services such as the Resource File Index (RFI), the *NACURH Network* (newsletter), the videotape library, and the "Official NACURH HomePage: http://www.nacurh.okstate.edu/" which includes numerous links to related web sites. By taking an active role in NACURH, and utilizing the resources of the NIC and other services, each residence hall student in a leadership position can help his or her respective institution and NACURH accomplish the basic goal of strengthening the residential environment.

Organizational Structure

NACURH is organizationally structured in two ways: geographically and corporately (Figure 1). Geographically, the continental United States is divided into eight regions. Canadian institutions affiliate with the region due south of the institutional location. Corporately, each of the regions elect, through a "popular vote," a director and one or two associate directors who represent their respective regions on the National Board of Directors (NBD).

The NBD is the governing body of NACURH, and is comprised of the eight Regional Directors and several ex-officio members including the NACURH Chairperson, the National Associate for Finance, the National Associate for Administration, the Directors of the NIC and the National Residence Hall Honorary (NRHH), the National Adviser, the Conference Resource Consultant (CRC), and the National Conference Chairperson (NCC). Although these individuals are considered part of the NBD, only the Regional Directors have voting privileges. This ensures that all key decisions are made by members through representative elections, and not arbitrarily by the governing body.

The NBD meets twice a year, once mid-year and once in May at the site of the annual conference. Although these meetings focus on numerous issues, the main objective is to discuss and act on ways that NACURH can further its purposes and become the best and most effective organization possible through the skills, talents, and leadership of the individuals serving on the NBD.

Organizational Strengths

An appropriate analogy for the history of NACURH would be to conceptualize the organization as a tapestry. Several common threads are identifiable and found throughout this tapestry. Those threads have been woven together over time and constitute the fundamental basis for the organization now known as NACURH. The common threads include (a) the pre-eminence of the annual conference in the life of the organization, (b) a predisposition toward inclusion, (c) the impact of individual leadership and the institutions these individuals represent, (d) accommodation to societal changes, (e) the struggle for continuity and stability in shaping organizational evolution, and (f) recognition and appreciation. A brief analysis of those six threads provides insights into the continuing success and endurance of NACURH over the years, plus an instructive foundation for comparative analysis with other student organizations.

Pre-eminence of the Annual Conference

Historically, the annual conferences have provided the most threads for the organizational fabric. The conference generates sustenance and strength for the following year; its energy radiates back to campuses through the individual representatives in attendance. New officers are selected annually and the next conference site is announced. An exceptionally strong annual conference with an outstanding program and good attendance virtually guarantees that a successful year will follow. Beginning in 1976, NACURH made an attempt to increase organizational continuity by selecting the Chairperson of the NBD at the mid-year meeting in January rather than at the annual conference. It was envisioned that overlapping officers between the conferences would provide additional organizational stability. However, academic years were also overlapped and the turnover of officers was unprecedented. Further, a "changing of the guard" between conferences failed to provide either the "jump-start" or the closure critical to the success of student organizations, and the idea was abandoned in May 1979. A chronological listing of the annual conference sites follows, with a thumbnail sketch of organizational changes, conference attendance, and other noteworthy events.

Predisposition toward Inclusion

NACURH was founded at Iowa State University in 1954. Prior to that, an informal association of residence hall students among the Big Ten schools had begun to meet to exchange communications and ideas. Students from Iowa State were interested in participating in those meetings, and inquired into the possibility of expanding the network base being established within the Big Ten schools. This tentative overture was rejected, and the students from Iowa State University decided to contact some of their sister schools in Iowa as well as their Big Seven (later Big Eight, and now Big Twelve) Conference friends to see if a meeting among residence hall student leaders from a group of schools might be mutually beneficial. The response was encouraging, and four schools met on the campus of Iowa State University in 1954. The name of the association was initially established as the Mid-West Dormitory Conference.

From the inception of the organization, the NACURH leadership has always found ways to include new institutions and has actively resisted notions of exclusivity. Thus, all institutions with a resident population have been invited to join. Over the years, the organization expanded to include large and small institutions, as well as public and private, religious and nonsectarian, military, predominantly Black, single-sex, and international institutions. The inclusive thrust of the organization applied not only to institutions but also to individuals as well. Indeed, before "equal opportunity" and "affirmative action" became terms commonly used on campuses across the country, this fledgling organization in 1957 elected Haile Clay, an African American, as President. To this day, the organizational constitution emphasizes openness to all individuals and institutions and NACURH is unalterably linked with a commitment to diversity which constitutes another series of threads woven throughout the organizational fabric.

Individual and Institutional Leadership

NACURH's tapestry of history also has been inextricably woven by unique threads of individual leadership coupled with the institutional support received from those leaders' respective campuses. To date, Bob LeVand from Ferris State University is the only individual to serve back-to-back terms as President of the Association. The individual efforts of Zack Cooper from Oklahoma State University not only brought corporate status to NACURH but also initiated organizational involvement with vendors and corporate partners interested in the collegiate market. Don Steeples from Kansas State University possessed the vision that brought the first Canadian schools into the Association, formalized contacts with Congressional representatives, and stimulated tremendous growth in membership. Cathie Crouch from the University of Mississippi was inducted as Chairperson of the NBD at the Silver Anniversary Conference hosted by Kansas State University in 1979; her enthusiasm and organizational skills provided a foundation for growth and success that continues today, almost two decades later. Also during her tenure, a permanent relationship was established with the Association of College and University Housing Officers-International (ACUHO-I).

Several institutions also have consistently provided leadership. Iowa State University hosted the first conference, encouraged the first President, provided the first Adviser, and supported the first NIC. Similarly, Oklahoma State University has been consistently strong over the years, hosting the annual conference three times, providing the Association with four presidents or NBD Chairs, hosting the NIC for six years, and winning the School of the Year (SOY) Award three times. The University of Northern Colorado must also be mentioned, claiming three NBD Chairs, hosting the NIC for four years (as well as one annual conference), providing a CRC, and winning SOY honors twice. In addition, enthusiastic leadership from smaller schools (such as St. Mary's College of Maryland, Whittier College, and Winthrop College) and medium-sized schools (such as Eastern Illinois University, Mankato State University, Sonoma State University, and the University of Akron) will not be forgotten.

Accommodation of Societal Changes

As with institutions of higher education, the history of NACURH has reflected the social trends and issues of the time. In the 1950s, more men than women attended institutions of higher education. Indeed, for the first decade of NACURH's existence, all 10 presidents were men. In the last 10 years (1987 through 1997) five NBD chairpersons were women. As the organization has matured, more upper-class and graduate students have accepted leadership positions than in the organization's formative years. This organizational maturation reflects similar development of student organizations on campuses.

The Civil Rights movement, the age of majority and voting rights, plus the war in Vietnam all had a tremendous impact on the attitudes and approaches of student leaders of the 1960s. The emphasis on inclusion incorporated at the inception of the organization positioned NACURH well for surviving the social difficulties of that decade. One positive outcome was NACURH's endorsement of the Joint Statement on Rights and Freedoms of Students in 1970 (ACUHO-I, 1970). The 1970s were uncertain and disjointed; this was reflected in NACURH by the tremendous turnover of officers. Following the intensity of the 1960s, this search for meaning and purpose and re-establishing the organization in the 1970s was predictable. The 1980s were marked by a period of stability and tremendous organizational growth. The organization's adaptability and resilience over the years provides another complement of threads to the organizational tapestry.

Struggle for Continuity and Stability

In the early years, during its struggle for organizational survival, NACURH tenaciously clung to life, as metaphorically represented by worn threads in the organizational tapestry. However, those worn areas also symbolize organizational victories and learning opportunities which provided meaning and strengthened the significance of the organization. Today, after 45 consecutive years, NACURH is the longest continuously functioning student-led organization in North America.

Continuity was enhanced when the organization achieved corporate status. With this change, the Chairperson of the NBD began to be selected (promoted) from the ranks of existing Regional Directors and other national officers, guaranteeing at least one year of organizational experience prior to assuming leadership of NACURH. Several individuals changed institutions to begin graduate school upon completing their terms as Regional Directors and accepting the role of Chair of the NBD. Scott Miller from San Diego State University and Cathie Crouch from the University of Mississippi both transferred to the University of Georgia, Gene Zdziarski from Oklahoma State University transferred to the University of Tennessee, and Charlotte Rasche from Stephen F. Austin State University and Barbara Olson from the University of Houston both transferred to Oklahoma State University. Prerequisite leadership within the organization and the involvement of career-directed and professionally oriented graduate students further enhanced organizational stability.

History and Services of NACURH

The stability and depth of NACURH was enhanced tremendously over the years by the development of new programs, enabled by the ability and willingness of NACURH to reorganize and empower. Reorganization is seen as a legitimate means to foster continuity and stability. Often, new positions have developed through executive initiative as new programs grew and became more complex. Initially, the President of NACURH was an organizational convener serving as the conference host and chair of the business meetings held at the conference. In 1956, after only two years of organizational existence, the Presidential and conference host roles were separated. For several years there was an adviser to the President who was appointed by the institution where the President was located. In 1960, the first organizational Adviser was appointed, whose tenure was envisioned to span several years. The idea for NRHH was enthusiastically received by the NBD and, in 1964, led to the creation of separate office to handle the annual obligations of the NRHH. Similarly, in 1969, when member expectations of information sharing could no longer be handled solely by the executive office, the NIC was created. To gain continuity in advising the annual conference, the CRC position was created in 1974. The desire for continuing involvement in the association by past officers and other interested "friends and alumni" resulted in the establishment of the AAFN in 1982.

Occasionally, attempts to strengthen NACURH through reorganization did not evolve as envisioned. For example, the continuing growth in publication responsibilities of the NIC led to the creation of the National Publications Office (NPO) in 1992. Designed to separate printing tasks and obligations from the NIC, this particular reorganization proved unworkable and, in 1993, the NPO ceased to exist and those duties were reassumed by personnel in the NIC. Even failed initiatives have promoted learning and strengthened NACURH. However, for the most part, spreading organizational duties and significant leadership functions among many capable leaders has augmented continuity and stability while also providing a series of checks and balances among the officers; the occasional weak link in any one position of leadership is never catastrophic as the other organizational leaders pull together in compensation for deficiencies.

Another important contributor to organizational continuity and stability relates to the truism that "good followers and good leaders are flip sides of the same coin." Individuals who accept responsibility for mundane organizational duties perform valuable services, which not only adds continuity and stability but also strengthens the organization. These efforts often evolve into solid programmatic enhancements that provide additional leadership opportunities for others. Those who complete assigned tasks thoroughly and on time are good followers — and good followers often become good leaders. The NACURH leadership seems to understand that the organization moves forward by incorporating individuals who can be good followers and good leaders. Thus the NRHH began when an individual stepped forward with a willingness to enlist NACURH members schools in a recognition effort and to send certificates to new inductees. The NIC began with the willingness of an individual to catalogue a variety of conference materials collected by past officers and to duplicate those materials for member institutions. The NRHH and NIC began as clerical functions which evolved into positions of organizational leadership and offices with significant responsibilities. Tremendous talent and leadership capabilities exist on every campus in the country. It is a testimony to those who stepped forward "to follow, or to lead" as well as to the personnel at institutions that encouraged, nurtured, and supported these good followers and good leaders in strengthening NACURH.

Initially, NACURH did not have a resource base sufficient to sustain even the meager financial needs of the organization. With relatively minor financial needs, the organization survived from year to year on the good will of the institutions from which the officers were elected. The financial setback suffered at the 1973 conference re-emphasized the precarious financial position of NACURH and resulted in the creation of the first contingency fund and the CRC position. Although the contingency fund was created, it was impossible to guarantee or protect the funds from use over the next few years. As the CRC position developed, hosting conferences became a more routine and manageable event and the numbers attending the conferences continued to grow throughout the 1980s. This resulted in some financial surpluses from the conferences which made the goal of establishing a permanent reserve a reality. The creation of the AAFN in 1982 included a trust to protect contingency funds as well as the principal amount collected from individual donors. The stability of the organization has never been more promising. NACURH has become financially independent from the host institutions of both the national officers and conference sites and subsequently the organization has managed to obtain an admirable degree of stability and financial security.

The appointment of J. Albin Yokie as the organization's first Adviser in 1960 was an additional plus in the quest for organizational continuity and stability. Even though Mr. Yokie changed institutions twice during his 11-year tenure, the continuity and perspective he provided was indispensable. Subsequent Advisers have also served extended terms and added strength to the organization. The CRC was originally envisioned as a student-held position to provide support to those hosting NACURH national or regional conferences. This position evolved into a second advisory position to NACURH. As in the case with the Adviser, the CRC is employed full time within the profession at a member institution of NACURH. The tenure of the CRC also has evolved to span several years, again increasing the continuity and strengthening the organization.

Recognition and Appreciation

NACURH has truly institutionalized the belief that recognition and appreciation are basic to communication and progress. The organization thrives on the recognition of participating individuals and institutions. NACURH facilitates recognition of individuals at a variety of levels. At the institutional level, NRHH and AAFN provide two excellent mechanisms for recognizing individuals on campus. Virtually all regions have an NCC of the Month and Year, a Program of the Month and Year, a School of the Month and Year, an Adviser of the Month and Year, plus a variety of other recognitions, including Silver Pins and regionally specific recognitions such as MACURH's Dennis Lynch Scholarship and the Mabel Strong Award. Similarly, at the national level, NACURH also offers the same "of the Month" and "of the Year" awards. At the annual conference, the closing banquet and the annual corporate business meeting are laced with recognitions. Gold Pins are awarded at the national level. Numerous institutional awards are announced, including Best School Display, Most Spirited Delegation,

School of the Year, Program of the Year, and a variety of other annual service awards. Continuous contributions are recognized through a variety of longevity awards such as the Life Member Award established in 1972, which later evolved into an award called the Four-Year Pin.

Appreciation of corporate sponsors also has been expressed over the years by naming specific awards for these companies, such as the Swank Service Award which existed during that corporate relationship, and now the regional and national Campus Fund Raisers Outstanding Service Awards in acknowledgment of this current corporate sponsor. Occasionally awards are named for specific individuals in recognition of their special relationships with the organization. The Program of the Year Award was renamed in 1992 in recognition of the late Daniel A. Siler from the University of Wisconsin-Whitewater who regularly presented exceptional programs for delegates attending the annual conference. Likewise, the Daniel A. Hallenbeck Outstanding Service Award and the Kenneth L. Stoner Distinguished Service Award, named in honor of past Advisers of NACURH, both recognize continuous service over the years.

The organizational tapestry is still being woven; the fundamental success of NACURH can be credited to the unique philosophy and operational approaches which constitute the six threads found throughout the organizational fabric. Indeed, most successful organizations acknowledge the importance of attending regular meetings and supporting annual renewal, insisting on inclusion, facilitating mutually beneficial individual and institutional support mechanisms, sharing leadership and distributing executive power, recognizing individuals and their achievements as both leaders and followers, developing leadership, accommodating societal changes, and adapting to difficult times and circumstances (Stoner, Spain, Rasche, & Horton, 1993). Any organization whose fabric is woven from these threads will provide meaningful participation, learning opportunities, and noteworthy accomplishments for the membership.

Association of Alumni and Friends of NACURH (AAFN)

Another organizational initiative, considered to be a modest proposal at the time, evolved into the Association of Alumni and Friends of NACURH (AAFN). The desire for continuing involvement in the association by past officers and other interested "friends and alumni" resulted in the establishment of AAFN in January 1982. At the mid-year meeting, the NBD approved a resolution authorizing the creation of a NACURH alumni association. For a minimum contribution of $100 to a NACURH reserve fund, any individual could join the association. A commitment was made to not spend contributions (principal monies); however, investment earnings (interest monies) generated from this reserve fund were made available to fund current programs and activities, as necessary or as decided by the NBD. In 1982, it was anticipated that interest monies ultimately would be used for leadership development and recognition scholarships once the initial membership goal of 120 was realized.

The primary benefit to any individual choosing to join was conceptualized to be personal and public recognition of support by the NACURH leadership. It was agreed that the individual's name, institution of choice, and year of personal affiliation with NACURH would be published as part of the conference program, along with appropriate recognition given as part of the closing awards banquet at the annual conference each year. In addition, a membership brochure was to be updated annually, distributed at national and regional conferences, and sent to all individuals on the AAFN mailing list. It was anticipated that this initiative would generate both symbolic and actual support from individuals who had been active in NACURH as well as from other professionals who were once active as advisers but who had been promoted to other positions within the educational environment or for other reasons no longer participated in NACURH or attended annual conferences. In addition, members of the AAFN were to be sent invitations to attend and be recognized at each annual conference.

The initial goal of 120 members was established in anticipation that a modest return from investment of these funds would yield additional organizational income in excess of $100 per month. After approving the idea in January of 1982, five members were recognized at the annual conference in May 1982 at the University of Wisconsin-Whitewater. At the 1983 annual conference at Penn State, 27 individuals were recognized. The 1984 conference at the University of Colorado acknowledged 51 members; 77 individuals were recognized at the 1985 meeting at the University of Florida; 110 were honored at the University of San Francisco; and 133 members were recognized at the 1987 conference at Central Michigan University.

Although the initial membership goal was realized at CMU in 1987, AAFN continued to grow, with 171 members recognized at the University of Wisconsin-LaCrosse as part of the 1988 annual conference. The ranks grew to 210 by the 1989 conference at the University of Northern Colorado, and to 234 in 1990 at Southwest Missouri State University. In 1991, 254 members were recognized at Arizona State University, 287 in 1992 at the University of North Dakota, 320 in 1993 at the University of South Carolina, 368 at Northern Arizona University in 1994, 405 at Virginia Polytechnic University in 1995, 450 at the University of Oklahoma in 1996, and 492 alumni and friends were recognized at the 1997 conference at Ball State University. With good reason, it is anticipated that the list of AAFN inductees will continue to grow.

As promised, AAFN has faithfully protected the principal and contributions have never been spent. Over the years, interest monies grew until all AAFN expenses could be paid from the proceeds; these expenses included purchase and distribution of recognition paperweights, printing of the annual brochure, postage for individual and mass mailings to AAFN members, and shipping of brochures to the regional and national offices. In addition to protecting alumni contributions, AAFN accepted responsibility for investing organizational reserves. Surplus funds from regional or national conferences with attendance above projections required to meet the base conference budget were transferred to AAFN. Thus, over time, AAFN evolved beyond the original vision of a self-sufficient and self-sustaining program into a broader role that included investment of funds to generate interest monies as an income supplement to the annual budgets of the regions and various NACURH offices.

AAFN is one of the more complex organizational arrangements maintained by NACURH. In 1971, NACURH officially received nonprofit corporation status from the State of Oklahoma; however, as an Oklahoma corporation, NACURH was still taxable under Internal Revenue Service Code Section 11(a). Obtaining tax-exempt status under Section 501(c)(3) of the Code proved elusive. With the creation of AAFN in 1982, NACURH again recognized that tax-exempt status was essential if AAFN were to survive in any permanent organizational form. Without tax-exempt status, alumni could not claim contributions as tax deductions. Further, by NACURH internal policy, the portfolio of investment opportunities was limited to nontaxable options which have lower yield rates and earning power. Without either an internal policy or tax-exempt status, NACURH would have been liable for taxes according to applicable state and federal laws. The quest for tax-exempt status took 15 years; in 1997, approximately $180,000 from AAFN was transferred to accounts established to accommodate the newly obtained tax-exempt status of NACURH. Achievement of tax-exempt status with the Internal Revenue Service after 15 years and three separate filing initiatives is a testament to the ability and tenacity of individuals who continue to build on the efforts of previous officers and their leadership initiatives.

During the first thirty years of existence, NACURH did not have a resource base sufficient to sustain even the meager financial needs of the organization. The officers and the national offices were frequently subsidized by the host institutions and regional and national conferences covered expenses at best. As the membership grew, economies of scale were realized and conferences became large enough to generate additional surplus funds. NACURH has become financially independent from the host institutions of both the national officers and the conference sites; subsequently the organization has managed to achieve an admirable degree of stability and financial security. AAFN assisted NACURH in fund management until tax-exempt status was obtained.

NACURH and ACUHO-I

NACURH and ACUHO-I have enjoyed a long, positive, and mutually productive organizational relationship. Both organizations serve identical constituencies (residents living in facilities operated by institutions of higher education) although the institutional membership list does vary somewhat between the two. Housing officers generally hold either institutional or individual membership with ACUHO-I as their professional association of choice. Campuses with active student leadership in RHAs are almost always affiliated with NACURH. The two associations are independent entities; however, the common constituency has fostered numerous collaborative efforts over the years as illustrated by the examples provided in the following paragraphs.

Beginning in the mid-1960s, both organizations began the practice of sending representatives to the national conference of the other association. As opportunity allowed, NACURH adjusted regional boundaries to be in closer alignment with ACUHO-I regional boundaries in order to facilitate a similar exchange of officers at regional conferences. Following the lead of ACUHO-I, NACURH archived historical records with Bowling Green State University. Between 1968 and 1970, both organizations endorsed the Joint Statement on Rights and Freedoms of Students (ACUHO-I, 1970). In 1979, the "NACURH/ACUHO-I Program of the Year" was created to provide the opportunity for an outstanding program developed by students at a NACURH member institution to be shared at the annual ACUHO-I Conference attended by professional housing officers.

In 1985, formalization of the organizational liaison was approved by ACUHO-I at their annual business meeting. Also, in 1985, both associations endorsed the *Statement of Alcohol Policy for Institutions of Higher Education* (Inter-Association Task Force on Alcohol Issues, 1985). At their mid-year meeting in 1988, the NBD endorsed

Wirag's (1988) chapter on AIDS on the college campus as a reasonable set of guidelines for student housing facilities to consider in developing policies related to AIDS. The Executive Board of ACUHO-I passed a similar endorsement at their 1990 Spring meeting.

NACURH developed the policy for evaluating programs during the conference and re-offering, in a final program slot held open for that purpose, those "Top Ten" conference programs rated as "the best." NACURH established track programming to assist students and advisers in selecting conference programs geared to their specific needs. The practice of closing the final conference banquet with a grand finale slide show or video of conference activities was instituted by NACURH. All of these initiatives were borrowed from NACURH by ACUHO-I.

In addition, a cursory review of host institutions and officers from NACURH, ACUHO-I, and their respective regions, will quickly reveal that many of the same institutions have served as host sites for both organizations as well as for numerous individuals who have been active in both associations. Indeed, individual involvement in NACURH or one of its eight regional associations has proven to be one of the best "feeder experiences" leading into the profession as a housing officer.

Organizational Chronology with Annual Conference Host Institution

The remainder of this chapter is devoted to highlighting the activities and accomplishments of NACURH in chronological order.

1954 — Iowa State University. The first meeting was scheduled in 1954 when the leadership of the Iowa State student residence hall government felt that such an organization was needed to encourage the exchange of ideas and information. Four schools (Iowa State University, University of Colorado, University of Missouri, and University of Northern Iowa) were in attendance at this first conference and participated in founding the Midwest Dormitory Conference. During the first two formative years, presidential duties included serving as the annual conference host. Dick Wiggins from Iowa State University was the first President of the Association; a complete listing of the organizational presidents, later to evolve into the Chairperson of the NBD, follows at the end of the chapter.

1955 — University of Missouri. The name of the organization was changed to the Association of College and University Residence Halls (ACURH). Steps were taken at this conference to broaden the scope of the organization.

1956 — University of Colorado. ACURH had six institutional members by this conference. There were 100 delegates representing 17 institutions (the six member institutions plus an additional 11 nonmember institutions) in attendance. At this conference, presidential duties were separated from those of host committee responsibilities.

1957 — University of Nebraska. ACURH had grown to 11 institutional members.

1958 — Iowa State University. One hundred twenty-four delegates from 10 institutions were in attendance.

1959 — University of Missouri. One hundred ninety-two delegates from 17 institutions were in attendance. Twelve institutions were members of ACURH. The organization continued to broaden its scope by establishing its first newsletter and publishing its first promotional brochure.

1960 — Southern Illinois University. ACURH had 13 member schools, and 12 institutions in attendance at the conference. The Adviser position was created, and J. Albin Yokie began his term as the organization's first Adviser. A listing of the organizational advisers is appended to this chapter.

1961 — Oklahoma State University. During this conference, the Inter-Mountain Residence Hall Association (IMRHA) affiliated with ACURH, and the organizational name was changed to the National Association of College and University Residence Halls (NACURH). A constitution was ratified and two regional organizations were created within NACURH: the Intermountain Association of College and University Residence Halls (IACURH) and the Midwest Association of College and University Residence Halls (MACURH).

1962 — Montana State University. At this conference, 15 institutions were in attendance.

1963 — University of Arizona. At the Tenth Annual Conference, over 50,000 students living in residence halls were represented by the delegates from the 26 institutions attending. NACURH membership had also grown to 26 institutions.

1964 — University of Denver. NACURH's membership remained stable at 26 institutions; 247 delegates from 29 institutions attended the conference. NACURH was listed as an educational organization with the Department of Health, Education, and Welfare, and the National Residence Hall Honorary (NRHH) was founded. A listing of the NRHH Directors and their host institutions is included at the end of this chapter. In addition, three new regional organizations were created "on paper" to plan for expansion: the Pacific Association of College and University Residence Halls (PACURH), the North Atlantic Association of College and University Residence Halls (NAACURH), and the South Atlantic Association of College and University Residence Halls (SAACURH).

1965 — Washington State University. Two hundred eight delegates representing 35 colleges and universities were in attendance at this conference. Institutional membership had grown to 41. April was designated as National Residence Hall Month and a major constitutional revision was completed.

1966 — Southern Illinois University.

1967 — University of Kansas. Representatives from NACURH twice attempted to get Congress to pass a bill declaring April as National Residence Hall Month. Membership was 41, with the first Canadian institutions joining. NACURH ended the year with the first organizational surplus; monies were utilized to purchase a photocopier for duplicating articles and files being requested from the national officers. The NACURH President participated on panel discussions at both ACUHO and NASPA annual conferences. The first mid-year meeting of the Executive Board was held at Kansas State University.

1968 — Pennsylvania State University. Over 500 delegates from 82 institutions were in attendance. Institutional membership had more than tripled, with 130 schools now affiliated with NACURH. During the year, NACURH's first promotional film was produced. Although orchestrated at the national level, it was at the 1968 MACURH Conference that the Great Lakes region (GLACURH) was established by dividing MACURH and taking Ohio from NAACURH. SAACURH scheduled its first conference. All six regions hosted a conference in 1968. NACURH's mailing list included member institutions or contacts in all 50 states plus several Canadian institutions.

1969 — California State College-Long Beach. Five hundred fifty-two delegates from 81 schools were in attendance, with 88 institutional members. National dues were increased from $25.00 to $50.00, and the word "dorm" was replaced by "residence hall" in the constitution. A proposal to establish graduated dues based on institution size was rejected. Conference host institutions had to begin limiting delegations from large member institutions to provide for adequate representation from all NACURH member institutions. The NIC was begun when resource files were moved from the office of the National President to a separate office at Iowa State University. A list of NIC Directors and host institutions is appended to the end of this chapter. In addition, the Educational Facilities Laboratories awarded NACURH a $12,000 grant to study architectural facilities in the residence halls. The receipt of this grant generated positive national media coverage for the organization. In April 1969, the Big Ten Residence Hall Association merged with NACURH. The Vietnam War and the age of majority were issues of concern to college-age students and both of these topics were debated extensively throughout the year and at the national conference. However, representatives voted not to politicize the organization, opting instead to focus on communication of all perspectives and to be supportive of personal initiatives on matters of principal or conscience.

1970 — Texas Tech University. Over 800 delegates were in attendance at the Seventeenth Annual Conference. Membership included 125 institutions. NACURH joined a number of other national student and professional organizations in endorsing the Joint Statement on Rights and Freedoms of Students, first published in 1967.

1971 — Oklahoma State University. At this conference, the articles of incorporation and national bylaws were approved and the NIC was formally established as the National Office for NACURH. In addition, NACURH and the SWANK Motion Picture Company signed a contract for mutual services, and the first *NACURH Review* (newsmagazine) was published. Dr. Dan Hallenbeck was selected to serve as the second NACURH Adviser, replacing Mr. Yokie who resigned after 11 years of faithful service.

1972 — University of Wisconsin-Stevens Point. On November 16, 1971, NACURH was officially recognized by Oklahoma's Secretary of State as a nonprofit corporation with an NBD. The regional associations became regional affiliates of NACURH. The SOY Award was established, with Oklahoma State University as the first recipient. A listing of institutional recipients of the SOY is attached. Over 350 delegates from 61 institutions attended the conference. In February 1972, the colors of blue and white, along with a logo representing the structural form of the many varied facilities and housing units of the organization, were officially accepted by the NBD to symbolize NACURH.

1973 — University of Delaware. The conference staff planned for over 600 delegates, but due to mitigating circumstances, only 196 delegates from 56 institutions were in attendance. This caused severe financial problems for the organization and the first contingency fund was created. The Gold and Silver Pin Awards were established to recognize service at the national and regional levels respectively.

1974 — Illinois State University. Fifty-five institutions and 322 delegates were in attendance. The organizational structure and functions of NACURH were decentralized by the NBD to better serve the educational needs of the residents at member institutions. The opportunity to host the NIC in its new form, containing more than the resource files, was bid for the first time. During the reorganization, the leadership positions of President and Vice President were changed to Chairperson and Secretary/Treasurer, respectively, of the NBD. Also, the CRC position was established to assist institutions with regional and national conference bids and conference planning. Tony Warner from Western Illinois University was the first CRC elected by the NBD; a complete listing of CRCs is found at the end of this chapter. Due to the poor financial condition of the corporation, the NBD recommended that the traditional semiannual meeting in January be canceled. The NBD met in August at Kansas State University to establish a plan to alleviate the financial problems. The possibility of lobbying at government levels was considered but the NBD decided that such a move would be inconsistent with the goals of the organization.

1975 — University of Wisconsin-Stevens Point. Three hundred six delegates from 48 institutions were in attendance. The first annual corporate business meeting was held, with discussion concerning an NBD Handbook. NRHH restructuring resulted in an expansion of chapter memberships. The NBD unanimously endorsed and supported the creation of ongoing relationships with Commission III of American College Personnel Association (ACPA) and with ACUHO-I. These relationships were developed to promote information and program exchange among the student and professional organizations.

The realignment of the PACURH region into the Pacific North (PNACURH) and Southern Pacific (SPACURH) regions brought the regional total to seven. In September 1974, the MACURH region instituted the first School of the Month (SOM) program to recognize outstanding efforts within the region. The Best School Display Award and the School Spirit Award were established, with Eastern Illinois University and Emporia State University, respectively, as the first winners. A listing of the annual institutional recipients of the School Spirit Award is located at the end of the chapter.

1976 — Mississippi State University. Over 500 delegates attended, representing 61 institutions. By this conference, all regions had implemented SOM programs to recognize member institutions for outstanding programming efforts. The first NBD Handbook was published. Members of Congress were contacted again about designating April as National Residence Hall Month.

1977 — Oklahoma State University. Realignment of NACURH was studied but no action was taken.

1978 — Ball State University. Institutional membership was at 79, with 58 institutions attending the conference. The NBD began investigating disclaimers that would alleviate the liability of the organization. During this conference a foreword and preamble were added to the bylaws, and NIC document guidelines were re-established to facilitate the submission of reports. With the desire of the NBD to be aware of regional activities and financial status, it was decided that each Regional Director would submit a written report, including a financial statement, at each NBD meeting. A letter-writing campaign was initiated in yet another effort to have Congress designate April as National Residence Hall Month.

1979 — Kansas State University. Over 900 delegates attended the Silver Anniversary Conference. NACURH's membership grew to 113 institutions. Oklahoma

State University received a special Anniversary Award for dedicated service to the organization. A recommendation was made to investigate the possibility of videotaping sessions at the national conference. When concern about liability was expressed once again, the consensus of the NBD was to have delegates sign a waiver prior to attending a conference. In other business, the NBD voted to move the election of officers from January to May, and the Pacific North (PNACURH) and the Southern Pacific (SPACURH) regions were again merged to form the Pacific Affiliate of College and University Residence Halls (PACURH), reducing the total number of regions to six. In addition, policy and procedures sections were added to the NBD Handbook. In an effort to strengthen the relationship between NACURH and ACUHO-I, the NACURH/ACUHO-I Program of the Year (POY) Award was created to provide an opportunity for an outstanding student-developed program by a NACURH member school to be recognized and shared with residence hall student leaders in NACURH and the professional housing officers in ACUHO-I. A Life Member Award was established.

1980 — University of North Carolina-Chapel Hill. Over 1000 delegates from 90 institutions were in attendance. Institutional membership increased to 135. NACURH was once again realigned, with the Midwest (MACURH) region divided into MACURH and the new Southwest (SWACURH) region, again taking the regional total up to seven. Ken Stoner was selected to serve as the NACURH Adviser when "Dr. Dan" resigned after nine years of exemplary service. The "Satellite Groups in Residence Halls" program from the University of Cincinnati was selected as the first POY; a listing of the institutional POY recipients is found at the end of the chapter.

1981 — Texas A & M University. Institutional membership had grown to 151, with 967 delegates from 94 institutions in attendance at the conference. During the year, NACURH affiliated with the Free University Network.

1982 — University of Wisconsin-Whitewater. Membership had grown by 30, with institutional membership now at 181. One thousand ninety-seven delegates from 106 institutions attended the conference. In January, the NBD approved a resolution authorizing the Association of Alumni and Friends of NACURH (AAFN); an initial goal of 120 members was established. It was anticipated that the AAFN would provide recognition of, and generate symbolic as well as actual support of NACURH and its programs from, individuals who were once involved with NACURH. The minimum contribution of $100 was to be placed in a reserve fund and not spent; interest generated from this fund was to be used to increase financial solvency and for leadership development and recognition scholarships.

1983 — Pennsylvania State University. While the conference maintained its size, with 1083 delegates from 128 institutions attending, institutional membership reached 205. AAFN recognized 27 individuals. The *NACURH Network* was published, constituting a second attempt at an organizational newsmagazine; this publication continues today more in the form of an informative newsletter.

1984 — University of Colorado-Boulder. One thousand eighty-four delegates representing 125 institutions were in attendance. The first organizational scholarship was awarded, and national and regional membership recruitment packets were combined.

1985 — University of Florida. This was a record-setting conference with 1725 delegates from 138 institutions in attendance. Institutional membership reached 208. Oklahoma State University was awarded the first Research Project Award (RPA), co-sponsored with ACPA, for their Resident Lifestyle Survey. A listing of institutions receiving the RPA is attached at the end of this chapter.

1986 — University of San Francisco. Institutional membership grew to 220, with 1521 delegates from 128 institutions in attendance at the conference. The NBD approved a contract with Campus Fund Raisers (CFR) and endorsed their Exam Support Basket program. The CFR Outstanding Service Award (given to a student) and the Daniel A. Hallenbeck Outstanding Service Award (given to a non-student), honoring the former NACURH Adviser, were established. In addition, the videotape library, a component of the NIC, was established.

1987 — Central Michigan University. Over 1500 delegates from 157 institutions were present. NACURH now included 241 institutional members. One hundred thirty-three individuals were members of the AAFN, surpassing the initial goal, set in 1982, of 120 members. Three documents were prepared by members of the NBD on strategic planning, long range goals, and the future of NACURH. The historical reference portions of the NIC files were sent to the National Student Affairs Archives at Bowling Green State University.

1988 — University of Wisconsin-LaCrosse. One thousand eight hundred fifty-six delegates were in attendance. The NBD updated the policy book, endorsed the CFR Welcome Kit, and established a contract with Collegiate Carpets. With ACUHO-I, the NBD jointly endorsed a resolution on AIDS. Judy Spain was selected as NACURH Adviser when Ken Stoner resigned after eight years of service. AAFN was organizationally assigned to report through the Adviser, and Ken Stoner agreed to continue handling AAFN duties.

1989 — University of Northern Colorado. This conference had the distinction of being first, and only (to date), to be co-hosted by two institutions, the University of Northern Colorado and Colorado State University. Two thousand one hundred twenty-one delegates attended the annual meeting featuring 361 program sessions plus an optional day at Estes Park. The RPA jointly established in 1985 with ACPA was modified and became the Student Award for Leadership Training (SALT); the emphasis of the award was changed from research to leadership training. A listing of institutional recipients of SALT is included at the end of the chapter.

1990 — Southwest Missouri State University. Two thousand one hundred five delegates representing 198 institutions were in attendance at the annual meeting. The Dr. Kenneth L. Stoner Distinguished Service Award was created to recognize continuous dedication, commitment and achievement with NACURH. Ken Stoner and Bob Tattershall were the first two recipients of this award, announced at the closing banquet of the conference. Bob Tattershall stepped down as CRC after seven years of exemplary service; Beth Hellwig-Olson from Colorado State University was selected as the new CRC.

1991 — Arizona State University. Two thousand one hundred fifty-one delegates from 220 institutions were represented at the annual conference. NACURH established a collaborative relationship with Eastern Michigan University (EMU) to create the Student Action Team Network (SATN), which trains peers to programmatically educate on responsible alcohol use; the first SATN Training Conference was held in January at EMU. The duties of Secretary/Treasurer were divided into two positions entitled National Associate for Administration and National Associate for Finance. A small-school category was added to the Best School Display Award, with Eastern Montana College selected as the first recipient. A diversity statement was incorporated into the bylaws, and the contract with Campus Fund raisers was renewed for another five years.

1992 — University of North Dakota. One thousand seven hundred twenty-eight delegates representing 206 institutions attended the national conference. A number of changes investigated in the previous year were implemented including: the NAACURH Region formally split into the Northeast Atlantic (NEACURH) and the Central Atlantic (CAACURH) regions, bringing the total number of regional organizations to eight; and the National Publications Office was established with Laurie Aaronson from the University of Southern California selected as the first Director. To improve the financial accountability among the regions, the first annual Financial Officers Training Conference (FOTC) was hosted by the University of Northern Colorado. The POY was renamed in honor of the late Daniel A. Siler from the University of Wisconsin-Whitewater, and Mark Hudson from the University of North Dakota received the Ken Stoner Award.

1993 — University of South Carolina. Following the expiration of the original FIPSE Grant, NACURH assumed sole responsibility for continuing SATN. To accomplish this, an Education Coordinator Position was created and the SATN training was incorporated into the annual conference. The Four Year Pin was created to give national recognition to residence hall students who dedicated four years or more of service within the halls. The Critical Issues Months Program was adopted at the national level to provide resources to member schools for addressing a different issue impacting residence hall students each month. NACURH began to consider the Freshman Year Experience program as an opportunity for developing tomorrow's residence hall leaders. NACURH worked cooperatively with the ACUHO-I Research and Educational Foundation to publish *Advice for Advisors: The Development of an Effective Residence Hall Association,* edited by Norbert W. Dunkel and Cindy L. Spencer.

1994 — Northern Arizona University. Approximately 2400 individuals attended the annual conference; 334 institutions were members of NACURH. The first Student Action Team (SAT) office was appointed, with New Mexico State University as the host. The NBD began a long-term discussion of the effect of having half of the regional affiliates with terms of office running from May to May and the other half running from November to November. The organization also began a serious discussion regarding simplifying the organizational policies and reducing the number of officer attendees at the semi-annual and annual business meetings. Judy Spain from the University of Wisconsin-Stout was honored by the NBD with the Ken Stoner Award when she stepped down as NACURH Adviser and was replaced by Bob Tattershall from Washington State University.

1995 — Virginia Polytechnic Institute and State University. Approximately 2500 people attended the conference, with 356 member institutions. NACURH began the arduous process of obtaining tax-exempt status by hiring a CPA in the state of Oklahoma and filing the necessary fees and applications. Other major accomplishments during the year included the selection of a new CRC (Cindy Spencer from Ball State University, who replaced Beth Hellwig-Olson from the University of Northern Colorado), and the selection of MicroFridge, Inc., as a corporate partner. Beth Hellwig-Olson was honored by the NBD with the Ken Stoner Award.

1996 — University of Oklahoma. Approximately 2100 people attended the 1996 conference. As of the May meeting, 366 institutions were members of NACURH. The NBD began to use a more cooperative approach during board meetings. Their approach was to utilize small group discussions to accomplish dialogue about the issues and problems facing NACURH. The organization continued to work toward tax-exempt status and fiscal responsibility. This included a formula for investment of conference surpluses which addressed technology and financial stability for the life of the organization. NACURH signed another five-year agreement endorsing Campus Fund Raisers as a corporate partner. The affiliation of 180 NRHH chapters was achieved. New host sites for the NIC and NRHH National Office were selected.

1997 — Ball State University. Approximately 2475 people from over 250 institutions attended the 1997 conference. NACURH reached a high of 380 member institutions during this year. This was a landmark year for the organization. For over 20 years, NACURH sought tax-exempt status and finally it was obtained. This new status will have lasting effects on the organization, including investment benefits, corporate partners liabilities, and fiscal responsibility of financial officers. Due to the increase in monetary flexibility, the office of the AAFN was eliminated and the various tasks associated were reassigned to the NRHH, the NIC, and the Adviser. As of May 1997, the organization had more than $180,000 in reserves. During the semi-annual conference the organization decided that the SAT Office would best be served if it was housed at the NIC with regional representatives. Critical Issue Packets were changed to Critical Resource Packets and were made available to member institutions at no charge. NACURH signed another five-year agreement endorsing On-Campus Marketing as a corporate partner.

1998 — University of Nebraska.

1999 — University of Wisconsin-La Crosse. The history of NACURH continues to be written even as this chapter is "in press."

References

Association of College and University Housing Officers-International. (1970). *ACUHO-I statement of students' rights and responsibilities.* Muncie, IN: Author.

Dunkel, N. W., & Spencer, C. L. (Eds.). (1993). *Advice for advisors: The development of an effective residence hall association.* Columbus, OH: ACUHO-I.

Inter-Association Task Force on Alcohol Issues. (1985). *Statement of alcohol policy for institutions of higher education.*

NACURH (1997). *National Association of College and University Residence Halls, Inc., articles of incorporation.* Stillwater, OK: Author.

Stoner, K., Spain, J., Rasche, C., & Horton R. (1993). History and services of NACURH, Inc. In N. W. Dunkel & C. L. Spencer (Eds.), *Advice for advisors: The development of an effective residence hall association* (pp. 161-185). Columbus, OH: Association of College and University Housing Officers-International.

Wirag, R. J. (1988). AIDS on the college campus. Columbus, OH: ACUHO-I.

Wyatt, K., & Stoner, K (1984). A NACURH "White Paper" on residence hall government. *Journal of College and University Student Housing, 14*(1), 3-6.

NACURH PRESIDENTS/NBD CHAIRS & HOST INSTITUTIONS

Year	Chairperson	Institution
1954-1955	Dick Wiggins	Iowa State University
1955-1956	Carl Wesemann	University of Missouri
1956-1957	Len Froyen	University of Northern Iowa
1957-1958	Haile Clay	University of Missouri
1958-1959	Bruce Garver	University of Colorado
1959-1960	Fred Swartz	University of Northern Iowa
1960-1961	Myron Diebel	Montana State University
1961-1962	John Oakland	Iowa State University
1962-1963	James Petty	Southern Illinois University
1963-1964	Torlof Nelson	University of Idaho
1964-1965	Jim Tschechtelin	University of Kansas
1965-1966	Dick Haasnoot	Pennsylvania State University
1966-1967	Don Steeples	Kansas State University
1967-1968	Ken Stoner	Kansas State University
1968-1969	George Lease	University of Arkansas
1969-1970	Terry Serie	St. Cloud State University
1970-1971	Tom "Zack" Cooper	Oklahoma State University
1971-1972	Brad Johnson	Pennsylvania State University
1972-1974	Bob LeVand	Ferris State University

During a reorganization of NACURH, the leadership positions of the NBD were changed from President and Vice-President to Chairperson and Secretary/Treasurer, respectively.

Year	Chairperson	Institution
1974-1975	Mary Jacqmin	University of Wisconsin-Stevens Point
May-Dec. 1975	Kirk House	Indiana University of Pennsylvania
Jan.-Dec. 1976	Ron Wilson	Eastern Illinois University

Jan.-May 1977	Don Steffan	Iowa State University
May-Dec. 1977	Scott Miller	San Diego State University
Jan.-Aug. 1978	Basil Daley	Mississippi State University
Aug.-Dec. 1978	Scott Miller	University of Georgia
Jan.-May 1979	Steve Zuelhke	Colorado State University
1979-1980	Cathie Crouch	University of Georgia
1980-1981	Deb Lancello	University of Wisconsin-Stout
1981-1982	Kevin Wyatt	Oklahoma State University
1982-1983	Dwayne Wilder	Texas Tech University
1983-1984	Gene Zdziarski	University of Tennessee
1984-1985	Larry Speaker	University of Colorado
1985-1986	Laura Christianson	Iowa State University
1986-1987	Corrinne Shearer	University of Northern Colorado
1987-1988	Charlotte Rasche	Oklahoma State University
1988-1989	Allan Blattner	San Diego State University
1989-1990	Barb Olson	Oklahoma State University
1990-1991	Jeff Cullen	Colorado State University
1991-1992	Amy Stockly	Sonoma State University
1992-1993	Ray Horton	University of Idaho
1994-1995	Rich Ruscitti	Eastern Illinois University
1995-1996	Tyson Milanovich	Arizona State University
1996-1997	Krista Berry	University of Northern Colorado
1997-1998	Gretchen Vogel	University of Northern Colorado
1998-1999	Dave O'Brien	University of Wisconsin-Madison

NATIONAL RESIDENCE HALL HONORARY (NRHH) HOST INSTITUTIONS & DIRECTORS

Year	Institution	Director
1964-1965	University of Utah	Marge Cook
1965-1966	University of Kansas	Sherry Ball
1966-1968	University of Kansas	Barbara Nottago
1973-1974	Virginia Commonwealth University	Wendy Winters
1974-1975	Illinois State University	Phil Tripp
1975-1976	Illinois State University	Mary Lou Emmerick
1976-1977	University of Wyoming	Tom Owen
1977-1978	Oklahoma State University	Paula Bland
1978-1979	Kansas State University	Curtis Rath
1979-1981	Mississippi State University	Tammy Dearing
1981-1983	Eastern Illinois University	Mark Hudson & Wendy Tommas
1984-1986	Western Washington University	Dana Wilson
1986-1988	University of Wisconsin-Whitewater	Dan Millot
1988-1990	Texas A & M University	Darby Roberts
1990-1992	Colorado State University	Julie Love
1992-1993	University of Tennessee	Loy Carney

1993-1994	University of Tennessee	Mike Baker
1994-1995	University of Wisconsin-Eau Claire	Bryan Mueller
1995-1996	University of Wisconsin-Eau Claire	James Martin
1996-1997	Western Illinois University	Mishelle Banas
1997-1998	Western Illinois University	James Edlin
1998-1999	University of North Dakota	Michael Grosz

NATIONAL INFORMATION CENTER (NIC) HOST INSTITUTIONS & DIRECTORS

Year	Institution	Director
1969-1971	Iowa State University	Ken Stoner
1971-1973	Pennsylvania State University	Ron Erret
1973-1974	Pennsylvania State University	Carol Carberry
1974-1976	Eastern Illinois University	Craig Ullom
1976-1978	Iowa State University	Denise Gaumer
1978-1979	University of Illinois at Champaign-Urbana	Mike Inglimo
1979-1981	Oklahoma State University	Kevin Wyatt
1981-1983	Oklahoma State University	Gene Zdziarski
1983-1985	University of Wisconsin-Whitewater	Joe Candella
1985-1987	University of Wisconsin-Whitewater	Cathy Buyarski
1987-1988	Oklahoma State University	Stephanie Carnahan
1988-1989	Oklahoma State University	Chris Ferguson & Dana Stockton
1989-1991	University of Wyoming	Justin Wilke
1991-1994	University of Northern Colorado	Cheryl Fulmer
1994-1996	University of Northern Colorado	Krista Berry
1996-1997	Oklahoma State University	Laurie McCormick
1997-1998	Oklahoma State University	Robert Kesterson
1998-1999	Oklahoma State University	Robert Kesterson

NACURH ADVISERS AND HOST INSTITUTIONS

Year	National Adviser	Institution
1960-1971	J. Albin Yokie	Iowa State University Southern Illinois University Marquette University
1971-1980	Dan Hallenbeck	Iowa State University University of Georgia
1980-1988	Ken Stoner	University of Tennessee University of Kansas
1988-1994	Judy Spain	University of Wisconsin-Stout
1994-Present	Bob Tattershall	Washington State University

Year	CRC	Institution
1974-1976	Tony Warner	Western Illinois University
1976-1977	Mary Jacqmin	Western Illinois University
1977-1983	Craig Ullom	Radford College
		University of Georgia
1983-1990	Bob Tattershall	University of California-Santa Barbara
		San Jose State University
		Washington State University
1990-1995	Beth Hellwig-Olson	Colorado State University
		University of Northern Colorado
1995-Present	Cindy Spencer	Ball State University

Year	AAFN	Institution
1982-1997	Ken Stoner	University of Tennessee
		University of Kansas

NACURH/ACUHO-I
PROGRAM OF THE YEAR (POY) AWARD WINNERS

1979-1980	University of Cincinnati: "Satellite Groups in Residence Halls"
1980-1981	Eastern Illinois University: "How to S.C.O.R.E. with Scholarships"
1981-1982	Western Michigan University: "Bronco Buddies"
1982-1983	University of Maryland-College Park: "Spirit Semester"
1983-1984	Pennsylvania State University: "Fire Safety Committee"
1984-1985	Eastern Illinois University: "Rookie Runners"
1985-1986	Western Michigan University: "Ackley/Shilling Pursuit"
1986-1987	Texas A & M University: "Freshman Leadership Program"
1987-1988	University of Wisconsin-Whitewater: "C.O.W. (Celebrating Our World) Week"
1988-1989	University of Georgia: "S.C.O.A.R. (Student Committee On Acquaintance Rape)"
1989-1990	Miami University of Ohio: "AIDS Awareness Week"
1990-1991	Colorado State University: "Look out any Window: Homelessness Awareness Week"
1991-1992	University of North Dakota: "Hall Orientation Teams"
1993-1994	University of Northern Colorado: "Rockies to the River"
1994-1995	Western Illinois University: "Tunnel of Oppression"
1995-1996	University of California - Santa Barbara: "Project CARE"
1996-1997	Franklin and Marshall: "Our Neighbors, Ourselves"
1997-1998	Indiana University of Pennsylvannia: "FLUSH: Friends Living Under Serious Hardships"

NACURH/ACPA RESEARCH PROJECT AWARD (RPA) WINNERS

1985 Oklahoma State University: "Resident Lifestyle Survey"
1986 Oklahoma State University "Resident Lifestyle Survey" (continued)
1987 George Washington University: "Alcohol Research Project"
1988 Virginia Polytechnic University: "Institutional Support as Perceived by RHA Presidents"

STUDENT AWARD FOR LEADERSHIP TRAINING (SALT) WINNERS

1989 Texas A & M University: "FISH Leadership Camp"
1990 Fordham University: "We Can Move Mountains"
1991 University of Akron: "Summer Leadership Series"
1992 University of Northern Colorado: "Leaders at the Helm ... Steering into the Future"
1993 University of Washington: "Park Forest Student Leadership Retreat"
1994 University of Akron: "Building a Neighborhood Together"
1995 University of Vermont: "Going for the Gold ... A Celebration of Our Olympic Leaders"
1996 Ball State University: "It's in the Cards"
1997 University of Akron: "LEAP: Leadership, Education, and People"

SCHOOL OF THE YEAR (SOY) AWARD WINNERS

1972 Oklahoma State University
1973 Iowa State University
1974 University of Northern Iowa
1975 Mississippi State University
1976 Kansas State University
1977 Oklahoma State University
1978 University of Wisconsin-Stevens Point
1979 Duquesne University
1980 Montana State University
1981 Oklahoma State University
1982 Southwest Missouri State University
1983 University of Wisconsin-Whitewater
1984 Murray State University
1985 San Diego State University
1986 University of California-Santa Barbara
1987 University of Northern Colorado
1988 San Diego State University
1989 Occidental College
1990 University of North Dakota
1991 George Washington University
1992 University of Akron
1994 Oklahoma State University

1995 DePaul University
1996 Western Illinois University
1997 University of Michigan
1998 State University of New York at Geneseo

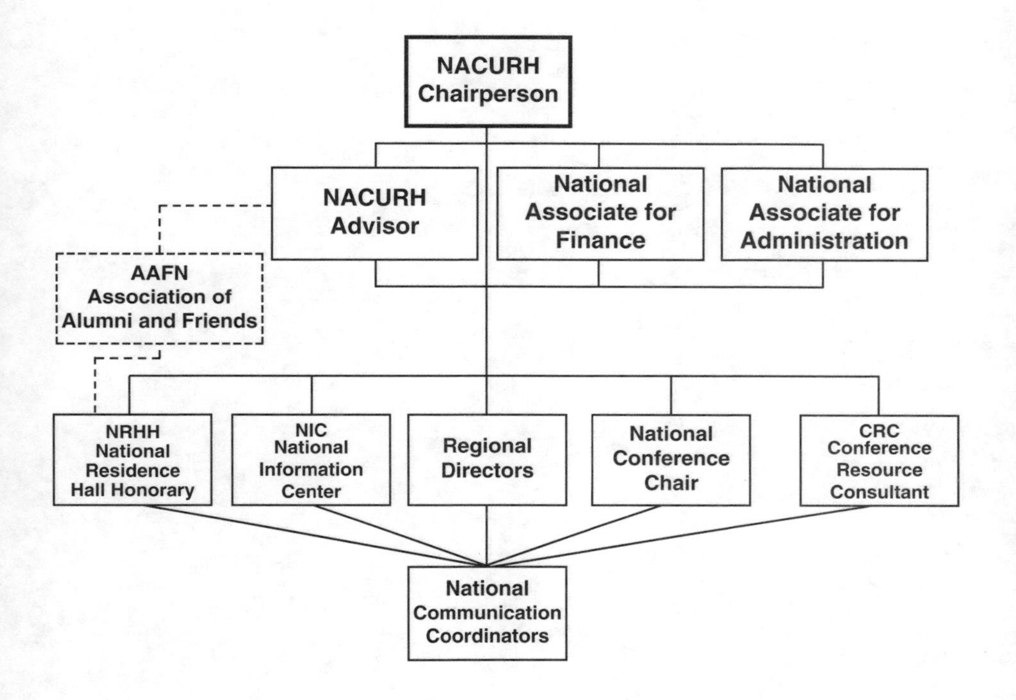

Figure 1. The organizational chart provided above reflects the current organizational arrangement of NACURH.

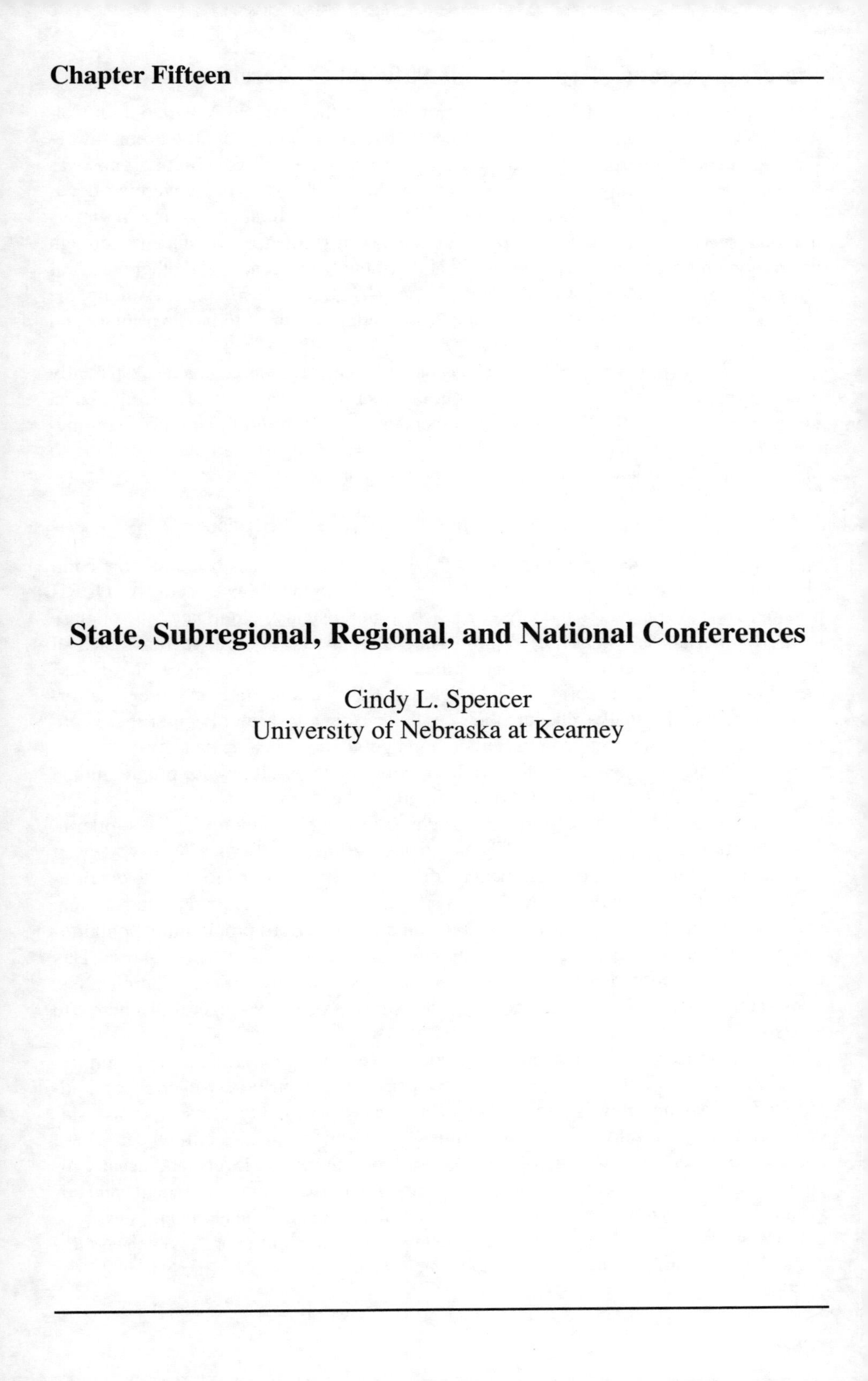

Chapter Fifteen

State, Subregional, Regional, and National Conferences

Cindy L. Spencer
University of Nebraska at Kearney

State, Subregional, Regional, and National Conferences

Conferences have always been a major focus of the National Association of College and University Residence Halls, Inc. (NACURH) since its inception. From this beginning, the stated purpose of such gatherings of residence hall governing groups was to share ideas, problems, and solutions. In Article II of NACURH's governing documents, the purpose of the organization is "to design and facilitate programs and informational services to promote the educational goals of residence hall students through discussion groups, seminars, and speakers at the annual conferences and other means of informational exchange throughout the year" (NACURH, 1997, p. 2). Among the myriad services offered to its membership, conferences continue to be the primary and most utilized service of NACURH.

The process by which NACURH has met this objective has changed substantially over the years. From its inception, with four member institutions at the first conference, to the present day, when NACURH membership is close to 400 institutions and national conference attendance averages close to 2,500 delegates, advisers continue to play an important role in the conference experience of their students.

Conference Structure, Format, and Purpose

As NACURH has grown and as leadership development has become more complex, the number of conferences offered has increased to meet those needs. NACURH organizes one annual national conference each spring (usually held in late May or close to the Memorial Day weekend). Within NACURH there are eight regions, each of which organizes an annual conference in the fall. Each region also holds a "No-Frills" or miniconference in the spring. In addition, there are various state or subregional organizations which usually schedule their conferences in the spring. Each of these conferences has its own format with different target populations in attendance.

The NACURH annual conference usually offers three full days of programming. At the conference students have the opportunity to hear from various guest speakers and to attend additional programming sessions. The programming topics are similar to those mentioned previously, the difference being the increased scope of new ideas at the national level. As with other student conferences there is a trend to include opportunities for small group dialogues relating to specific topics or interest areas. In addition, national conference host staff have continued to provide various programming opportunities for advisers. Because most students are not in class during the Memorial Day weekend, many conferences offer an "optional day" activity for an additional fee. These activities usually involve various local activities or historical sites of interest to tourists.

Because they are held during the academic year when classes are in session, regional and state or subregional conferences usually begin on Friday evening and adjourn on Sunday morning. These weekend conferences are usually a less expensive student leadership development opportunities than the national conference. These conferences offer programming on a variety of topics at several levels, and usually include one keynote or guest speaker in addition to the presentations by students and advisers. Topics may relate to leadership development, personal development, new programming ideas, gender issues, fund-raising, current events, or advising issues. "Track" programming may be targeted to specific audiences, such as the National Residence Hall Honorary (NRHH), Student Action Team (SAT), RHA presidents, National Communication Coordinators (NCCs), and advisers. In addition, many small group discussions or roundtable topic programs allow delegates to have an interactive learning experience.

During these conferences, the NCC or NRHH representatives from each institution will attend business meetings which may conflict with certain programming sessions. It is important that the adviser be aware of these meetings and attend them if possible. The adviser's role can vary greatly. It might be helpful to have conversations with the students as well as other advisers at the conference to determine the advising role at business meetings.

While the primary focus of the conferences is programming and leadership development, various social and entertainment options are available, such as movies, dances, karaoke, hospitality lounges with refreshments, and various games. Additionally, with all NACURH affiliated conferences, no alcohol is allowed.

Regional "No-Frills" or miniconferences have a considerably different format. The primary focus is organizational business. These conferences usually do not offer structured programming opportunities. They may offer roundtable discussions for NRHH and SAT representatives or RHA Presidents, and dialogue opportunities for advisers. As the title implies, these conferences usually do not offer many "frills."

The various conferences could be viewed as a pyramid of leadership experiences. The state or subregional conferences serve as the base or foundation of leadership development, followed by the regional conferences and then the national conference, all building on the leadership developed at the local level.

At the fall regional conference, students can be introduced to NACURH. Attending this conference can motivate new student leaders to continue the programming ideas on their own campuses, setting new goals based on what they learn from peers. Because they interact with students from various states or regions they have the opportunity to meet a more diverse group of students than they would at state or subregional conferences. This conference can be a good beginning for those mid-level leaders prior to attending a national conference. Regional conferences provide the opportunity for students to develop a network of their peers while still retaining a sense of familiarity with other student leaders with whom they have attended other conferences, had campus exchanges, and so forth.

Spring semester can be a challenging time to keep students motivated and excited about activities on their home campus. State and subregional conferences held during the spring semester not only serve as catalysts to spark interest in students seeking leadership roles for the following year but also re-energize "seasoned" leaders.

The national conference is designed to meet the needs of experienced leaders and students who have attended past regional and state or subregional conferences. With strong advising and thorough preparation on what can be expected, the national conference can be a rewarding experience. Students who have significant experience in RHAs, NRHH, SAT, or other campus leadership roles will be exposed to ideas from all over the nation. Delegates will find that the quality of the programs may not differ greatly from that of a regional conference, but the quantity and variety of topics will offer greater depth.

Conference Costs

As the number of conferences has increased, this has brought a significant question for advisers in deciding with their students which conference best meets their needs, given the financial resources available for conference attendance. State and subregional conferences are usually the most economical conference with regards to registration costs, travel costs, and time. Regional conferences currently have registration fees ranging from $100-$150 per delegate. National conference fees currently range from $130-$170 per delegate. Those fees include housing and meals. Adviser registration fees are on the average $10-$30 higher than student delegate fees. This additional cost difference is primarily due to the difference in adviser housing options.

In addition to registration costs, transportation costs can affect decisions about attendance. Transportation costs can range from $10-$100 per delegate for a regional conference, depending upon the proximity of the conference to one's institution. National conferences may involve up to 24 hours of ground travel or the cost of air travel, again depending on the proximity of the institution to the host site. As the cost of conference fees and transportation has increased, more institutions are working together to share economical modes of transportation, including charter buses or air travel for delegations within states or sub-regions.

Bidding for Awards

While the primary focus of the conferences is directed at programming and leadership development, another focus is challenging students to take risks and gain recognition. Numerous awards are distributed at the various conference levels. Awards include individual as well as institutional recognition, such as Student of the Year, School of the Year (SOY), Program of the Year (POY), NCC of the Year, Advisor of the Year, and NRHH Chapter of the Year. One award that is given only at the national level is the NACURH/ACPA Student Award for Leadership Training (SALT). Each region has specific guidelines and policies for the bid process, available from the institution's NCC or the NACURH Regional Director. Information regarding the SALT and POY awards at the national level is available from the NACURH Conference Resource Consultant (CRC).

Pre-Conference Preparation

Before the conference, there are a number of important topics and tasks that need to be addressed and completed. Most of these tasks are completed by the NCC. However, it is important that the adviser work with the NCC to provide the support and knowledge needed. This can be particularly important in reviewing program proposals and arranging travel plans. These tasks include:

1. Determine delegation size and make-up following guidelines or delegation caps determined by the conference staff.
2. Develop a process for selection of the delegation and outline the criteria that will be utilized to determine who will serve as delegates.
3. Market the conference to potential delegates. This can begin prior to receiving the conference registration information. Most conferences provide newsletters, web

pages, and other information a few months prior to the distribution of registration information.

4. Select delegates as soon as possible once registration information has been received. It is recommended that a few alternate delegates also be selected, giving the NCC options from which to fill spaces if students cancel.

5. Recruit program proposals to be presented at the conference. One proposal for every five delegates is recommended.

6. Send registration information to conference host site. Be sure to follow the established timeline to meet all deadlines.

7. Meet with the delegation to allow them to get to know each other. This will give them opportunities to develop committees that can assist the NCC with some of the responsibilities in preparing for the conference. This will also provide opportunities for the group to have discussions and collectively make certain decisions.

8. Identify fund-raising projects (if needed) to pay for conference expenses.

9. Determine the mode of transportation and make necessary arrangements.

10. Make plans for roll call. The guidelines for this may be determined by the conference host. For the national conference roll call is coordinated at the regional level.

11. Institutional displays are optional; however, this is an opportunity for students to showcase their institution. Often displays coordinate with the conference theme.

12. Collect items to trade, such as shirts, hats, signs, noise makers, and so forth. Items are usually symbols of delegation spirit and pride that reflect the conference theme or campus traditions.

13. Create a means of communication with delegates for information they will need to know prior to leaving for the conference.

Preparing for a conference and completing the tasks outlined requires students and advisers to work together, establish goals and priorities, set deadlines, and most importantly plan and follow through on preparations. The learning experience of being a part of a conference delegation and preparing for the conference often can be as beneficial as attending the conference itself.

Role of the Adviser: Responsibilities and Delegate Accountability

The conference delegation adviser needs ensure that the NCC clearly understands his or her responsibility to the delegation and develops a clear and consistent line of communication with the conference delegation, the adviser, and the conference host staff. It is recommended that the adviser and NCC establish and communicate their expectations of each other and of the delegates. Self (1992) offered several suggestions for advisers that might be included in a regional newsletter:

1. Assist in organizing a delegation. Work with residence hall leaders in planning strategies to recruit students to attend the conference. It is a good idea to have students who have attended previous conferences talk with student groups to share their experiences. As the time for the conference approaches, assistance may be needed in requesting approval from professors for students to miss classes or change exams.

2. Ensure that conference information is communicated. The NCC receives a variety of mailings from the conference office which need to be communicated to the delegation. Deadline dates, registration instructions, and other important information should be double-checked with the NCC. All the administrative necessities need to be taken care of on time and in the correct manner.

3. Help students assess their personal and organizational needs. Before the delegation leaves for the conference, students should assess how they, as individuals and as a group, can get the most out of the conference. Pre-planning will give students a lead on looking for conference programs which can help them in their work on campus.

4. Plan conference program attendance. Once the group arrives at the conference, the conference program should be reviewed with the delegation. Students can maximize their conference dollars by having representation at a variety of workshops.

5. Process information from the conference. Many institutions have a plan to help students be accountable for sharing the information they gather with the students unable to attend the conference.

6. Prepare students to take risks. NACURH and the state associations have a strong history of recognizing students and their accomplishments. Students take a risk by presenting bids to be evaluated. It is imperative that students be prepared for the possibility of not being selected to receive awards and bids. It is a great achievement to be strong enough to take a risk in the first place to bid for an award. It is not unusual for students to be devastated upon hearing news that they were not selected for the recognition they sought. Advisers can play an important role in setting an appropriate tone regarding awards and recognition.

Hosting Conferences

Role of the Adviser

An adviser can assist students in determining whether the monumental task of hosting a conference is realistic. It is essential that advisers empower students to make important decisions, to learn about failure, and to acquire leadership experience throughout the conference planning process. It is equally important that the adviser not assume the role of conference chairperson. An adviser may be aware of many more global issues and legal liabilities with regard to conference hosting. Training, challenging, and showing support are all still critical roles for the adviser to perform throughout the planning process. It is important for advisers to assess the needs of those they advise before committing to formally organize a bid.

Feasibility Issues

Hellwig-Olson and Tattershall (1993) identified criteria for hosting a conference and provided information on submitting conference bids. An adviser can assist students with executing a feasibility study before submitting a conference bid. Several questions should be answered during this analysis:

1. Who is the catalyst for hosting a conference?
2. What is the motivation for hosting a conference?

3. Does a core group of students exist who are interested in planning, writing a conference bid, and implementing a conference?

4. Is there support from the chief housing officer? He or she must sign a host acknowledgment form for NACURH-affiliated conferences.

5. Does the institution or the community have the appropriate facilities to support the size of the conference?

6. Is the institution willing to assume part of the financial responsibility in the event of a financial loss?

7. Are the conference dates compatible with other events on the host campus?

8. Do sufficient resources exist in the area of housing, food service, transportation, financial support, workshop presenters, and volunteers?

9. Does the campus RHA support the concept of hosting a conference?

10. Is there a willingness to be sensitive to issues of diversity in all areas when planning the conference?

11. Can support be gained from essential nonhousing departments on the campus? Other important areas include police, conferences, parking, management, catering, student center, and so forth.

12. Can the institution host a conference on its own or would it be more feasible to co-sponsor a conference with other institutions?

Criteria for Hosting a Conference

To be eligible to host a regional or national conference, an institution is required to be in good standing with NACURH. Dues to NACURH are required each year in order to remain in good standing financially with all other national and regional offices. An annual report submitted to the National Information Center (NIC) is also required.

Resources and Services

Conference Resource Consultant (CRC)

The purpose of the CRC is to assist institutions in conference bid preparation, implementation, and evaluation. The individual who holds this position is a full-time housing professional with experience in advising students on conference planning. In most cases, the CRC will have had first-hand experience with the implementation of a regional or national conference. Any institution interested in hosting a conference is encouraged to contact the CRC and inquire about bid materials, policies, past conference reports, and any general questions. The CRC also works extensively with institutions after receiving the bid and entering the preparations and hosting phase.

National Information Center (NIC)

The NIC is a clearinghouse for information from member institutions. The NIC houses bids from past years for "No-Frills," regional, and national conferences. Member institutions may access information from the NIC; the first 100 pages are free and thereafter a minimal fee is charged. The NIC also processes all member registration forms. The NIC can create a master mailing list of current members for institutions hosting conferences. The updated lists make it easier for conference hosts to distribute materials informing students about important items. The NIC rotates on a three- to six-year basis. The NCC on each campus receives information regarding the location of the NIC when they attend the national conference. For institutions not attending the national conference information from the conference is mailed to them from the NIC.

Conference attendance is a significant milestone in student leadership development. Students gain information about programs, speakers, and activities to take back to their institutions. It is vital for advisers to possess knowledge of conferences and their benefits in order to maximize students' experiences.

References

Hellwig-Olson, B., & Tattershall, B. (1993). Conferences: Attendance, structure, and benefits. In N. W. Dunkel & C. L. Spencer (Eds.), *Advice for advisors: The development of an effective residence hall association* (pp. 187-196). Columbus, OH: Association of College and University Housing Officers-International.

NACURH. (1997). *National Association for College and University Residence Halls, Inc., articles of incorporation.* Stillwater, OK: Author.

Self, C. (1992, October). Role of a conference delegation advisor. *Intermountain Affiliate of College and University Residence Halls Newsletter.*

Professional Development for RHA Advisers

Valerie S. Averill
Kansas State University

Patrick Bradley
Central Missouri State University

Professional Development for RHA Advisers

Introduction

The support of the adviser is one of five components critical for a successful and effective residence hall association (RHA; Wyatt & Stoner, 1984; see also Chapter One in this volume). "Without a doubt, the most effective means of administrative support is the leadership and commitment provided by the professional staff member serving in the role of adviser to the RHA" (Wyatt & Stoner, 1984, p. 4). The role of the adviser was also one of five areas identified as key to the RHA's effectiveness in a study by Komives and Tucker (1993). Advisers of student groups owe it to their students and institutions to be current and proficient in the theories and practices which maximize the potential of the RHA and each member.

Professional Development Defined

Professional development is an ongoing, lifelong process with stages similar to Erickson's stages of human development. "The professional development of student affairs practitioners might be a subset of general human development, related to age as much as to a particular field of employment" (Young, 1987, p. 21).

Professional development is "a planned experience designed to change behavior and result in professional and/or personal growth and improved organizational effectiveness" (Merkle & Artman, 1983, p. 55). As advocates of intentional and purposeful development, we further define it as the learning process one pursues in an effort to develop, refine, and master skills and knowledge that will enhance one's job performance, namely the advising role.

A Review of the Literature

Higher education literature contains many articles on student development, the importance of student involvement in the residential and academic community, and the training of successful academic advisers. The literature on student personnel and higher education gives little insight, however, into the collective knowledge and skills needed to be an effective and successful RHA adviser, nor does the literature provide direction for the professional development of student group advisers.

Professional organizations have identified standards of practice and professional competence for student housing departments and their staff. The American College Personnel Association (ACPA; 1993), the Association of College and University Housing Officers-International (ACUHO-I; 1991), and the Council for the Advancement of Standards for Student Services/Development Programs (1986) have all published standards and guidelines. These documents provide valuable information against which to evaluate departmental activities, functions, and quality of service, and they provide information on the types and levels of education and experience recommended for various staff positions. For example, the ACUHO-I Standards (1991) include a functional area called Education/Programming, which states that "the residential learning community provides educational opportunities for students and other members of the campus community. Staff involvement in educational opportunities ensures that learning experiences are oriented toward promoting maturity and are grounded in human/student development theory and research" (p. 7). The subsections of Educational Opportunities and Staff Activities include examples of the types of activities and experiences that should be available to students, and of the activities and functions expected of the staff.

Chief housing officers have been surveyed to rank order lists of competencies gleaned from the literature that they believe to be important in young professionals (Dunkel & Schreiber, 1992; Ostroth, 1981). These surveys provide a valuable inventory of skills upon which to focus training efforts, including interpersonal communication and leadership, as well as the ability to work cooperatively and effectively with a wide range of individuals and the ability to assess student needs and interests. Although 78.2% of the respondents in Ostroth's (1981) survey ranked the ability to advise groups as an important competency, nowhere can one find a prescription for the training and development of the RHA adviser.

The Role of the Adviser

The adviser's roles and responsibilities have been addressed by several authors (Averill, 1993; Boersig, 1993; see also Chapter 3 in this volume) and generally fall into the categories of (a) educator/trainer, (b) historian, (c) fiscal agent, (d) group development coordinator, (e) liaison and resource person, and (f) counselor and confidant. In addition, Cuyjet (1996) asserted that "as advisers to student organizations, their members, and their leaders, student affairs educators need to be competent programmers, and they need to be able to effectively transfer these abilities to students who come to them for advice and mentoring" (p. 397).

Certainly many of the skills identified by the professional associations and affirmed by the studies of Dunkel and Schreiber (1992) and Ostroth (1981) are important to the successful fulfillment of the above-mentioned advising roles. In addition, Cuyjet (1996) believed that "it is critical to focus on the development of the relationship between advisers and groups in order to maximize their effective interaction.... Formal training for advisers is an excellent medium for building these relationships. Such a program provides an opportunity for the campus activities office or the dean of students office to provide tangible support for organizational well-being" (p. 408). To successfully fill these diverse responsibilities, ongoing professional development and training for the adviser is essential.

Purposeful and Intentional Development

Dunkel and Schreiber (1992) suggested that a formal plan of professional development be created. Despite the attempt to formalize this concept, for many student personnel professionals the plan is usually hit-or-miss. Little thought goes into decisions concerning how much money to spend and where to focus one's attention. Many young professionals rely primarily on training given during their orientation or through departmental staff development sessions.

The first step should be to determine one's strengths and weaknesses as an adviser. How current is the adviser's knowledge of student and group development? Is the adviser aware of legal issues which affect student groups and their advisers? Whether the adviser is in the first year of advising or the tenth, a critical review of knowledge and skills is important in order to create an appropriate and effective plan.

Professional Development Opportunities

M. Dannells (personal communication, October 8, 1997) categorized professional development activities into conventional and unconventional. The conventional category includes professional associations; national, regional, and state workshops and conferences; graduate courses; and scholarly reading and research (see Bibliography).

Professional Associations

Four key objectives of professional associations are "to advance understanding, recognition, and knowledge in the field; to develop and promulgate standards for professional practice; to serve the public interest; and to provide professionals with a peer group that promotes a sense of unity" (Nuss, 1993, p. 365). Many housing and residence life professionals rely on their involvement in one or more professional organizations to meet their ongoing professional development needs. According to a recent survey, 354 of 905 respondents (39.12%) cited professional growth opportunities as the single most important factor that caused them to affiliate with ACUHO-I (Moser, 1993). Moser also found that 342 of 926 respondents (36.93%) identified the opportunity for professional networking as the leading reason for continued affiliation with ACUHO-I.

Several organizations cater to the needs of higher education professionals. A brief description of the four major organizations (one student association and three professional associations) related to housing and residence life is appended. In addition, Bradley (1993) identified four other organizations which serve certain groups or interests in higher education, including the National Association for Campus Activities (NACA), BACCHUS (Boost Alcohol Consciousness Concerning the Health of University Students) and GAMMA (Greeks Advocating the Mature Management of Alcohol) Peer Education Network, the National Association for Equal Opportunity (NAFEO), and the National Association for Women in Education (NAWE).

Creative Strategies for Professional Development

It is easy to chart a professional development course when money is not an obstacle. The ability to attend conferences sponsored by the above-mentioned associations and to order the latest scholarly books could go a long way toward fulfilling professional development. However, many student group advisers find themselves challenged when the need or desire to pursue professional development conflicts with the financial resources available. Housing and residence life departments take a variety of different approaches to the ongoing training and development of staff. Financial restraints often limit the number of staff who attend conferences, and whether those conferences are national, regional, or state-wide gatherings. Some departments create their own series of training workshops, either using their own staff or hiring consultants, in order to provide information on topics they deem important to their entire department. Other departments make sure their in-house library contains the latest scholarly work on the profession so that staff may be current in the knowledge and use of various theories and practices.

In addition to, or regardless of, the number and type of professional development opportunities provided by one's department, meaningful development is limited only by creativity and time. The following list of unconventional activities is certainly not exhaustive, but is offered as a springboard for your own ideas.

1. Spend a day in the RHA office.
2. Keep a journal of advising activities and experiences.
3. Ask RHA officers and members to ask you "Why?"
4. Visit a neighboring campus to meet with the RHA adviser and perhaps attend an executive board or general membership meeting.
5. Acquire syllabi from student personnel graduate courses and read the assigned books and articles.
6. Attend free teleconferences.
7. If other departments on campus subscribe to publications which carry articles related to advising, make arrangements to read them (NACA's The Programmer is an excellent example).
8. Volunteer to teach a class on campus and become a student of student behavior.
9. Create a support network and learning group by having a regularly scheduled "brown bag" lunch with colleagues who also advise student groups.
10. Join a list service or electronic bulletin board to communicate with advising colleagues around the country.
11. Research one aspect of the advising role and write an article for a professional or student newsletter.
12. Offer to present a professional development session on advising student groups to the residence life department or student affairs division. We learn best what we teach.
13. Work with your RHA to plan a leadership retreat.
14. If free course hours are part of your benefit package, enroll in a student personnel graduate class. If that program is not offered, choose a class of interest.
15. Create a file folder or binder of advising articles and other resources. Soon you'll have your own library of helpful information to use and to share.
16. Offer to be a guest speaker to student organizations on campus.

Summary and Conclusion

To identify areas for professional development and training, the key roles and responsibilities of the RHA adviser were listed, as well as some skills and competencies seen as important in housing professionals. Many of the skills mentioned in this chapter are taught in graduate programs, but not usually in the context of advising student organizations. For advisers who graduated a few years ago, a whole new body of research and knowledge is being taught today.

By attending national and regional conferences and/or being involved in professional associations, RHA advisers can learn from and network with advising colleagues and professionals on the cutting edge. While conference attendance costs money, meaningful involvement can sometimes be acquired for only the cost of membership. Regardless of the opportunities to attend conferences, investment in professional development should not end there. Just as a successful recipe requires multiple ingredients, a meaningful plan of professional development incorporates many strategies, including the effective, yet low cost, ideas for development listed above.

Advisers must take responsibility for their own training and development. Before one can make good use of these resources, skills and strengths should be identified, as well as areas in need of attention. The Adviser Inventory and Professional Development Plan at the end of the chapter is designed to help readers identify training needs in order to maximize their resources. The goal, of course, is to be well rounded in one's skills and abilities. Advisers owe this to themselves, to the profession, and to the students.

Adviser Inventory and Professional Development Plan

Successful professional development is the result of an intentional plan. Advisers are encouraged to take this opportunity to reflect on their strengths and areas in need of improvement regarding advising responsibilities, and to make a plan to expand and enhance their knowledge and skills.

Experience Assessment and Reflection

1. I have been a student group adviser for : _______________ (years and/or months).
2. I have served as adviser for the following types of groups:
3. I enjoy these aspects of advising:
4. I am challenged by these aspects of advising:

Skills Assessment

5. I know the following skills, theories, and concepts are important to a successful adviser:
6. I believe I am proficient in the following areas, and I know this because:
7. I need to improve my skills or knowledge in these areas:

Development Plan

A. Development area:
   Strategies for Improvement:
   Time Frame and Evaluation:
B. Development area:
   Strategies for Improvement:
   Time Frame and Evaluation:
C. Development area:
   Strategies for Improvement:
   Time Frame and Evaluation:
D. Development area:
   Strategies for Improvement:
   Time Frame and Evaluation:

References

American College Personnel Association. (1993). *Statement of ethical principles and standards.* Washington, DC: Author.

American College Personnel Association. (1996). *Member resource directory.* Washington, DC: Author.

Association of College and University Housing Officers-International. (1991). *Ethical principles and standards for college and university student housing professionals.* Columbus, OH: Author.

Averill, V. (1993). Responsibilities of an RHA adviser. In N. W. Dunkel & C. L. Spencer (Eds.), *Advice for advisors: The development of an effective residence hall association* (pp. 20-26). Columbus, OH: ACUHO-I.

Boersig, P. (1993). The first advising position. In N. W. Dunkel & C. L. Spencer (Eds.), *Advice for advisors: The development of an effective residence hall association* (pp. 10-18). Columbus, OH: ACUHO-I.

Bradley, P. (1993). Professional development for advisors. In N. W. Dunkel & C. L. Spencer (Eds.), *Advice for advisors: The development of an effective residence hall association* (pp. 198-207). Columbus, OH: ACUHO-I.

Council for the Advancement of Standards for Student Services/Development Programs. (1986). *CAS standards and guidelines for student services/development programs.* Washington, DC: Author.

Cuyjet, M. J. (1996). Program development and group advising. In S. R. Komives & D. B. Woodard, Jr. (Eds.), *Student services: A handbook for the profession* (3rd ed., pp. 397-414). San Francisco: Jossey-Bass.

Dunkel, N. W., & Schreiber, P. J. (1992). Competency development of housing professionals. *Journal of College and University Student Housing, 22*(2), 19-23.

Komives, S., & Tucker, G. (1993). Successful residence hall government: Themes from a national study of select hall government structures. In N. W. Dunkel & C. L. Spencer (Eds.), *Advice for advisors: The development of an effective residence hall association* (pp. 28-41). Columbus, OH: ACUHO-I.

Merkle, H. B., & Artman, R. B. (1983). Staff development: A systematic process for student affairs leaders. *NASPA Journal, 21*(1), 55-63.

Moser, R. (1993). *ACUHO-I member satisfaction and needs assessment.* Columbus, OH: ACUHO-I Member Needs and Services Task Force.

National Association of Student Personnel Administrators. (1998). *Member handbook.* Washington, DC: Author.

Nuss, E. M. (1993). The role of professional associations. In M. J. Barr (Ed.), *The handbook of student affairs administration* (pp. 364-377). San Francisco: Jossey-Bass.

Ostroth, D. D. (1981). Selecting competent residence hall staff. In G. S. Blimling & J. H. Schuh (Eds.), *Increasing the educational role of residence halls* (pp. 65-80). New Directions for Student Services, No. 13. San Francisco: Jossey-Bass.

South Atlantic Affiliate of College and University Residence Halls (SAACURH). (1997). *The ART institute constitution.* Mississippi State, MS: Author.

Wyatt, K., & Stoner, K. (1984). A NACURH "White Paper" on residence hall government. *Journal of College and University Student Housing, 14*(1), 3-6.

Young, R. B. (1987). A model of professional education. In L. V. Moore & R. B. Young (Eds.), *Expanding opportunities for professional education* (pp. 19-25). New Directions for Student Services, No. 37. San Francisco: Jossey-Bass.

Bibliography

Advising

Dunkel, N. W., & Schuh, J. H. (1998). *Advising student groups and organizations.* San Francisco: Jossey-Bass.

Dunkel, N. W., & Spencer, C. L. (1993). *Advice for advisors: The development of an effective residence hall association.* Columbus, OH: ACUHO-I.

Schuh, J. H. (Ed.). (1987). *A handbook for student group advisers.* Alexandria, VA: ACPA.

Housing Operations

Schroeder, C. C., & Mable, P., (Eds.).(1994). *Realizing the educational potential of residence halls.* San Francisco: Jossey-Bass.

Winston, R. B., Jr., & Anchors, S., (Eds.). (1993). *Student housing and residential life.* San Francisco: Jossey-Bass.

Student Personnel and Higher Education

Astin, A. W. (1993). *What matters in college: Four critical years revisited.* San Francisco: Jossey-Bass.

Barr, M J. (Ed.). (1988). *Student services and the law.* San Francisco: Jossey-Bass.

Barr, M. J. (Ed.). (1993). *The handbook of student affairs administration.* San Francisco: Jossey-Bass.

Chickering, A. W., & Reisser, L. (1993). *Education and identity.* San Francisco: Jossey-Bass.

Komives, S. R., & Woodard, D. B., Jr. (Eds.). (1996). *Student services: A handbook for the profession* (3rd ed.). San Francisco: Jossey-Bass.

Pascarella, E. T., & Terenzini, P. T. (1991). *How college affects students.* San Francisco: Jossey-Bass.

American College Personnel Association (ACPA)

Mission: To provide professional programs and services for educators who are committed to the overall development of students in post-secondary education (ACPA, 1996).

*Membership:*General, Associate, Student, and Emeritus membership categories.

Cost: 1998 membership rates are $90 for General, $34 for Student, $90 for Associate, and $45 for Emeritus status.

Involvement: ACPA offers 16 Commissions, generally based on functional areas, and five Standing Committees, organized around special interest groups. Members are encouraged to join as many as their interest indicates. ACPA also has state divisions under the auspices of the national organization which allows for additional involvement at a more local level.

Benefits: Members receive the *Journal of College Student Development* six times per year; *About Campus: Enriching the Student Learning Experience,* published bimonthly; and ACPA *Developments,* the quarterly news publication. Members also receive reduced rates on conference registration.

Contact: American College Personnel Association
One Dupont Circle, N.W.
Suite 300
Washington, DC 20036-1110
Phone: (202) 835-2272
Fax: (202) 274-4540
E-Mail: info@acpa.nche.edu
Web Site: http://www.acpa.nche.edu

Professional Development for RHA Advisers

Association of College and University Housing Officers-International (ACUHO-I)

Mission: To bring college and university staff members who have responsibility covering any of the various aspects of student residence, food service, developmental programming, administration, and related operations into meaningful association (ACUHO-I, 1991).

Membership: Institutional membership; individual affiliate membership categories are available for professionals, students, associates, emeritus; sustaining memberships (corporate or business) with varying degrees of costs and benefits.

Cost: In 1998, institutional memberships ranged from $150 to $925, associate memberships were $99, and student memberships cost $28.

Benefits: The chief housing officer receives the *Journal of College and University Student Housing,* published twice a year; the ACUHO-I *Talking Stick,* published eight times per year; and the ACUHO-I Directory. Members also receive reduced rates for national and regional conferences, which often include programs on advising residence hall student groups.

Involvement: Members can participate in many activities and committee opportunities at the state, regional, and national levels. ACUHO-I is committed to the development of new professionals and endorses and sponsors the annual National Housing Training Institute (NHTI) for professionals with three to five years of experience.

Contact: ACUHO-International
364 W. Lane Avenue, Suite C
Columbus, OH 43201-1062
Phone: (614) 292-0099
Fax: (614) 202-3205
E-Mail: osuacuho@postbox.acs.ohio-state.edu
Web Site: http://www.acuho.ohio-state.edu

National Association of College and University Residence Halls, Inc. (NACURH)

NACURH is the largest student-run, tax-exempt organization in the country. The national organization and its eight regional affiliates offer adviser track programs at their annual national and regional conferences.

The South Atlantic Affiliate of College and University Residence Halls (SAACURH), which represents the South Atlantic region of NACURH, has joined forces with the Southeastern Association of Housing Officers (SEAHO) to create "The ART Institute" — The Adviser Recognition and Training curriculum. Its purpose is to:

> provide a regional forum for the education and mentoring of new residence hall organization advisers, to provide continuing education for veteran ... advisers, to promote residence hall organization advising within the housing profession, and to improve the state of residence hall organization advising through education, mentoring, and research. (SAACURH, 1997, p. 1).

NACURH's National Board of Directors are students, and most terms of office expire each May; therefore inquiries should be made to the National Adviser.

Contact: Bob Tattershall
Washington State University
c/o Housing Services - WSU
P. O. Box 641726
Pullman, WA 99164-1726
Phone: (509) 335-7732
E-Mail: tattersh@wsu.edu
NACURH Web Site: http://www.nacurh.okstate.edu/

National Association of Student Personnel Administrators (NASPA)

Mission: To serve student affairs administrators who bring an institutional perspective to work with students in higher education (NASPA, 1998).

Membership: Institutional dues are charged based on a matrix that considers the institution's full time enrollment and total educational and general fund expenditures. Individual memberships are available for those working at nonmember schools and are categorized as Associate, Faculty, and Emeritus Affiliations. Student Affiliations are available for graduate students not employed full time at any institution.

Cost: In 1998, institutional dues ranged from $264 to $1217. For persons employed at member institutions, Professional Affiliate dues are $52. For persons employed at nonmember institutions, Associate Affiliate dues are $156, and Faculty Affiliate dues are $52. Student Affiliate dues are $31, and Emeritus Affiliate dues are $42.

Benefits: Members receive the *NASPA Journal,* published quarterly; and the *NASPA Forum,* published monthly. Members also received reduced conference registration fees.

Involvement: NASPA invites members to become involved through any of its 16 "Networks," which are organized around functional areas, institutional type, or special interests.

Contact: NASPA
1875 Connecticut Ave. NW
Suite 418
Washington, DC 20009-5728
Phone: (202) 265-7500
Fax: (202) 797-1157
E-mail: office@naspa.org
Web Site: http://www.naspa.org

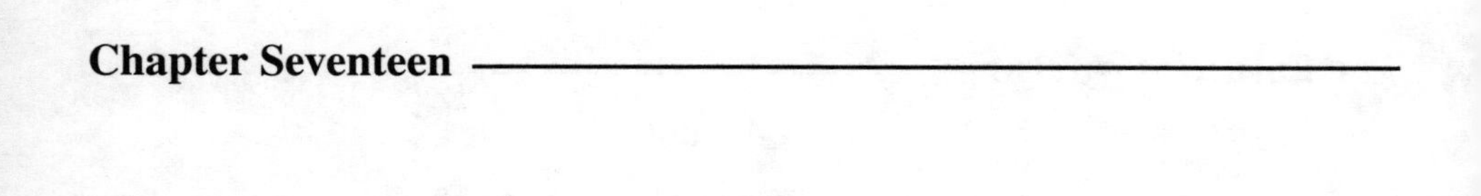

Chapter Seventeen

The Future of Advising

Norbert W. Dunkel
University of Florida

Introduction

Advisers do not have a crystal ball to see into the future of their profession. However, with research, literature, observation, and experience, advisers can draw conclusions as to where the advising profession may be headed. It is exciting to be an active adviser and continue to observe students develop and transition in their lives. When speaking to housing professionals, many will state that their motivation to serve as an adviser is to be able to work with students, to feel a sense of collegiality, to understand current fads and trends, to be close to the energy students possess, and to experience the gratification that hall governance brings an education through to the students that can be transferred to their careers. It is equally exciting to have colleagues create the advising literature. Advising literature in the past five years has included the publication of three books and numerous refereed and nonrefereed articles. Additionally, several regional and national studies on advising have provided quantitative and qualitative data to support many observations and beliefs. This literature and research has been presented and published to a broad audience through state, regional, and national conferences and publications. This information provides additional techniques, activities, and knowledge to aspiring and seasoned advisers as they continue to search for new approaches to work with students and organizations. This chapter will provide a look forward to the adviser's role in working with students in the next millennium.

Quality Advising

Appointing staff to serve as student governance advisers ensures the organization that there is an individual to approach when seeking guidance and direction. How do housing staff know that the advising is of high quality? How do they know that advisers are providing the right information for any given situation? How do they know that the organization is better because of the adviser? How does the adviser know that members are effectively meeting the organization's mission and purpose? In the future, advisers and housing staff will be more accountable for finances and legal issues. This book has provided detailed information on the pitfalls of poor financial management and difficulties in group development, as well as information on avoiding legal problems. An institution places responsibility upon the organization's adviser to insure that financial and legal complications are minimized. Is there a way to know that the advice provided by the adviser is correct? Housing staff must turn to evaluation to answer many of the questions that have been posed. "Evaluation is any effort to use assessment evidence to improve institutional, departmental, divisional, or agency effectiveness" (Upcraft & Schuh, 1996, p. 19).

The adviser's effectiveness, as well as the organization's, should be evaluated. Evaluating the latter currently is difficult without an instrument to use. However, Gardiner Tucker from Colorado State University is developing an instrument to determine an RHA's effectiveness. His research is being supported by the ACUHO-I Research and Educational Foundation and NACURH. His instrument will be completed by RHA members and scored locally to determine the level of the organization's effectiveness. The future will bring more certainty to an area of evaluation that currently possesses little reliable information. Until the instrument is available for institutional use, advisers can still facilitate discussion of several questions among RHA members. First, "one of the best ways to look at an organization is to review its stated goals and objectives. These are articulated in the constitution and bylaws and should be used to frame the activities of the group" (Dunkel & Schuh, 1998, p. 219). Does the RHA program and design activities around the organization's goals? Does the RHA get involved and discuss issues beyond its goals? Does the RHA change the stated organizational goals during the academic year to fit what members want? Additionally, are members enjoying their involvement in the RHA? Do members rise through the various leadership positions? Does the RHA receive respect and admiration from the institutional administration? These questions assist in determining whether the RHA is fulfilling the members' desired needs as well as meeting the organization's goals and objectives.

To determine their own effectiveness, advisers should ask self-evaluative questions and allow RHA members to answer similar questions. Questions the adviser should ask are: Do I know the goals and objectives of the RHA? Do I meet regularly with the executive board and members? Do I understand the RHA constitution and bylaws? Do I motivate and encourage the executive board and membership? Do I attend student conferences with the RHA? Do I attend activities and programs designed and developed by the members? Do I make myself available to answer questions and provide direction? Do I audit financial records? Do I assist the membership in dealing with difficult situations of group development and leadership?

Similarly, there are several questions RHA members can answer: Does the adviser attend activities and programs? Does the adviser know the members? Does the adviser allow members to make decisions or make decisions for them? Does the adviser understand the history and culture of the RHA? Does the adviser appear to be excited and motivated to be a part of the RHA? Can the adviser answer questions regarding policies, rules, and processes? Do members find the adviser accessible to talk with about career, professional, or personal topics? Do members consider the adviser a mentor?

These types of questions provide excellent feedback to the adviser regarding his or her effectiveness and knowledge of the organization. The future will bring validated instruments advisers can use to determine the effectiveness of the organization and of themselves. For accountability, budget rationale, and organizational effectiveness, it is incumbent upon advisers to set up a formal plan of evaluation with members of the RHA.

The Changing Campus Climate

The residential nexus (ACUHO-I, 1996) was published to challenge housing officers to consider their institutional academic role. "A renewed commitment has emerged toward developing campus community, reforming undergraduate education, and placing the focus of the educational enterprise on its core mission — student learning. As housing and residence education professionals, we must strive to be an integral part of this movement" (ACUHO-I, 1996, p. 6). With this statement, ACUHO-I emphasized need for housing officers to create a new role in forming partnerships, programs, and services with the academic community.

Given this evolving role of housing, RHA members also need to examine their governing documents to determine whether their role should be adjusted accordingly.

The Future of Advising

Perhaps RHAs should be more involved in the academic nature of their communities. Certainly, a few RHAs currently develop academically related programs and services (e.g., tutors, study halls, faculty speakers, etc.). However, these types of programs appear to be secondary to the members' need for social programs. The challenge for RHAs is to include new positions and facilitate discussions within their organizations that reflect a renewed sense of academic commitment. For instance, new positions may include an academic liaison with the campus undergraduate advisory council; a board of college councils representative with voting privileges in the RHA; or a student academic coordinator whose task it would be to develop tutorial programs, speakers, psychoeducational programs, and so forth. A committee of representatives could work with selected faculty and housing staff to examine the academic commitment, to open discussions on distance education and how the RHA could participate, to assist in recommending academic theme houses on campus and providing the house a voting seat in the RHA, or to publish a newsletter for faculty and administrators that highlights the academic commitment and involvements of the RHA.

Similarly, many institutions are experiencing renewed residential growth and renovation. RHAs must participate in the feedback process to assist the planning and development of new and renovated facilities. Institutional and housing officials must recognize the value and benefit of involving residents in the planning process. The architectural design, interiors, furnishings, aesthetics, and access all influence the learning style differences of students. Some students study better individually than in groups or "differences may occur around ethnic or cultural issues, nationality differences, and gender differences" (ACUHO-I, 1996, p. 8). Students must be able to provide input into the creation of their learning space. RHAs should establish work groups to collaborate with institutional and housing planners and to create a close working relationship with key housing officers. A work group could use furnishings for a semester that are being considered for future purchase or offer feedback on schematic designs, color selection, or case goods. With the increased use of computers and the need for Internet access, RHAs could provide representatives to housing committees to assist with deciding where to place computer outlets, what types of desks and chairs to purchase to support computer equipment, what types of lighting would augment their study, or how to secure the computer equipment. It is vital that advisers work with students to encourage their participation in the process of academic retooling.

Campus climates are diverse. RHA members and leaders should develop a means to select representatives that reflect the diverse nature of the students living in housing. RHAs should establish a position of diversity educator who will (a) develop programs for members regarding diversity in housing, on campus, and in the greater community; (b) develop multicultural programming; (c) develop agenda lines to provide information from traditional campus organizations such as institutes of Black culture, Hispanic or Latino culture, and so forth; and (d) coordinate sending representatives to the same organizations to bring information regarding housing.

The adviser's role is to challenge the RHA membership to discuss and consider their governing documents, to recognize the implications of construction and renovation, and to realize the diversity of the institution and students living in housing.

Budgets

Komives and Tucker (1993) maintained that in order for an RHA to be successful "there is a clear source of adequate funding and budget authority ... resources were developed from a variety of sources, including activity cards, allocations from rental income, vending percentages, hall dues, and allocations from the department of residential life" (p. 38). The underlying meaning of this statement is that an RHA must receive multiple-source funding, including money from the housing operation. It is difficult for an RHA to spent inordinate amounts of time fund-raising when members could be planning and designing programs for residents. Having a commitment from the chief housing officer (CHO) is important to an RHA's success.

A CHO committed to student involvement in the governance process will attempt to insure the housing allocation. CHOs with less commitment who are pressured to find money for housing projects may decrease or eliminate the allocation to the RHA. It is important for advisers to work with students to establish a good relationship with the CHO. The CHO who does not serve as the RHA adviser and yet is knowledgeable of the organization's purpose, plans, and involvement will demonstrate a greater commitment to its mission. Housing money alone does not determine success. In the future, advisers must guide students to establish multiple-source funding through programs currently offered yet not utilized, as well as discover new, innovative funding and budget strategies.

Staff Selection

In Chapter 4, Tucker and Komives identified several common themes of successful RHAs. One theme, the role, placement, and commitment of the RHA adviser, is key to understanding that staff selection is important in the overall quality of the RHA. Komives and Tucker (1993) believed that the RHA adviser should be a member of the central housing office staff. This staff member would be at a level high enough to "insure access to information concerning the department and to receive and carry student feedback forward" (p. 33). Osteen and Tucker (1997) proposed a model of parallel relationships between hall governance and housing operations. They maintained that for the greatest accountability and authority on process issues and program content, the staffing and student governance structures must be considered. Osteen and Tucker (1997) believed that at the floor or house level, the resident assistant should advise the student group; at the area or hall level, the area director or resident director should advise the student group; and at the campus-wide level, a member of the central housing office should advise the RHA. Komives and Tucker (1993) found that all of the 12 most successful large and small institution RHAs implemented the model proposed by Osteen and Tucker (1997).

The appointment of a central housing office staff member to serve as an RHA adviser is generally conducted by choice of the staff member or by appointment from a supervisor. When appointing a staff member as an adviser to the floor, area, or campus-wide student governance, prior experience and knowledge of the purpose of student governance is vital to determining the staff member's ability to perform the adviser responsibilities. An adviser must possess the interest and energy to fulfill the responsibilities. When a current member of the staff indicates an interest in serving as an adviser, that individual's qualifications are generally understood. If the staff member who has the added responsibility of advising is interviewing for a vacant position, it is recommended that questions be integrated into the interview process to determine the level of knowledge and interest in advising. The following are sample questions that can be incorporated into an interview for a staff member who will serve as an RHA adviser.

1. What is the purpose of student governance in the residential setting?
2. What skills are acquired by residents involved in student governance that can be transferred to their select profession?
3. Have you served as an adviser to a residential organization or to any other group or organization?
4. What kind of relationship would you like to establish with the executive board of the organization? With the organization's membership?
5. How involved should you be with training of the executive board and membership?
6. How do you integrate education into the role of adviser when working with student governance?
7. What developmental issues do you believe an RHA experiences from the beginning of the term (point of new elections) to the end of the term (closing banquet)?

It is important to include questions regarding advising for all residence life vacancies. The staff member may not be the adviser to an organization; however he or she may supervise the graduate adviser or the entry-level staff member who advises an area council. Residence life staff who understand the purpose and value of student governance will provide support to the students and staff. Care must be taken when hiring staff who have been highly engaged as students or who perhaps served as graduate advisers, to provide them with supervision of advisers or advisory experience. The problem that can arise is hiring staff who all have a great interest in hall governance and want involvement and participation without enough opportunities for all of them.

In the future, housing personnel must be more intentional regarding not only the staff hired to fulfill advising responsibilities but also the placement of the staff member in relation to the level of student governance.

Adviser Preparation

For many years hall government, area council, or RHA advisers began their duties with a file passed on from the previous adviser or perhaps with a notebook of activities and programs found on the shelf. They may have received a few kind words of encouragement from a supervisor who was "pleased to provide this professional development opportunity" to the staff member, or they may have begun with no written materials or verbal support. For many advisers, learning on the job has been their introduction to their responsibilities.

Advising is a complicated responsibility full of policies, procedures, rules, theories, and concepts. Within the past ten years conference program planners have started including adviser tracks, individuals to speak on topics pertinent to advisers, and workshops designed to meet advisers' needs. This intentional planning to provide information and knowledge to advisers has been received warmly by many advisers who have searched for information to apply to the RHA they advise. As the level of accountability rises for advisers, the need for specialized information and resources becomes greater.

In 1996, Ed Grandpré from Mississippi State University proposed a program entitled A.R.T. (Adviser Training and Recognition). He conceptualized an intentionally structured program to train new advisers and seasoned advisers. Utilizing Grandpré's model, Dunkel and Porter (in press) received support from SAACURH and the Southeastern Association of Housing Officers (SEAHO) for their training curriculum for advisers based upon their 1996 national study of adviser responsibilities. They proposed to establish five core programs and four elective programs. The core programs included presentations on: (a) recruitment and retention of members, (b) working with an executive board, (c) student and group development models and theories, (d) roles and responsibilities of the adviser, and (e) the adviser as an information resource person for campus, state, regional, and national services and organizations. The elective programs included presentations on: (a) how diversity affects the RHA, (b) conferencing (membership and dues, election procedures, bid processes, NACURH, forming a delegations, etc.), (c) the motivation, encouragement, and recognition of students, and (d) legal issues.

SAACURH embraced Grandpré's model and with the curriculum established a regional adviser training model that recognized the needs and experiences of new and seasoned advisers. The core and elective programs are offered at regional and national conferences and, when combined with years of experience and business meeting attendance, apply towards a "certification" of advisers who complete the program.

This intentional adviser training will continue to grow not only on the regional and national levels but on the local level with hall government and area council adviser training. Educational programmers are developing hall- and area-level adviser training programs for graduate students and post-Masters' professionals. These training programs are presented simultaneously with beginning-of-term training. It is quite difficult to schedule an adequate amount of time to cover the many topics and issues necessary to feel comfortable as an adviser. In the future, housing officers will need to discuss their training approaches and provide skill development as transferable to supervising or advising versus training to be a supervisor separate from training to be adviser. The similarities between advising and supervising are many and with discussion the proper training will suffice for both roles.

Transitions

Dunkel and Porter (in press) determined that one of the greatest problems RHA members faced in 1996 was the controlling nature of their advisers. Advisers ran the executive board elections, made decisions on which conferences students would attend, decided which students and which programs would be presented at student conferences, maintained the budget, approved all checks, sat at the head table during RHA meetings and answered all the questions, and so forth. Clearly, the students' comments were quite revealing of the controlling nature of their RHA advisers.

The transition from student to adviser is a difficult step for many to make. Generally, this step is from a highly engaged, high-performing student to a graduate position where the individual is advising a hall government or area council. Similarly, graduate students who make the decision to continue in the housing profession may then advance and be appointed the RHA adviser. This transition from advising a local hall government or area council to advising a campus-wide organization is equally difficult. In the future professionals working with ACUHO-I and NACURH must study these transitions to provide (a) recommendations on how best to develop programs or services that assist the transition, (b) training approaches that reduce the anxiety of role changes, and (c) literature that provides information to better understand the different roles.

Adviser Experience

Dunkel and Porter (in press) conducted a national study of adviser responsibilities. The 1996 study was the first comprehensive research conducted with RHA advisers and RHA presidents. Of the 137 advisers that participated in the study, two were undergraduate students, nine were graduate students, 112 were full-time housing professionals, and 14 were CHOs. RHA advisers generally believed that ten years ago many more graduate students and fewer CHOs served as RHA advisers. However, there is no research to support that belief. Chief student affairs officers (CSAO) are asking CHOs to find their customers. The CSAO wants housing operations to seek feedback from the resident student regarding issues of campus satisfaction, rules and regulation changes, tuition and room and board rates, contracted services, and so forth. With resident students as its customers, the RHA is best positioned and organized to obtain that feedback. The adviser is in an excellent position to educate the RHA on housing budgets, services, rules and regulations, rental rates, and so forth. The better understanding the RHA membership possesses regarding these aspects, the better relationship the student might have with housing and student affairs administrators.

As housing staff continue to seek feedback from their customers, many more CHOs will consider becoming RHA advisers to increase their involvement in the education and development process of students. The national study determined that RHA advisers averaged 4.1 years of experience in 1996. As more CHOs elect to serve as advisers, the years of experience will increase due to the continuity of a CHO versus a mid-level housing professional. This CHO continuity brings the RHA a consistent and knowledgeable individual who understands the culture, history, traditions, and values of the organization. Additionally, just as an RHA serves the campus-wide constituency, the CHO serves as the leader of the campus-wide housing operation. Communications and decisions flow more easily at that level than through supervisory lines to the CHO.

Compensation

Advisers of hall governments, area councils, or RHAs generally have their role as an added responsibility. In Chapter 10, Schuh alluded to the need to include this role in the staff members' position description or to receive a letter of appointment outlining the additional duties. The adding of advising responsibilities to a staff member's duties should also merit additional compensation. For instance, the graduate student whose sole responsibility is advising a hall governance organization receives compensation for those duties. What kind of like compensation or considerations are provided to the graduate staff who have advising as an added responsibility? In recognition of this added responsibility, some institutions have (a) adjusted the duty schedule to allow staff to have first pick for weekend duty or to be exempt from holiday duties, (b) provided them with extra money on a meal card, (c) provided support to attend a professional conference, or (d) removed a duty from their position description to provide equity in the amount of time spent in their position. For professional housing staff who advise the RHA, several forms of compensation are possible: (a) reimbursement of out-of-pocket expenses to attend student conferences, (b) creation of a graduate assistant or practicum student position to provide assistance, (c) salary augmentation, (d) a meal card, or (e) a title change and/or promotion due to the added responsibilities. The point is that serving as an adviser entails investing considerable time meeting with the executive board, members, participating in activities, and attending conferences. In the future, housing officers need to intentionally evaluate the benefits and value of staff members who serve as effective advisers and compensate them accordingly.

Conclusion

This chapter has provided several challenges to advisers and housing officers to consider in the future based upon current practices and research. The outlook for all levels of student residence hall governance looks good. Research is being generated, aggressive training programs are being developed, compensation issues are being discussed, and staff selection that considers advising as an integral skill is being practiced. There are still many more challenges ahead and many questions and concerns needing study and research.

References

ACUHO-I (1996). The residential nexus: A focus on student learning. *Talking Stick, 13*(7), 6-10.

Dunkel, N. W., & Porter, J. D. (in press). Residence hall association adviser responsibilities. *Journal of College and University Student Housing.*

Dunkel, N. W., & Schuh, J. H. (1998). *Advising student groups and organizations.* San Francisco: Jossey-Bass.

Grandpré, E. (1996). *The adviser training and recognition program (A.R.T.).* Unpublished manuscript.

Komives, S., & Tucker, G. L. (1993). Successful residence hall government: Themes from a national study of select hall government structures. In N. W. Dunkel & C. L. Spencer (Eds.), *Advice for advisors: The development of an effective residence hall association* (pp. 27-43). Columbus, OH: ACUHO-I.

Osteen, J. M., & Tucker, G. L. (1997). Authority, accountability, and advice: Understanding the unique roles of residence life staff and hall government leaders. *Journal of College and University Student Housing, 27*(1), 34-40.

Upcraft, M. L., & Schuh, J. H. (1996). *Assessment in student affairs: A guide for practitioners.* San Francisco: Jossey-Bass.